A

Matthew Manning is a world-famous healer who lectures and demonstrates his techniques all over the world. He has been involved in more scientific research and testing than any other healer in the world and has addressed the Royal Society of Medicine and spoken to MPs in the Houses of Parliament about his healing work. Regularly featured in the media, he is the author of *One Foot in the Stars*, his autobiography, *No Faith Required* and *The Link*. Matthew Manning has a healing practice in Suffolk, where he lives with his two children and his wife Gig.

The
HEALING
JOURNEY

MATTHEW MANNING

The HEALING JOURNEY

A Complete Guide to Healing Yourself and Others

Foreword by Professor Karol Sikora

PIATKUS

Copyright © 2001 Matthew Manning

First published in 2001 by
Judy Piatkus (Publishers) Limited
5 Windmill Street
London W1T 2JA
e-mail: info@piatkus.co.uk

The moral rights of the author have been asserted

A catalogue record for this book is available from the British Library

ISBN 0 7499 2244 3

Edited by Lizzie Hutchins
Text design by Sara Kidd

This book has been printed on paper manufactured with respect for the environment
using wood from managed sustainable resources

CONTENTS

Disclaimer

The Healing Journey does not replace normal allopathic medical treatment. It is a means of supporting and complementing such medical treatment. If you have any acute or chronic disease you should seek medical attention from a qualified doctor. The author and publisher accept no liability for damage of any nature resulting directly or indirectly from the application or use of information in this book.

Acknowledgements

I would like to thank John and Inger Fredriksen for the tranquillity of La Paloma where I gathered my thoughts for *The Healing Journey*, and Pat Clarke and Jane and Catriona MacFarlane for all their help with my research and work on the manuscript. I am also very grateful to Dr Greg Morley for taking the time to check the material for medical accuracy, and Patrick Holford for fine-tuning the chapters on nutrition.

My greatest appreciation and thanks go to my wife, Gig, whose illness inadvertently led to this book and who then happily encouraged me to spend evenings and weekends writing whilst she became a 'writer's widow'!

And finally, to Pat Metheny, who reminded us in our more difficult times that *'The Truth Will Always Be'*.

FOREWORD

Karol Sikora, MB, MA, PhD, FRCP, FRCR, is Professor of Cancer Medicine at Imperial College and Consultant Oncologist at Hammersmith Hospital, London. He was Chief of the World Health Organisation's Cancer Programme and has been involved in designing cancer services in different cultures and economic environments.

C ancer is an increasingly common problem. One in three Europeans will develop the disease and this will rise to one in two by 2020. Due to painstaking laboratory research there has been a dramatic increase in our understanding of the disease. We now understand the molecules that control the growth and division of cells. These vital cogs determine the intricate balance of cell behaviour. Changes in the structure or function of these vital components lead to abnormal growth and the ability of a cell to migrate and divide in other parts of the body. Cancer can arise in any organ, leading to a plethora of clinical patterns of the disease.

Science will provide a complete understanding of the disease within the next few years. With this will come new treatments – almost certainly tablets to control abnormal growth and the spread of cancer. Already we are seeing the fruits of a more targeted approach to cancer drug design. These new drugs will be far less unpleasant and used earlier in the natural history of the illness. Surgery and radiotherapy will become less important as we enter the next decade, but will still be used to reduce the burden of disease in the body. The future at a technological level is very exciting.

But perhaps the most challenging area of medicine is dealing with the interaction of mind, body and spirit. This is important in all healthcare, not just the treatment of cancer. The decline of traditional religious structures and the break-up of previously close-knit families and indeed communities have led to the isolation of many individuals who face, often for the first time, a life-threatening illness. And yet traditional healthcare systems and their practitioners spend little time trying to find the best ways to convey the ability to cope with the new challenges faced by patients.

Healing is nature's way of helping us cope. Matthew Manning has a remarkable track record of working at the interface between body and soul. His knowledge is outstanding in both breadth and detail. This book puts together in a very readable format a concise review of healing. It is full of practical advice of ways to regain control of your life and how to use an illness as a lever to a more fulfilled existence.

There are several intriguing exercises to follow. Many patients become overwhelmed and emotionally overloaded, which leads them to focus on the intricate details of their treatment, becoming obsessed with blood counts, X-rays and clinic visits. And yet developing an effective coping strategy for life, whether by laughter, relaxation, diet or simply love, is far more important. This is an enormously difficult area to study using conventional scientific methods, but you will see that there is abundant evidence of benefit.

Modern medicine increasingly uses guidelines to ensure patients get optimal treatment. So far none has been produced for emotional care. Faith, hope and love are too personal to standardise. Instead we all have to find our own way through the maze. Matthew has provided a map. I can thoroughly recommend this book to every patient, regardless of their problem, and to their loved ones.

Karol Sikora

INTRODUCTION

Gerry Jampolski, the founding father of what is now known as 'attitudinal healing', once said that we tend to teach what we want to learn.
This book represents much of what I have known for many years in my work as a healer but as I have researched and written it, I have learned so much more. I believe that as a result of this I have become better at what I do and am better able to give balanced advice to my patients.

I decided to write this book in 1998 after my wife Gig had been diagnosed with cancer and well-meaning friends and patients had deluged us with books, papers, suggestions and recommendations about all manner of therapies. I had quickly amassed a small library of books and documents that spread right across the back wall of my office. Having worked in the field of complementary medicine for over twenty years, I thought I was fairly familiar with different treatments and therapies.

As I began sifting through all the material I had now collected, I realised that many of the books were written by zealous alternative practitioners who railed against all orthodox medical treatment and gave dire warnings of its side-effects, if not immediate then undoubtedly future. I found that many of them, although well-intentioned, were extremely limited in their knowledge of cancer and that, as a group, they tended to be enormously critical of conventional medicine and as fixed in their own beliefs as they accused the medical profession of being. Many of their books made what I felt were highly spurious, and sometimes very misleading, claims for alternative therapies that had not been properly tested or evaluated, still less reported in any form of scientific or reputable journal. There were also books written by doctors who had a completely myopic and often hostile stance to anything other than orthodox medicine.

It felt as if we were being fed information from doctors and alternative practitioners all speaking completely different languages, unwilling or unable to understand each other. So many of the books seemed to be mutually exclusive and everybody seemed to have their own particular belief system, axe to grind or product to sell. If I had difficulty in making any sense out of all this disparate and conflicting information, how would a layperson, without my years of experience, cope?

Anyone who has ever been diagnosed with a serious or possibly life-threatening illness will probably have experienced the same fears, conflicts and stresses that we went through. Although this book was inspired by Gig's successful battle with cancer, and although much of my work is with cancer patients, this is not just a book about this particular disease. As you will discover, I have included a great deal of material about other problems, such as multiple sclerosis, arthritis, heart disease and even the common cold! The principles are the same whatever the problem. So many illnesses are caused by a breakdown in immune functioning and so much of our lifestyle and attitude can potentially weaken our immunity, making us more susceptible to disease.

Gig and I spent a long time wondering why she had become ill and we asked every doctor we met the same question. Nobody could ever give us an answer. However, I now believe that it is probably unusual for disease to be caused by one particular event. Accordingly, I have covered a wide range of topics, from emotional and psychological influences to stress and nutrition, faith and prayer. If, for example, you have a poor diet, live under great stress, lack assertiveness and frequently denigrate yourself with internal self-talk, you are perhaps more likely to suffer from health difficulties than if you are merely under stress or happen not to eat well.

In an effort to create a bridge between orthodox and complementary therapies, I have drawn not only on journals of medicine, psychiatry, psychotherapy, nutrition or other similarly scientifically sound publications, but also on my own work with hundreds of patients. Every statement or claim that I have made is numbered so that by checking the references at the end of the book you can find the original publication source.

While I was researching and writing, it became clear that often I was barely scraping the surface of a particular topic and indeed many of the chapters could have been turned into books by themselves. In the past I have heard reports being dismissed because 'It was only reported once and nobody else has ever been able to replicate it,' yet this was clearly untrue, as I discovered that sometimes contentious findings *had* been repeated and reported several times, but not always in an English language journal.

I think there is perhaps a tendency for doctors to read their national journals and not be so aware of what is published abroad. An example of this concerns an all-natural mushroom extract nicknamed 'Turkey Tail' in some Western countries. Although there are scant references to it in British medical journals and it is not really known here, based solely on Japanese sales it is the top-selling anti-cancer agent in the world, with over 400 reports of clinical trials published in medical journals, predominantly those of the Far East. I have tried to look at a larger picture and have drawn from journals published not only in Britain and the United States but also Europe, Russia and Japan.

So, whether you are looking for ways to help your own healing process or you want to help heal someone you love, this book contains a wealth of material that has been tried and tested by my own patients and in hundreds of clinical studies around the world. There is an enormous range of practices and techniques that you can use to your advantage. If you are ill, you may well find that simply doing something for yourself has a very empowering effect by making you realise that you are no longer a powerless victim of an illness that is treated by others. Patients, doctors, therapists, family members and friends can all help each other on the healing journey.

Chapter 1

THE HEALING JOURNEY

For almost all of my adult life I have worked as a healer. To be honest I don't really consider it to be either 'work' or 'a job', but almost a vocation or calling. I also realise how fortunate I am to be able to do something that gives me so much pleasure and others so much benefit. However, I can still get somewhat self-conscious when one of my patients expresses great gratitude for the help that I have been able to give them and I'll jokingly reply that 'It's just my job!'

Although I work from home, in the middle of the Suffolk country-side, my patients come from every part of Britain, all over Europe and as far away as the United States and Australia. They also come from every walk of life, demonstrating that illness is one of the greatest levellers. The fact that they are so motivated makes my time with them easier. They *want* to learn and to be helped. Occasionally, though, I do get an enquiry from somebody living just ten miles away, but they feel it is too far for them to travel – which says a lot about their level of motivation!

Some people are frightened and disorientated, others are angry and resentful; some are resigned, while others are filled with determination and hope. Almost all of them want to know what they can do to give themselves the greatest chance of beating their disease. Over the decades I have learned that there is much, much more to healing than the simple act of physically placing my hands on them.

My healing sessions generally last for half an hour, although they will often run for longer when I first meet somebody because I want to get to know them and offer the best advice, whether it is about a medical treatment that they have not heard of, supplements that might help them or self-help ideas that have been successful with other patients with the same problem. I may see some people just a few times for healing sessions and others on a regular basis, perhaps monthly, over a longer period of time.

Unfortunately, I cannot tell you how many sessions you may need and neither can I tell you whether my efforts are working. However, I hope to be honest and straightforward with my patients, although I sometimes find myself walking a fine line between encouraging hope and optimism, which you will see are so important to the healing process, and being realistic by avoiding excessive claims. I have always known that my work carries a great responsibility and that ill-chosen words can be harmful.

My healing room is bright and cheerful, being dominated by a warm yellow wallpaper with gold stars that leads many people to say what a beautifully sunny room it is, even when it is dull, grey and raining outside! From the outset, I hope to guide my patient towards a positive frame of mind.

When I am healing, I nearly always start by placing my hands on the patient's neck and shoulders. They might immediately feel great heat, perhaps accompanied by a tingling sensation, but may also feel nothing in particular, which does not mean that nothing is happening, as countless people have discovered. During those first few minutes, I am trying to gain what I call 'a sense of connection' with the person. I am aware that my breathing and my heartbeat slow down, that I become mostly unaware of the external environment and eventually I sense that somehow the patient and I have become linked together as one.

Now I will move my hands to the area or point that I intuitively become drawn to. While this is often the place of pain or disease, it may be to a quite different place. I have learned over the years to trust my guiding intuition and not to be concerned about the logical part of my brain telling me that I have got my hands on the wrong spot. I am sure there are connections between healing and acupuncture in so far as both would appear to be using energy meridian lines within the body. If you go to an acupuncturist with a problem in your liver, he may stick a needle in your ear, and the same applies to my healing work.

While I am working I will nearly always get sensations of heat and a tingling rather like a mild electric current, as well as what I can best describe as great energy surges which flow throughout by body. I also experience vivid images that are sometimes very abstract, at other times more literal, which have the quality of what is termed a 'waking dream state'. As I will explain in Chapter 8, music is an integral part of my healing sessions and I am aware that sometimes these images seem to be initiated by the music. I always know when the healing has come to an end because the physical sensations start to weaken and my imagery is replaced by conscious thought processes.

Everybody reacts differently to their sessions with me. You might find that quite unexpectedly you have a huge emotional outpouring and that tears are flowing down your cheeks, but you might just as easily find yourself sitting in my chair with a big blissful smile on your face! You might find, as many people seem to, that you go off into an almost dream-like state but you might also find yourself imagining a healthy future and setting goals for yourself. Sometimes somebody will tell me that they didn't feel or experience very much at all during the healing but that some hours or even days later emotions were released and pains eased.

Since I always work the same way, I have always been interested in why healing works sometimes, either partially or completely, while at other times it seems to be of little obvious benefit. Obviously, there are times when a disease is so aggressive and virulent that any amount of positive thinking and healing is going to have a limited physical effect. However, I am quite certain that the majority of the people with whom I have worked successfully have also played a substantial role in their own recovery through their own efforts.

I hope that the experiences and case histories that I am going to share with you will be helpful in understanding your own problems. Learning from the experiences of Gig and myself, my patients and medical researchers will be a major factor in maintaining your health. Self-healing requires us to take responsibility for our health and make a commitment to carry out what is needed to maintain it.

In the Laboratory

My journey as a healer began in the laboratory in the 1970s when I volunteered to participate in a wide range of experiments designed to test what effect, if any, my thoughts would have on a wide range of biological systems. Although I took part in many different tests, there were two that provided particularly striking results which showed it was clearly possible to demonstrate healing under scientifically controlled conditions in a laboratory.

If red blood cells are put in ordinary tap water the red corpuscles will expand and eventually burst, releasing haemoglobin. This process is known as haemolysis. However, if that water is made slightly saline, the red corpuscles are buffered and will remain intact for longer. As haemolysis proceeds, the blood-saline solution changes from cloudy to clear, so providing researchers with a measure of the rate of decay.

This particular experiment consisted of ten trials, each one measuring the rate of haemolysis of ten blood samples. Five of these were control samples and five were samples that I attempted to influence. During the control trials I tried not to think of the test tube of blood cells. When I was trying to heal, I placed my hands above the tube without touching it while imagining the cells surrounded by a brilliant white light. I assured the cells that the light and energy would protect them and that they would remain intact and resistant to the surrounding solution. The test results showed that the cells remained intact four times longer in the experiments in which I tried to heal than they did in the trials where I removed my influence. Dr William Braud, one of the scientists involved in the experiment, later told a newspaper:

By concentrating his mind on the test tube of blood, Matthew was able to slow down the death of the cells. Normally the blood cells would break down and die within a maximum of five minutes. But he was able to slow down the destruction so that the blood cells were still intact as long as twenty minutes later.

The second experiment was designed to discover whether I could disrupt the electrostatic charge on Hela cervical cancer cells in order to render them inactive. Named after Henrietta Lafayette, the black American woman from whom they were taken before her death in the 1950s, these cells are used extensively in cancer research laboratories around the world. The cells are grown in culture flasks (plastic containers which look similar to the cases of audio cassette tapes) in a liquid protein feed. When they are first placed in the flask they float in the liquid, but eventually they drop to the bottom of the flask, where they begin to grow. After several days the cells will cover the bottom surface of the flask, attaching themselves to the plastic by means of an electrostatic force produced by the positive/negative attraction between the cells and the flask. The cells themselves have a positive surface charge, while the flask has a negative charge. If that charge is broken, it causes the cell to float free in the medium in which it has been grown. In this state the cell is essentially inactive or dead.

Some cell death normally occurs in the tissue culture (usually in the order of about 1,000 cells per millilitre of liquid), so before each trial the researchers used a machine called a spectrophotometer to count the number of dead cancer cells to give them a control line or measure of the 'state of health' of the cultures. Each culture flask was then sealed with wax, to ensure that any attempt to physically break open the flask would be obvious, and placed on a level surface for me to heal. It was my job for the next twenty minutes to try to heal the cancer cells.

In some of the thirty trials I was permitted to hold the flask between my hands; in others I tried to influence the cells from a distance, while confined in an electrically shielded room. Somebody else who was not a healer was also given a flask of cells and had to mimic every movement I made. A third container was left in another part of the building and received no attention.

As with the blood cells, I tried to imagine the cancer cells surrounded by white light. After each trial the samples were placed again in the spectrophotometer and the cells were recounted. In each of the trials there was never any change in the number of dead cells in the flask that had been left in a different part of the building. Neither was there any change in the number of dead cells in the flask held by the control subject who tried to imitate my actions. However, in 27 out of the 30 trials there was a change in the number of cells in the flask I tried to influence, ranging in magnitude from 200 to 1,200 per cent changes. If at the beginning of the trial there was 1 dead cell per millilitre of liquid, after my healing intervention there were anything from 2 to 12 dead cells.

Dr William Braud, who observed these trials, described the results as 'impressive' and said, 'What Matthew has demonstrated is that he can influence cancer cells. There may be factors involved that could be used to heal oneself or heal others.'

I was interested to find out if this was correct. The answer, with a few provisos, was yes. By the early 1980s I had given up the research work, having been tested quite extensively over a five-year period, so that I could devote all my time to healing people rather than 'in vitro' samples.

Healing Others

Henrietta Trenner was one of my first patients. In 1981, she had been diagnosed with cancer of the pancreas, which generally has a poor prognosis, and her family had been told that she probably had about three months to live. In view of the advanced state of her disease, she received no medical treatment. After healing sessions with me all her symptoms disappeared. She finally died eighteen years later, in 1999, of heart failure at the age of seventy-seven.

In 1984, Dan, a fifty-five-year-old retired tax consultant, had been diagnosed with a rare form of cancer. He had a tumour the size of a small melon in his right adrenal gland and the cancer had also spread to his liver. He had lost six stone in weight; he felt constantly tired and was by his own admission 'in a very low state indeed'.

'Statistics showed that nobody with this form of cancer had survived. They said I would require an operation, and on being pressed they admitted the chances of a successful operation were about one in a hundred. Without the operation they told me I could put my affairs in order and look forward to about six months.' Dan declined the surgery. I felt, and Dan agreed, that he was so weak and ill that it would be best if I started by treating him quite intensively. He came to see me twice a day, every day for a week. 'After each visit, I felt in a really relaxed state. After my first visit to Matthew, I got back to my car and found that I was carrying my stick and that my pain had mostly gone,' Dan said. After a few months of treatment, by which time I was only treating him a couple of times a month, his brother, who was a doctor, found him 'in a remarkably good state, so much so that he suggested that we went out for a walk. We walked and walked and discovered that we'd done about five miles over the Chiltern Hills. I felt wonderful!'

In 1992, eight years after I first treated him, Dan got an unexpected letter from the hospital that first diagnosed his cancer, offering him the chance of an MRI scan. Dan's name had come up on their computer records and they were obviously surprised that he was still alive. The scan showed the tumour had completely disappeared. At the time of writing, seventeen years later, Dan is still alive.

Sheila's troubles began in 1983 when her doctors told her that she had incurable cancer of the cervix. Although initial radiotherapy seemed to have a positive effect, six months later the cancer had spread to the lining of her bladder. Her doctors wanted to carry out radical surgery, involving a colostomy and removal of her bladder. After her first appointment with me, Sheila asked me for my advice. I have never felt it right to tell my patients to follow or decline medical treatment.

Sheila began questioning the surgeon about the operation and analysing his answers. He told her that the operation would be long and difficult. Her bladder and other major parts would be removed. Even then she would face many problems, but she would have between five and ten more years of life. Without surgery she could expect to live between eighteen months and two years. Instead, for the next eighteen months I treated Sheila on a monthly basis.

She said, 'I decided not to have the operation, and once I made up my mind I felt really elated.' The healing obviously had a profound effect on her cancer. Sheila has not been for hospital treatment since refusing surgery and at the time of writing, seventeen years later, she is still alive.

Tuire Huttenen worked as a nurse in a private clinic in Helsinki, Finland, where she joined my seminar. I chose her for a healing demonstration at the end of the day because she suffered from rheumatoid arthritis and had great difficulty moving either her neck or wrist. She was also unable to bend her back. Before and after my healing demonstration a medical doctor in the audience checked her. After twenty minutes of healing she was able to move her wrist, turn her neck and bend her back.

Two years later Tuire joined another of my seminars and received further healing, but this time her doctor had taken a blood test two days previously. He took another one immediately afterwards. Her sedimentation rate, which is a reflection of the level of inflammation in her joints, was 48 mm per hour before she left. After the seminar it had dropped to 18 mm per hour, showing that inflammation was greatly reduced. A similarly dramatic drop occurred in her haemoglobin levels. Before the seminar it was 100, which is quite normal for somebody suffering from rheumatoid arthritis, yet five days later it was up to 135. According to her doctor there was no medical treatment available that could account for such a dramatic change. Later that year she sent me a Christmas card telling me that her sedimentation level was now 12 and her haemoglobin was 180, indicating that the healing had continued for quite some time after the original session. Proof indeed, it seems, that what can be demonstrated in a laboratory test tube can also occur in a human subject.

Obviously, these are just four case histories from thousands over the past twenty years. I deliberately chose them from the distant past to show the healing was lasting and permanent.

My Strategy for Healing

Although healing does not work for everybody, for reasons I cannot always understand, it certainly helps a good many. I have always been honest with people. At the start of their healing sessions with me I tell them that there are four possible outcomes:

1 It may be that I cannot do anything to help. From many years of experience, I would ask that I be given two, or possibly three, sessions of healing with a patient. If there is no appreciable benefit, I probably cannot do any more. If I reach this point my patient will sometimes say, 'It may not have made any difference physically, and I am still deteriorating, but now I feel much calmer and better able to deal with the situation.'

2 It may be that while the disease does not get any better, it does not get any worse. That in itself can be an achievement. I have worked with numerous patients who have come to me with a very poor life expectancy. Some, having been given six months to live, are still alive five or ten years later, by which time, as some of my patients have discovered, a new treatment to help them may be available.

3 Some patients find that although they have not totally recovered, they have experienced a considerable improvement. If I work with someone whose joints have been extensively damaged by arthritis, there is a limit as to how far I can help. However, I have always believed that my role as a healer is to improve *quality* of life, and I can achieve this by reducing or eliminating pain.

4 I always hope for a complete and permanent healing, and this does happen, as you will discover from many of the stories in this book. There is no doubt in my mind that those patients who do the best, those who beat a pessimistic prognosis and those who go on to make a full recovery, are those who are also prepared to work on themselves with the exercises and techniques that I will share with you.

The Power of Compassion

I have always felt that as a healer I am only channelling some form of universal, unconditional love. Although it may sound corny, those are the best words I can find to describe the healing experience.

I have never felt any great need to surround myself with props or tools in my work, but if they give somebody else confidence that's fine. Let me give you an example. You may have been out shopping on a busy afternoon when you notice a young mother with small children, one of whom trips and grazes its knee on the pavement. As the child starts crying, its mother instinctively kneels down beside it and places her hand on the scraped knee, counting from one to ten as she does so. By the count of ten, the pain has magically disappeared. As far as I am concerned, that mother has carried out a simple act of healing yet she has not put on a white coat, placed crystals on her child's chakras and brought out a bowl of cold water and a pile of white towels! That's fine if it is your approach to healing, but I don't believe you need those props to make it work. Rather than focus on jargon or symbols of healing, we need to learn how to improve ourselves and develop our compassionate side.

The wonderful thing about compassion is that the more developed it becomes, the less need there is for external symbols or tools. It also helps to lead you out of suffering because it concentrates your attention on others. I have always felt that compassion is crucially important in the healing process. Most of us, unless we are trained in one of the caring professions, have very limited experience of helping someone who is very ill, frightened or in pain and distress. Typically, we react by feeling terribly sorry for the suffering person, and therein lies one of the healer's first mistakes. With that response, we are reacting sympathetically and are therefore allowing our emotions to become sympathetically involved.

A wonderful example of this was when the film *Lawrence of Arabia*, the desert classic starring Peter O'Toole, first came out, there were reports that concession stands were inundated at intermissions with demands for drinks despite the fact that many of the cinemas were air-conditioned or in cool climates. A thirst epidemic hit many filmgoers as they became immersed in the hot, sandy story they were watching on screen. The moral of this incident is that the influential and even life-changing forces we encounter are often not those things that are externally real.

If you strike a tuning fork against a table it will start to vibrate in a certain frequency. If you hold a second tuning fork close to the first one, it will start to vibrate in resonance with the first one. Healers need to develop the ability to change the vibration of the first tuning fork, rather than resonate in sympathy with it. They need to work from a position of compassion rather than sympathy. For me, sympathy means that I become involved with my patient on an emotional level, but if I respond with compassion I still care deeply what happens to them but I am able to help them from a point of emotional non-attachment. Also, the more compassion you feel, the more you exude it to others and the more benefit you feel.

Learning to Listen

I feel that a good healer must also learn to listen without judgement. Often just having someone to talk to allows space for healing. Perhaps that is why so many hard-pressed and over-worked doctors do not get the results that some complementary therapists achieve. When the average time that a GP can spend with a patient in surgery is just seven minutes, it should not be surprising that the therapist who acts as a listening post for an hour or more often gets better results.

I have learned that words are extraordinarily powerful and people, especially when ill or vulnerable, may attach great significance to something I may have said flippantly. Just as words can convey so much, so too can the gaps and things that are not said.

Doctors and healers alike need to help patients discover meaning in their suffering and to make them feel understood, cared about and special. This requires eye contact – the patient needs to see that they are being listened to intently. It also needs presence, which means the ability to *feel*, by a leap of empathy, into another's state of mind.

Professor Miles Little, an Australian surgeon, believes that true healing is a lot more than getting rid of objective disease and that an ill doctor, or wounded healer, ought to be able to provide what he calls a 'novelty of insight' into the experience of what it is to be ill. Having worked with thousands of ill people for twenty years, I was about to discover for myself just what he meant. Together with my wife, Gig, I found myself on a journey that would bring me to a far greater understanding.

My Healing Journey

The Diagnosis

I am not normally a superstitious person but I do know that 13 July, 1998 was one of the worst days of my life. It was the day that Gig was diagnosed with cancer. Somebody once said, rather aptly, that the experience of being diagnosed with cancer is comparable to being thrown out of a helicopter over a guerrilla war zone with a parachute but no compass, no weapons, no map and no training in survival. We can all pride ourselves on being understanding and compassionate, but none of us knows what someone else is going through until, filled with fear and confusion, we have gone through it ourselves.

At the beginning of 1998, Gig had developed what she thought were haemorrhoids and had started visiting different complementary practitioners for help. I had been rather sceptical about the wisdom of this without a proper medical diagnosis. Obviously, I am all for complementary therapies so long as they are proven and that the therapists know what they are dealing with. However, none of the remedies she tried was successful in healing the problem and she then began to develop worrying symptoms, including acute pain.

We were lucky in that we had an extremely good GP who, having carried out an examination, diagnosed thrombotic haemorrhoids, which he thought would have to be surgically removed. Within three days Gig was referred to a consultant at our local hospital who, although he didn't say it, obviously did not like the look of what he saw and arranged for a biopsy to be carried out under a general anaesthetic.

A few days later Gig and I returned to his office to find out the results. He had found, he explained, a tumour about the size of a large tomato and the biopsy had confirmed that it was malignant. My brain seemed numbed and paralysed and I simply couldn't think straight. I cancelled all my appointments for the week, as it would have been dishonourable for me to continue working with my patients when I couldn't even focus properly.

It was arranged that Gig and I should see an oncologist, a woman in her late thirties. For years I had heard my patients' complaints about doctors' lack of communication skills. This doctor had none at all and made no effort to disguise the fact. On the rare occasions that she made eye contact it was always with me, but mostly she directed her gaze away from us both. This was not a promising start, but as she talked it got worse. We wanted to know what might have caused the cancer. She said she didn't know, but it was a rare cancer affecting only about 300 people a year in Britain, of whom 200 are over the age of 70. In a handful of cases in men, it was AIDS related. This piece of information was tossed out almost as an aside and at this point Gig began to panic. The oncologist was oblivious to her reaction and ploughed on with her proposals for treatment.

This would involve chemotherapy and radiotherapy followed by a radioactive implant, known as a radioactive 'hedgehog'. Although we didn't know it at the time, and the oncologist did not tell us, we later discovered that the proposed procedure with the radioactive implant was part of a clinical trial.

Having already got a negative feeling about her, our attitude did not change after she had described the treatment. We both felt from the start that even if we were to follow the route she was suggesting, it would have to be with someone we could relate to and who acknowledged and understood our fears and anxieties. At this early stage I felt it was essential to get a second or even third opinion. We also wanted to find out just what alternatives, if any, were available.

First Steps

One of my patients had told me about a clinic in southern Germany that carried out numerous treatments, some controversial, which were not easily available in Britain. One of their treatments was based on the principle that cancerous tumours do not like changes in temperature, so if the temperature in the surrounding tissue can be either raised or lowered, the tumour tends to shrink. Gig and I wanted to visit this clinic before we made any decision about which treatment to follow. The oncologist was very sceptical and told us that this type of treatment had been known about since the eighteenth century. I asked if it would be safe for us to delay any treatment decision for two or three weeks and, although she agreed to this, she warned that she did not want to delay treatment any longer than that. The next day she telephoned me at home to say that it would not matter where we went in the world or whom we saw, because they would only suggest the same treatment that she was recommending. She then tried to persuade me into getting Gig to accept her proposed medical treatment.

A couple of days later we flew out to the German clinic with high hopes. We had heard good reports about it and by following this path Gig could avoid having chemotherapy and radiotherapy. However, it did not take long for us to realise that this was not the answer. The atmosphere was hard, almost military, we got no sense of care or compassion and there were desperately sick people everywhere, in corridors and on staircases, waiting for treatment. The German doctor we met wanted to use what he called 'galvo' treatment on Gig's tumour. This would involve passing an electric current directly into the tumour through a very fine wire. He assured us that it would be completely effective and the tumour would be gone after ten days. I trusted neither him nor his claim.

As we were waiting in the reception area just before we left, I struck up a conversation with a very pleasant and knowledgeable American doctor who had come over to look at the clinic with a view to possibly sending some of his patients there. I asked for his opinion on the treatment suggested by the clinic for Gig's tumour. He felt the cancer might temporarily disappear, but the treatments were stop-gaps and not cures. When we got back to England both Gig and I felt very low because we had thought that the clinic would provide the answer.

We had also heard about another doctor working in England who had claimed to have very good results with cancer patients. Now no longer working as a medical practioner, he was using a wide array of complementary therapies. We drove for three hours to meet him. He asked questions and listened attentively for over an hour and a half before saying that he was sure he could help.

He connected Gig to what he called a Vega testing machine. This apparently allowed him to measure the electrical resistance at acupuncture points. It is claimed that higher or lower readings than normal at a particular acupuncture point indicate a problem in the organ that corresponds to that point. To date there are over 2,000 such points that have been established as having specific relationships with internal organs. A skilled therapist can, in theory, discover not only which organs have problems, but also which part of the organ is malfunctioning and what other organs, if any, it is affecting. Thus it becomes possible to find the root of any problem. It is a form of electro-acupuncture biofeedback. It is also claimed that if the patient holds a sample homoeopathic solution of known disease substances such as bacteria, viruses, or diseased tissue, when they hold the one directly related to the cause of the problem, the reading on the Vega machine will return to normal. In this way it is supposed to be possible to detect almost every known disease, chemical toxin, food allergy and disregulation in organ and glandular systems. It can also be used to test various remedies to determine which medication will correct the problem.

Having prodded and probed various acupuncture points on Gig's hands and feet for another one-and-a-half hours, the medical practitioner announced that not only had the cancer been caused by an Epstein-Barre virus, but that he had the antidote for it and the cancer would be gone in a matter of weeks. I asked him what his level of success was in treating cancer. When he told me that it was 60 per cent, I wondered why this was not a standard form of cancer treatment.

We also heard of a herbal preparation that was made up to a secret formula for which great claims were made. Although Gig used it for a while, I think we both became rather suspicious when it emerged that in Britain alone there were four people selling this concoction, all claiming to have 'exclusive' access to the original formula. One of my patients was later told by one of the vendors of this preparation that it had a 98 per cent success rate. If this outrageous claim were true, there would be little further need for cancer research, chemotherapy, radio-therapy or surgery!

Treatment Decisions

Gig would have been happy to have let me give her healing and not to have had any medical treatment, but I was not prepared to take on that responsibility. I gave her healing each day and she decided that she would not follow any form of treatment or therapy that was exclusive to another, whether orthodox or complementary. I suppose we were much luckier than most because, by virtue of my work and contacts, I could find the people who could best advise us on the various options we had. In the end it was up to Gig to decide on the treatment she wanted.

I was becoming acutely aware that days and weeks were ticking by and that if we were to believe the first oncologist, time was not on our side. I suggested to Gig that we seek an appointment with Professor Karol Sikora at Hammersmith Hospital in London, the one person I would always go to if I were in Gig's situation.

I had first met Professor Sikora in the late 1980s when I had given a talk about my work to medical students at Hammersmith Hospital and had been very impressed by his relaxed manner and his receptiveness to different ideas. More recently he had been seconded to the World Health Organisation, where he was chief of their cancer programme, and was therefore only working part time at the Hammersmith. Gig was very lucky to get an appointment within three days of our GP writing and mentioning my name. It was also a significant turning-point.

Having studied the CAT (computerised axial tomography) scans and examined Gig, Professor Sikora advised us not to rush into any form of treatment. He thought the tumour might be operable, which from Gig's point of view might have been preferable to chemotherapy and radio-therapy. I asked him the same questions that I'd asked the first oncolo-gist: Why had this happened? What had caused it? He didn't know either and because it was such an unusual cancer, especially in someone of Gig's age, he could not draw any conclusions. He estimated that the tumour might have been there for up to five years. In his opinion, if anyone had to have cancer, this particular tumour was the best kind to have because it grows very slowly and tends not to spread. He advised us to talk to the surgeon before making any decisions. There was no rush and nothing untoward would happen with the cancer while we were making up our minds.

The difference between that meeting and the first one with the oncol-ogist was extraordinary. Both doctors were cancer specialists, so their depth of knowledge of the subject must be comparable. Yet one could have been forgiven for thinking that they were considering different cases. Why didn't the first oncologist tell us that the tumour had probably been there for five years, was very slow growing and was of a type that tends not to produce secondaries? Needlessly she had given us the impression that the prognosis was gloomy when in fact it was about as positive as any diagnosis of cancer can be.

We went to see the colo-rectal surgeon with our hopes high that this would avoid the need for chemotherapy and radiotherapy. We were to be disappointed, though, because in his opinion surgery was not the solution, unless Gig was prepared to have a permanent colostomy.

The consultant who had performed the first biopsy on Gig had warned us right at the start not to search for information on the Internet, as much of it was misleading or wrong. Having studiously followed his advice, several people then sent me information about anal cancer that they had found on the Internet. I realised then why we had been advised not to search there. I now read the figures and learned that with the kind of cancer Gig had there was a life expectancy of seventeen months. I was devastated. I was also very angry when I discovered that for $500 you could call up the doctor who published this information for further details.

Commonsense should have reminded me that such statistics are unhelpful and do not differentiate between types of tumour and their behaviour patterns. There are in fact about 200 different kinds of cancer. Like most people for whom cancer becomes a reality, the word does not reflect such distinctions and so one goes through a nightmare phase of being prey to one's worst fears. Once Gig opted for treatment at Hammersmith Hospital, I threw out much of the material.

There were books that really offered insight, help and inspiration by doctors such as Bernie Siegel and Andrew Weil, and these were much more helpful in directing us towards decisions and choices. In his wonderful book *Spontaneous Healing*, Andrew Weil had written:

> I maintain that the final common cause of all cures is the healing system, whether or not treatment is applied. When treatments work, they do so by activating innate healing mechanisms. Treatment – including drugs and surgery – can facilitate healing and remove obstacles to it, but treatment is not the same as healing. Treatment originates outside you; healing comes from within. Nonetheless, to refuse treatment while waiting for healing can be foolish.

The Treatment

We were told that Gig's proposed treatment would last seven weeks. The first stage would involve chemotherapy in weeks one and five and radiotherapy every day for five weeks. There would then be a break of two weeks, followed by two further weeks of radiotherapy.

One consultant oncologist handling Gig's treatment, a lovely and kind lady called Dr Pat Price, told us that the tumour would probably still be there after the seven weeks of treatment, but that the radiotherapy continues to work for months afterwards while the body breaks down and disposes of the dead tumour.

Like most other people in our predicament, we were both concerned that the chemotherapy would have unpleasant side-effects and that Gig would lose her hair. Thankfully, the drug she was given – 5FU (5-fluoro-uracil) – did not cause this to happen and there are many other forms of chemotherapy that do not either.

In addition to the conventional treatment, Gig took full advantage of the complementary therapies on offer at the hospital. These included aromatherapy, reflexology and massage, all of which the nurses had noticed were often better at controlling the side-effects of the medical treatment than anti-nausea drugs, for example. Gig had already contacted the Bristol Cancer Care Centre for advice on vitamins and minerals and began also taking these.

I know that healing does not cure every ill and when I began treating Gig I could no more guarantee her a successful outcome than I could any of my other patients, but I gave her healing every day until she began to experience the side-effects of the radiotherapy treatment.

Having completed the first five weeks of treatment at the Hammersmith, Gig was examined and given an X-ray. Although I was outside the X-ray room I knew that something had happened when I heard Gig shout in a positive and excited voice, 'YES!' The good news was that just this far through the treatment, the tumour had gone. The not such good news was that the doctors wanted her to complete the final two weeks of treatment. When you are in that situation you want to do all you can to ensure that not only has the cancer gone, but that it will never come back.

The final phase of the treatment was followed by a series of monthly check-ups and, at the end of April 1999, a CAT scan. We were lucky not to have to wait more than a few hours for the scan result. Pat Price came out of her office into the reception area where we were waiting, beamed at us and put both thumbs up. When she had finished explaining that the results were so good that there would be no need for further tests, she said to Gig, 'You are now an ex-cancer patient. Go home and get on with your life.'

Afterwards

Once life settled down to normal again I also spent a great deal of time thinking about our healing journey. More than anything, I realised how very difficult that same journey must be for anybody who is diagnosed with a serious or life-threatening illness simply because there is so much conflicting information and there are so many very seductive claims.

And yet, as I began to discover, there is a huge wealth of information on what you *can* do to help your own healing processes. Most of this is published in scientific journals. I felt there was a great need for a book for people who found themselves in our situation, based on what has already been established. You can waste an enormous amount of money and, more dangerously, time, on treatments that don't work and which have not stood up to any form of critical scrutiny. I have always believed that neither orthodox medicine nor complementary therapists such as myself necessarily have all the answers. This is one of the first things that I tell any new patient. The way ahead has to lie in cooperation rather than conflict.

How to Communicate with Your Doctor or Therapist

Whatever your illness, and whatever stage of your healing journey you are at, it might be helpful to consider the following points that Gig and I used:

○ If you are really going to work in partnership with your doctor, you must trust them. Communication skills are vital to this process. If you don't tell you doctor that you don't under-stand what they are telling you, they will be likely to repeat the same mistake each time you see them. Ask lots of questions before you have tests or treatment:

● What tests will I need?

● What do these tests involve?

● When do I get the results?

● What treatments are there to choose from?

● What are the risks or benefits of these treatments?

- How long will the treatments last?

- What have the results been in the longer term?

❍ You have a right to a second opinion. Although you may have to fight for it, do not let misguided loyalty or the fear of upsetting a doctor get in the way of what's best for *you*. Many doctors are involved in running clinical trials and you might be recommended a treatment that happens to relate to a current trial. As Gig and I discovered, you may not always be informed of this. If you are being rushed into a particular course of treatment, you should be cautious. You should always be clear about the pros and cons of various treatment options before coming to any decision.

❍ Treat with great caution any exaggerated or wild claims of complementary therapists. If they claim to have had many successes with treating a particular illness, ask if you could talk to a couple of former patients.

❍ Be very wary of any complementary therapist who says they can only treat you if you stop receiving medical treatment. Recently one of my patients embarked on a very strict diet recommended to her by a 'nutritionist'. After a couple of months it seemed to be having no beneficial effect and her therapist told her that it was because she was still taking prescribed medication. The diet, she was told, would only work if her anti-cancer drugs were not interfering with it. Foolishly, she stopped taking them and almost paid for the consequences with her life. She spent two weeks seriously ill in hospital and only started to recover again when she resumed her prescribed medication.

❍ Always check a therapist's credentials or qualifications and do not necessarily accept somebody else's recommendation of them.

❍ Learn to trust your own inner feelings about what is right for you and what is helping.

For most people, the diagnosis of a serious or life-threatening illness forces them to shake hands with chaos. You might perhaps wonder if God is punishing your wickedness or, more benignly, trying to encourage you to attend to the spiritual side of life. If you are more secular minded, you might find that psychology helps you. You might go back through your past, looking for childhood trauma or a pattern in your family history that has got you into this situation. If you are politically minded, your theme may be the damage of racism or another form of oppression. As a healer, I have learned over the past twenty-five years that people who can make sense of their illness, who can repair their life story, have a far better chance of healing, or else a far better death, which is the ultimate healing journey.

I have discovered that my patients need recognition, not just of themselves, but as people experiencing a threat to their lives. It is often difficult for someone else to understand such an important and frightening experience, but it is that understanding that the patient so often needs. Because we all have different life-stories and have developed different values, fears and prejudices, it can be difficult to experience what someone else may be going through. Yet at another level, close to healing, we can all aspire to understand the experience of illness because we all share the experience of living.

Chapter 2

THE IMMUNE SYSTEM

Inside your body is an amazing protection mechanism called the immune system. It is designed to defend you against millions of bacteria, microbes, viruses, toxins and parasites that would love to invade your body. It is a complex network of specialised cells and organs that has evolved to defend the body against attacks by 'foreign' invaders. When functioning properly it fights off infections by agents such as bacteria, viruses, fungi and parasites. When it malfunctions, it can unleash a torrent of diseases from allergy to arthritis to cancer to AIDS.

The immune system evolved because we live in a sea of microbes. Like man, these organisms are programmed to perpetuate themselves. The human body provides an ideal habitat for many of them and they try to break in, but because the presence of these organisms is often harmful, the body's immune system will try to block their entry or, failing that, to seek out and destroy them.

One of my passions in life is my garden, although during the summer months I do sometimes complain about having to cut the grass so often. I put the grass cuttings by the barrow-load onto the compost heap along with other garden waste. Within a couple of weeks the huge pile of cuttings has been reduced right down as nature starts turning the decomposed cuttings to mulch. We have many of those same forces acting on us but the reason we don't become mulch is that our immune system protects us.

The immune system is equal in complexity to the intricacies of the brain and nervous system and displays remarkable characteristics. It can distinguish between 'self' and 'non-self'. Not only is it able to recognise many millions of distinctive non-self molecules, but it can also produce molecules and cells to counteract each one of them. It is also able to remember previous experiences and react accordingly. Once you have had chicken pox, your immune system will prevent you from getting it again.

The success of this system in defending the body relies on an incredibly elaborate and dynamic regulatory-communications network. Millions and millions of cells, organised into sets and subsets, pass information back and forth like clouds of bees swarming around a hive. The result is a sensitive system of checks and balances that produce an immune response that is prompt, effective and self-limiting. It is when this breaks down that problems arise. So in order to know how you can help heal yourself, you need to know a little about how this system works.

The Discovery of the Immune System

From the middle of the nineteenth century, tens of thousands of people left their homes all over Europe in order to try to realise their dreams of wealth and fortune in America. In search of land and better prospects, the settlers began moving westward across North America, often finding themselves in far-flung places that lacked many of the necessities of life. Ministers, doctors, teachers, lawyers and other professional people were in short supply and self-appointed doctors became commonplace. Often these were men who had no medical training other than having spent some time working with a doctor. But a self-appointed doctor was better than no doctor at all.

One such 'doctor' and lay-healer was Dr H. C. F. Meyer, who hailed from Germany but found himself in a place called Pawnee in Nebraska. He almost certainly had no medical training and was probably illiterate. In 1886, he enthusiastically informed a Professor John King that he had been using a certain plant for the previous sixteen years and concluded that it was 'an antispasmodic and antidote for blood-poisoning'. Knowing nothing about the botany of the plant, he had been using it in a secret mixture with hops and wormwood. His many successes were widely reported and he quickly built up a reputation for healing cases as diverse as snakebites, diphtheria and other infections.

What was not clear was whether these successful treatments were the result of Meyer's healing abilities or the pills that he sold. Nevertheless, he recommended his wonder cure for almost every conceivable illness, calling it 'Meyer's Blood Purifier'. It contained a root extract that had, ironically, been used extensively by Native Americans who had found it healed abscesses, wounds, insect bites, burns, infections and joint pains. They also knew it as an antidote to rattlesnake bites. Indeed, Meyer claimed that he had allowed a rattlesnake to bite him, then bathed the bite with some of the tincture, drunk some of it and laid down and slept. Upon awaking, all traces of swelling had gone.

Although Meyer's patients and the Native Americans knew that the root extract worked, no one knew why. It would not be until early in the twentieth century that the mystery was solved.

In 1882, at about the same time as Meyer was proclaiming his 'blood purifier', a Ukrainian zoologist and microbiologist by the name of Elie Metchnikoff was on holiday in Italy off the coast of Sicily. He decided to collect some larvae from a species of small transparent starfish. Taking them back to his laboratory, he put them under his microscope and introduced some splinters and particles of vivid crimson dye into them. He then watched in amazement as a group of cells that were completely unconnected to the digestive system began to eat the dye and the splinters.

Not really sure of what he was witnessing, Metchnikoff then pricked the starfish with a thorn. He saw the primitive creature 'defend' itself against the invading thorn with a group of aggressive and war-like macrophages. These tiny swooping 'vacuum cleaner' cells became the start of the modern study of immunology and in 1908 Metchnikoff was awarded the Nobel Prize for Physiology and Medicine for his crucial discovery.

What We Know Today

A hundred years later we know far, far more than Metchnikoff would ever have dreamed of and yet there is still so much that remains a mystery. That is hardly surprising when you consider that the immune system alone is made up of a million million cells – or one million groups each with one million members. In 1984 the Danish scientist Niels Jerne was also awarded the Nobel Prize for his work in immunology. He envisioned the immune system as a massive orchestra, all playing together, but each member playing a different instrument – each cell reacting only to those body invaders that it alone could tackle. Jerne's 'network' theory suggested that the immune system cells, through a remarkable technique of cloning, alter themselves to meet whatever invader arrives on the scene and then shut themselves off when they are not needed.

Sadly, most of the information on the workings of our immune system tends to be technical, difficult to understand or in academic journals, which means that most of us have little idea of the amazing biological miracle that keep us healthy every moment of the day and night. We might have a general idea that our white blood cells make up our immune system, but it is far more complicated than that!

The Army within You

I have often observed in the countryside pubs around Suffolk old men, often well into their eighties, who have been smoking since they were about twelve years old. Yet most of them have not developed lung cancer. Likewise, I treat a number of people who are HIV-positive and none of them has yet gone on to develop any symptoms of AIDS because their immune systems are strong enough to prevent disease from taking hold. If the immune system is strong, people stay well.

In order to know how we can keep our immune system functioning, or to give it a boost, we need to know how it works. The immune system forms the most remarkable army, together with an extraordinary arsenal of weapons with which to fend off invaders.

How the Immune System Works

Basically, the blood circulating within our bodies consists of red blood cells, which mainly carry oxygen around the body, and white blood cells which defend us. Within those white blood cells is housed a variety of cells that make up the immune system – the macrophages, microphages, neutrophils, lymphocytes, granulocytes, B cells, T cells, natural killer cells, K cells, as well as cytokines, interleukins and immunoglobulins. Here is a brief summary of what they do:

Macrophages

Translated from its Greek name, this means 'big eater'. These are the generals of the army, highly intelligent and also great scavengers. On average there are around 100,000 macrophages per millilitre of blood.

Lymphocytes

Second in command are the lymphocytes, which are formed within our bone marrow. However, a remarkable phenomenon occurs as they leave there and move either to our thymus or to our intestine, where they will start to mature. Thus we have both T lymphocytes and B lymphocytes, each carrying out quite different functions.

T lymphocytes, known as T cells, mature in the thymus, a gland behind the breastbone, and learn to become 'helper cells', killing cells that are infected with viruses, alien cells from transplanted organs and abnormal cells. You can also imagine them as the sharpshooters of the army as they can zero in on an infected cell right next to a normal cell and destroy it without harming the healthy cell.

There are actually different types of T cells and they not only orchestrate many immune functions but are also a major factor in protecting us against the development of cancer, autoimmune disorders such as rheumatoid arthritis and allergies. There are helper T cells, which literally help other white blood cells to function; suppressor T cells, which inhibit white blood cell function; and cytoxic T cells, which attack and destroy foreign tissue, cancer cells and virus-infected cells.

The ratio of helper T cells to suppressor T cells is useful in determining the strength of the immune system. For example, AIDS is characterised by a very low ratio of helper T cells to suppressor T cells. With this ratio, autoimmune problems such as allergies, lupus and rheumatoid arthritis often occur.

B lymphocytes mature in the intestine and go on to mature into cells that secrete a number of different proteins, known as antibodies, that act like 'smart bombs' and interact with their target with extraordinary precision.

Granulocytes

Quite violent and blunt in their work, granulocytes shoot first and ask questions later. They circulate in the blood and enter tissue at the very first sign of infection. They maintain health in localised parts of the body, turning up almost like paramedics at accidents – the cuts, bruises and places infected by bacteria. They take their name from the fact that under a microscope you can see granules within the cell.

Neutrophils

Neutrophils literally try to neutralise invaders. They are the foot soldiers of our immune system who carry out the macrophage orders. They die within twenty-four hours and new recruits must then be brought in.

Natural killer cells

The natural killer cells can be seen as the immune system's elite SAS hit squad. First discovered in 1975, they are programmed to kill tumour cells on sight. They are a bad-tempered group who do not like viruses and hate tumours, the mere sight of which makes them attack. They are small and armed with granules inside the cell that, like bullets, penetrate the cancer cell and destroy it.

Internal Communication

So quite how do all these different regiments and platoons communicate with each other? The answer is by a complex method of chemical messengers. When the macrophages recognise bacteria, viruses or cancer cells, they release numerous chemicals known as a group as cytokines. Among these is yet another family called interleukins which cause immune cells to mature more quickly. They also produce inflammation, which increases blood flow and heat to the affected area, leading to those aches and pains you may get when you are coming down with something.

The B cells are also stimulated by interleukins and begin to confront the invader, ready to produce specific chemicals, or antibodies, which will combat disease. They then carry out what amounts to a wonderful 'sting operation' by coating the invading organism with a kind of chemical that attracts macrophages and granulocytes. It's rather like attracting wasps to a jar of honey. On finally meeting the invader, the B cells transform themselves into plasma cells, which in turn secrete substances known as immunoglobulins, which are a kind of 'smart bomb'.

There are five different kinds of B cell: IgG, IgA, IgM, IgE and IgD. Ig is the abbreviation for 'immunoglobulin', which is a synonym for 'antibody'. Many foreign invaders, disease-causing toxins and microorganisms are quickly made harmless by the simple attachment of these antibodies.

Once an attack on the body has been successfully repelled, not all of the immunoglobulins or antibodies disappear. Some of them will stay around, rather like a peacekeeping force after a war. The immune system never forgets an encounter, a skirmish or a battle and the information on how it dealt with it is stored away. If at a later time that same invader appears again, it knows exactly what to do. This of course is the principle behind vaccination: you are given a very mild dose of the disease so that should you ever encounter it again the immune system immediately launches a very powerful response.

When the Immune System Breaks Down

What happens, though, if there is a communications breakdown within the many regiments, platoons and foot soldiers of the immune system? Two of my patients, with quite different problems, found out.

Carole had suffered from systemic lupus for twenty years and she was rapidly deteriorating when I first met her in 1996. Lupus is a chronic disease that affects the connective tissue (tissue that binds and supports various structures of the body and also includes the blood). Carole was experiencing severe pain in various joints, and muscular contraction which had left her unable to walk unassisted. After I had given her healing sessions once a month for several months, most of her symptoms had gone and she was walking with ease and without pain.

Joshua was just three years old when his mother wrote to me in desperation about his multiple allergies, which seemed to have started shortly after he had had his vaccinations. He was suffering from severe food intolerances that were causing eczema, conjunctivitis, and flu-like symptoms, and worst of all a chronic cough that woke him up throughout the night.

'He cannot have any sweets, even honey, wheat, oats, corn or other glutens, any dairy foods or ice cream, no fast food or processed foods. During a flare-up, Joshua becomes very weepy, irrational and very hyperactive. I have a master's degree in Learning Disabilities and can tell you he is not hyperactive. He is just a different person during flare-ups. He also gets pimples and spots on his cheeks and on his back. It hurts me so much to see him unable to have a birthday cake or a sweet, and to hear him coughing non-stop,' his mother wrote.

After just one session many of Joshua's symptoms simply disappeared and after three or four sessions all his allergies had cleared. 'The result has been what we feared,' his father wrote tongue-in-cheek. 'Ice cream, French fries and sweets have become his favourite treats.' Of course, what child doesn't love going to MacDonald's? I was more than happy to help Joshua fulfil his dream!

For both Carole and Joshua, their immune system had turned from being their friend to being their foe. Suddenly the immune system defenders turned against their own body and became the enemy, leading to what is known as autoimmune disease. Examples of this are rheumatoid arthritis, systemic lupus erythematosus, allergies and multiple sclerosis.

In an inflamed arthritic joint, for example, there are increased levels of neutrophils that release an enzyme called myeloperoxidase as well as increased levels of cytokines. Quite why neutrophils gather in the joint is still not clearly understood, but it is thought that myeloperoxidase causes the macrophages to embark on a war of self-destruction.[1] Part of the macrophages' weaponry is the release of high levels of cytokines, including one known as tumour necrosis factor, which is pivotal in continuing the cycle of inflammation, experienced by those who suffer from rheumatoid arthritis. It starts a cytokine torrent that brings about a spiral of joint pain and destruction.

There are many different ways in which the immune system can turn against the body. In multiple sclerosis it attacks nerve cells and in systemic lupus it destroys many different cells throughout the body.

Immunity and the Nervous System

A startling breakthrough was to change the way that orthodox medicine understood the immune system with the publication of the groundbreaking work done by Robert Ader, a psychologist working at the School of Medicine and Dentistry at the University of Rochester, published in 1974. He discovered that our immune system, just like our brain, could learn! Prior to this, scientists believed that the immune system worked completely independently of any other system in the body. A suggestion that susceptibility to or recovery from disease might be linked with mental or emotional states had been curiously dismissed as unscientific and irrelevant.

Little had been known about how the brain communicated with the organs and cells of the body. Then David Felten, a colleague of Ader's, carried out further extensive research which revealed that our emotions have a very marked effect on the autonomic nervous system, which regulates many things in our body – from blood-pressure levels to the amount of insulin that is released. He and his colleagues discovered a meeting point where the autonomic nervous system is in communication directly with the lymphocytes and macrophages, the immune system. Using powerful electron microscopes they saw areas of contact between the two which were allowing the nerve cells to release neurotransmitters to regulate the immune cells and vice versa. It was another extraordinary finding that shook the scientific understanding of mind–body connections. Felten continued his research and came to the conclusion that the nervous system is also connected to the immune system and absolutely essential for normal immune function in animals.

An Australian scientific researcher, R. W. Bartrop, published the first work that showed a similar link between immunity and the nervous system in humans in the *Lancet* in 1975. He and his colleagues in New South Wales had been carefully studying the effects of bereavement and in particular its effect on physical health and immune function. They followed twenty-six surviving spouses of patients who had been either killed in accidents or died from natural causes.

As well as offering counselling to the bereaved, they recorded the changes in their immune functions in the weeks following the losses. By taking blood samples from the bereaved spouses and comparing them with samples from a non-bereaved group, they discovered that the immune systems of the grieving spouses showed a much-lowered activity of the T cells.[2] It was the very first time that anybody had been able to show a measurable depression of immune function following severe psychological real life stress.

In 1983 a group of researchers from the Mount Sinai School of Medicine in New York City published a paper in the *Journal of the American Medical Association* which supported the Australian findings, but took them further. Men who were married to women in the advanced stages of breast cancer showed a drop in the responsiveness of their lymphocytes after the deaths of their wives which continued for about two months. Soon after that their immune functions began to pick up again and between four and fourteen months after the deaths, the men began to recover their immune functioning and their feeling of bereavement lessened.[3]

By this time conventional medical authorities seemed to have fairly easily started to accept the idea that negative emotional states adversely affect the immune system, but for some reason they were initially sceptical about the idea that positive emotional states can actually enhance immune function. Immunologists were also sceptical about the suggestion that this sort of research result would have any relevance to immunology. Twenty years later we know they were wrong. It is now clear that not only does the brain communicate with the immune system, but the immune system also talks to the brain.

It would have been strange if there were no connection, since all the organs of immunity, such as the thymus gland, spleen and bone marrow, are covered with nerve endings that connect back to the brain. Intertwined with these pathways are many endocrine factors that control or improve both the brain's and the immune system's responses to infection, disease and recovery.

Discovery of the link between the two has led to a new scientific discipline called 'psychoneuroimmunology' – or the relationship between brain, behaviour and immunity. In order to better understand the importance of this and how it affects our health, we need to also look at our nervous system.

The Structure of the Nervous System

The nervous system is actually comprised of overlapping systems. The first is the central nervous system, which consists of the brain and the spinal cord. Then there is the peripheral nervous system, consisting of the autonomic nervous system, which is concerned with heart rate, glandular function and the smooth muscles of the digestive tract, over which we have little conscious control, and the voluntary nervous system, which connects the central nervous system to all the body tissues and voluntary muscles.

At this point it is the workings of the autonomic nervous system that are of interest to us. It has two arms, one known as the *sympathetic nervous system* and the other as the *parasympathetic nervous system*. The sympathetic nervous system prepares our internal organs for emergencies and times when extra demands are made on our body. It operates 'in sympathy' with our emotions and tends to be activated by excitement, ecstasy or emergency. It can be seen as an accelerator telling the body to act. It is now also known that stimulation of the sympathetic nervous system can lead to immune suppression.

The parasympathetic nervous system is more like a brake, in that it is much more conservative and is responsible for withdrawal and returning the body to normal after excitement or emergency. It also controls our bodily functions during times of rest, relaxation, sleep, visualisation or meditation. In the deepest stages of sleep, potent immune-enhancing chemicals are released and many immune functions are greatly increased.

Emotions and Immunity

Mental stress can bring about real physiological changes in our bodies in just the same way as a real physical stress. Whenever we are stressed, whatever the cause, early signals being sent by the brain cause a change in the body's physiology. Nerves release chemicals called adrenaline and noradrenaline which cause the heart to beat faster and blood pressure to rise, preparing the body to act. Blood vessels to the muscles are relaxed so there is the energy supply necessary to deal with a sudden burst of activity. Other blood vessels are reduced so that not so much blood reaches other parts of the body, like the gut. A flood of hormones is released into the blood, along with lymphocytes and granulocytes. The whole body is now primed to react to the stress.

Now we can start to get a better understanding of why the surviving partners of spouses who had died were found to have depressed immune-system functioning. When we become stressed and the level of the hormones cortisol and adrenaline rise, they start to adversely affect our lymphoid cells and to suppress our immune functions, bringing an increased susceptibility to disease. They also suppress the release of cytokines, the messengers used by the immune system cells, and they influence the production of immunoglobulin. So the stress reactions alter our immune functions. But, as we will see later, knowing how this works has enabled us to use it to heal ourselves.

In a well-known study, Paul Ekman from the University of California, San Francisco, showed that if you deliberately contort your facial muscles into expressions of fear, anger or happiness, you will soon start to *feel* those emotions.[4] However, researcher Nicholas Hall and his colleagues reported something even more dramatic, which could have important implications for all of us. They measured changes in the immune systems of two actors before, during and after they had performed in two plays. The first was a comedy called *Lucy Does a TV Commercial* and the second was a serious play whose main theme was depression, *It's Cold, Wanderer, It's Cold*, which was set in a prison cell on the eve of the execution of an assassin. The researchers began taking blood samples and measuring the heart rate of the two actors before they had even read the scripts. They were then monitored throughout their rehearsals and every subsequent performance. The actors performed at the same time each day for a fortnight before a different audience.

To their surprise, Hall and his colleagues found a direct correlation between the type of personality being performed and immune response. After the *Lucy* comedy, the female actress showed increases in her immune functions and after she performed a depressing role in the play, these functions were reduced. The male actor projected an anxious personality in the comedy as well as in the serious play. His immune function decreased after both performances.[5] If play-acting over a relatively short period of time can have such a marked and measurable impact on our immune system, what happens if we lead a life of anxiety and depression?

Over thirty years ago an American doctor, George F. Solomon, studied women with rheumatoid arthritis and their sisters who did not have the disease. As both sisters shared the similar genetic inheritance, which is known to play an important role in rheumatoid arthritis, Solomon was curious to find out if psychological differences between the sisters could explain why one became ill and the other didn't. Like Nicholas Hall, he got them to use role-play exercises and psychological tests in comparing the arthritic women with their healthy sisters. 'In every single case the healthy sibling was more assertive than the sister with arthritis,' he said.

In 1991 Solomon and Lydia Temoshok published another remarkable report after studying a group of patients with AIDS using very similar techniques. Looking at the group of longtime survivors of AIDS, all of whom had outlived their doctors' predictions, they discovered links between certain behaviour patterns and stronger immune cells. Group members who were more assertive and had the willingness 'to withdraw to nurture the self' had more T suppressor cells, which seem to play a key role in resistance to AIDS.[6] These same cells also help us to resist autoimmune diseases. Solomon and Temoshok's research seems to suggest that when we take care of our emotional needs, we also take care of our immune system. We will explore this in other chapters. But the immune system can also be strengthened by other means.

Echinacea – Nature's Greatest Immune System Booster

Elie Metchnikoff was astonished enough when he observed his starfish defending itself against an invading thorn by sending out aggressive macrophages. I wonder what he would have thought of the work of researchers such as George Solomon, Nicholas Hall and R. W. Bartrop. I think that H. C. F. Meyer would have been equally surprised if he had known that the essential ingredient of his 'blood purifying' pills would later be the subject of more than 350 scientific studies and make $1,000,000 a day in sales in the United States alone. The root extract that he had used came from a plant found widely in North America, from the Midwest right down to Texas, known as *Echinacea*. Although there are nine species of the plant, three are the most widely used as an herbal supplement – *E. angustifolia*, *E. purpurea* and *E. pallida*.

We now know that Echinacea has a remarkable ability to boost the immune system in a profound way. One particular component of the plant is a carbohydrate called inulin, which has now been found to increase the production of immune chemicals that activate macrophages. Once their activity is increased, so too is the production of T cells and natural killer cells, and the levels of neutrophils in the blood.[7]

Controlled studies have also shown that Echinacea strengthens the immune system in people who are perfectly healthy. In one trial a dose of 30 drops 3 times a day of the root extract of *E. purpurea* was given to healthy males for 5 days. The result was an astonishing increase of 120 per cent in the functioning of their leukocytes.[8] Another trial found that the freshly pressed juice of the same plant increased the migration of white blood cells to the scene of battle by 30 to 40 per cent.[9] Yet another study of patients undergoing radiotherapy treatment for cancer demonstrated that 85 per cent of 55 patients showed a stabilisation of their white blood cell counts after using the freshly pressed juice of *E. purpurea*, while a control group showed a marked and steady decline in their levels, starting from 6,000 and dropping to 2,500 after 6 weeks.[10]

Not surprisingly, sales of Echinacea are high. But *beware*. It is often believed that because a remedy has a herbal or botanical label and can easily be bought over the counter at your local pharmacy, it has no side-effects or interactions with conventional drugs, but it can. For example, Echinacea, used beyond eight weeks, has the potential to cause toxicity to the liver, especially if taken at the same time as other liver toxic drugs, for example anabolic steroids. As an immunostimulant, it should not be taken at the same time as immunosuppresants, such as corticosteroids and cyclosporin. Remember that many drugs are merely synthetic versions of what is found in botanical substances.

More Immune System Boosters

What you are now starting to see is that there is a wide array of foods, herbs and lifestyle factors that can have a powerful effect on your immune system and its ability to fight disease. Although I shall be giving you more information in other chapters, these are my suggestions for strengthening your immune system – and they have all been shown by scientific study to be effective:

Sleep If you are not getting enough sleep your immunity is probably compromised. Poor sleep is associated with lower immune system function and numbers of natural killer cells.

Social contact People who have a wide range of social contacts have been shown to have a better prognosis when faced with serious disease than those who do not.

Humour Most of my patients mention a sense of humour as one of their greatest coping strategies. It has also been demonstrated to be an immune system enhancer. (*See page 60.*)

Keep a diary Remarkable research has been carried out that clearly shows the benefits of recording your thoughts, feelings and emotions on a daily basis.

Keep the faith Scientific research has shown that if you have a strong religious or spiritual faith it will benefit your immunity. (*See page 235.*)

Herbs Apart from Echinacea, there are several other botanical extracts that also have a marked effect on the immune system, including ginseng, valerian and garlic. (*See page 157.*)

Get some culture It has been found that people who frequent cultural events such as concerts and museum exhibitions tend to live longer than their stay-at-home peers. People undergoing music therapy have significant increases in levels of antibodies that defend against infection and cancer.

Exercise Daily vigorous exercise such as a good walk can bolster your disease resistance. (*See page 145.*) However, don't overdo it – high-intensity exercise of more than an hour can *suppress* the immune system for up to twenty-four hours.

Vitamin C Studies have found a link between vitamin C and increased immune system response. You probably need 200 to 500 mg daily to get the effect, but don't overdose as 1,000 mg or more can cause kidney stones in susceptible people. (*See page 181.*)

Get a massage Massage has been shown to reduce anxiety and improve immune function considerably.

Chapter 3

HEALING HARMFUL EMOTIONS

The intimate connection between body, mind and spirit has been known and honoured in Eastern medicine for thousands of years, but only quite recently have we in the West begun to see that emotional health is directly connected to physical health. We now know that if you neglect your emotional and spiritual health, sooner or later it will take its toll on your physical body. Depression is a risk factor for heart attack, and vice versa. Anxiety can provoke digestive and skin disorders; self-centredness may increase your risk of stroke or heart disease. But there is an even deeper calling urging us to pay attention to our emotional health. Ultimately the deepest satisfaction, or greatest misery, comes from our ability to live authentically, deeply and intimately with others.

Emotions are mysterious and often dangerous things. Hostility, anxiety, stored-up resentment, guilt and hopelessness can all disrupt your immune system and drastically change your hormone levels. But emotions are what make life worth living. They are indescribable experiences. Emotions also have long-lasting effects on us; they are what make those landmark events from childhood so memorable.

Emotional experiences make us who we are; they are our own personal histories woven into the fabric of our brains. But it is not just moments of extreme emotion that leave their mark. Every day the aftershocks of past emotional upheavals are influencing our actions and silently nudging us towards decisions. Although we may be oblivious to this process, in every moment of our lives we are influenced by the resonance of our past.

The Power of Emotions

Since the 1960s, Western psychotherapists working with people suffering from serious, even life-threatening, illnesses have acknowledged the power of emotions as a contribution to the disease process. Later, in the 1970s, research in the field of psychoneuroimmunology documented direct links between emotions and biochemical events in the body, reinforcing what healers have always known: emotions can manifest themselves as physical symptoms.

Well-known women's health expert Dr Christiane Northrup first used the phrase 'toxic emotions' to indicate the powerful, strongly held and often unconsciously active beliefs and emotions that help to generate symptoms that keep illnesses in place. Dr Northrup explains that if we do not work through our emotional distress, which includes damaging beliefs and unexpressed emotions, we set up the body for physical distress. She believes that our personal histories become 'lodged and stored' throughout the body, and that beliefs and emotions can be legitimate toxins, contributing to an overall weakening of the immune system.

Many of my patients have either completely recovered or gone on to live way beyond their medical prognosis once they have learned to express their emotions, turn negatives into positives and set themselves goals.

Gill first came to me for healing in 1979. Some years earlier she had been diagnosed with breast cancer that had been treated surgically by a mastectomy and follow-up chemotherapy, from which she had recovered and 'led a totally ordinary life without thinking about the cancer'. Some years later she developed secondary cancer, or metastases, in her lungs. At the time she told me that she believed that the cancer had come back because of an accumulation of stress: her husband's business had not been doing very well, she had started a new teaching job and a close friend had died.

Although Gill knew that the situation was 'pretty bad', her husband had in fact been told by her doctors that she had probably just three months to live. Gill was determined to do all she could to help herself. She began by revising her diet, taking exercise where she could and listening to my relaxation and self-healing tapes. She then began coming to me for personal healing sessions on a monthly basis. 'When it got to Christmas I felt very emotional because I had not expected to live that long,' she later explained. 'Although I was very positive, deep down I did wonder whether it was going to be my last Christmas. I wanted to get all the family round. I felt as if it was probably the last one.'

Fourteen months after the disastrous prognosis divulged to her husband, Gill asked to have another scan because instead of feeling worse she was feeling stronger and better with each day that passed. When she went to see her consultant for the results, she found him seated behind his desk, his attention shifting alternately between her new scan images, her notes and herself on the other side of his desk.

'I've got good news for you and I've got bad news for you,' he eventually said. 'Which would you prefer first?'

Having spent over a year on positive self-help for herself, Gill asked to hear the good news first.

'The good news is that I have your latest scan results, and having looked at your lungs, your liver, your brain and your bones, you are completely clear. We can't see any trace of the disease anywhere. I don't know what you've done, but you can ask your husband, I told him last year that I thought you had only three months to live.'

Gill said, 'That's fantastic, isn't it? But if that's the good news, what's the bad news?'

'The bad news,' he said, drawing in a deep breath, 'is that you must live with the knowledge that, unfortunately, it will come back again.'

At this point Gill did something that she later told me was quite out of character for her. She was so utterly incensed by the consultant's negativity that she leapt out of her seat, banged her fists down on his desk, and shouted, 'The hell it will!'

'Why couldn't he have said to me, "You're in remission. Let's hope it lasts"?' she asked me. Many other people would have been so emotionally upset by this experience that I wonder what the eventual physical effect of such a comment really is. However, for Gill, the consultant's statement became the motivating factor that kept her going. She was simply determined to prove him wrong and she used it as a springboard from which she launched a wonderful cancer self-help group in Loughborough.

'I felt all along that there was some strong purpose behind it all,' she said. 'I think I've been the catalyst in bringing together the people that helped me . . . At the time I felt very over-privileged that so many people wanted to help me. I thought, "What have I done to deserve all these people helping me?" I felt I must give something back. My whole attitude has changed. It sounds a very strange thing to say, but having cancer has taught me so much that I wouldn't have missed the experience.'

Ironically, after she established her cancer support group, the consultant who had so angered Gill sent many of his patients to her.

Gill always said that she was determined to die of something else to prove him wrong. The cancer did, sadly, return and she died in September 1997. However, she had an additional eighteen years of life from her three-month prognosis in 1979 and I believe that the techniques she used, some of them perhaps unwittingly, gave her that extra time.

Conversely, there are those for whom illness sometimes seems to be a way out of dealing with what they feel are insoluble and insurmountable problems.

Celia also came to me having recently undergone surgery to remove a breast tumour and several infected lymph nodes under her arm. Like Gill, she had also gone through a course of chemotherapy and had been told that she was clear of cancer and only needed regular check-ups.

From her first visit she was completely convinced that the cancer would recur and that it was going to kill her. As she talked to me over several sessions I could hear Basil Fawlty telling me that she would die of 'terminal negativity'! She was resentful that she had had to give up work to look after children, she was resentful of her husband enjoying his job and she felt she had no friends and no one to talk to or confide in. She seemed to find it difficult to find a flicker of enthusiasm about anything in her life, and any suggestions I made to help her see things more positively were cursorily dismissed. Her thoughts seemed to be a stream of self-criticism and she felt there was no point at all in looking forward to the future, as there might not be a future. Perhaps not surprisingly, Celia had developed secondary cancer within four months and died not long afterwards.

Some Suggestions for Handling Emotions

Accept that your emotions are your own You cannot blame them on anyone else. They are all yours. External stresses are far less important than how you deal with them, and if you look to yourself as the source of your own feelings you have made the all-important step towards healing. Instead of saying to someone, 'You made me angry' (or jealous or afraid or resentful), change your reaction to: 'This situation is causing me feelings of anger.' It's not just a formula – it's the truth.

Focus on the sensation of the emotion, not its content All emotions have physical results, which is why they can make us ill. But we tend to focus instead on the who, why, what, when and where of a feeling. This is called rationalisation. Fortunately, the mind can't pay attention to two things at once, so if you stop thinking about who stressed you out and why, but instead put your attention on your body to feel where the discomfort lies, you break the cycle of obsessive thinking that makes a 'toxic' emotion keep going long after it should. You don't need to analyse your emotions so much as dissipate their harmful energy.

Label your emotions on two levels The first level is obvious – you know when you are unhappy or angry. However, at a deeper level, there is always a second emotion. If you are habitually caught in a situation that makes you feel stressed, ask what lies behind the mask of the first emotion. Do you feel that nobody is listening? Is your anger a cover-up for insecurity? Are you secretly afraid? Until you get to the second level of the emotion, you are not dealing with the toxic part. In my experience with hundreds of patients, if they trace their feelings somewhere in their body, inevitably the second level of emotion lies in the heart or stomach. This is where the emotional glue causes negativity to stick to you. Just as inevitably, the second-level emotions are recurrent. People carry around resentment or anxiety for many years. When you see that your patterns have been with you for a long time, it is easier to see that they belong to you, not to those you blame.

Express all your emotions Do this without exception, but through a healthy outlet. Emotions want to move, but their natural flow can be halted by denial and repression. Keeping a journal of feelings every day has proved extremely helpful for many people, since no one lives in an environment where all emotions can be outwardly expressed. In any event, don't aim your emotion at anyone. If you feel terribly hurt or mistreated by someone else, write down every detail of that feeling in a long letter. Don't leave out any scrap of resentment, hatred, jealousy or hurt. Leave it for a day then check it to make sure it is complete and then throw it away. You need to express your emotions to yourself first of all, not to others.

Release your emotions in a significant way In other words, don't just pass them off. Your body wants to know that you are aware of your feelings, so talk to it. Tell it that you are going to deal with a sudden outburst of negativity, even if you have to postpone your reaction until later. And keep your promise. If you need a walk outside, or time alone, or a few moments to vent in private, then carry out those intentions. The important thing is to discover your own process or ritual for releasing an emotion. You might choose exercise, praying, laughing or deep breathing – all of which I will cover later in the book.

Find the lesson As soon as you find the lesson that your negativity can teach you, it becomes positive. Perhaps you feel deep down that anger is always wrong or that you must not face guilt. It is your belief system that makes these emotions 'bad' and therefore toxic. You can choose to change these beliefs.

Share your process with a loved one This is the crucial step that makes all emotions positive. Every emotion you deal with makes you a healer. Share that with your spouse or closest friend. Let that person into your process and you will find that negativity begins to lose its grip much more quickly.

Take a step toward personal freedom Instead of your emotions using you, you are learning to use them. That is a cause for celebration and you shouldn't miss that moment of victory. When you let go of negativity, fill the space by congratulating yourself and allowing healthy pride, satisfaction and self esteem to fill the gap. This is just as important as getting rid of the toxic emotions. When you see your emotions as the best part of yourself, you have become a true self-healer.

The Benefit of Support Groups

The medical profession has, of course, long been sceptical – even hostile – towards the idea that our emotions or attitudes have any bearing on either the cause of disease or its control. One such person was David Spiegel, a psychiatrist working at the Stanford University Medical School in California. He had become so annoyed by claims that psychological treatments could extend life expectancy for cancer patients that he devised a study with the intention of exploding the myth. Not only was he shocked by his own results but also they were published in the *Lancet* with an editorial praising his scientific methods.[1]

Spiegel had set up a group therapy programme for women with advanced metatastic cancer. These women had been through initial treatment, often including surgery, but now had secondary cancer that was spreading through their bodies. None of them was expected to live. Spiegel compared the women receiving his group therapy, who were chosen at random, with a control group who did not take part but who were receiving the same medical care. In the group sessions the women were able to express their fears, their pain and their anger with others who understood their situation. Often this was the only place where they could be really open about these emotions because other people in their lives were too frightened to talk to them about the cancer or the possibility of their dying.

Both groups were followed for ten years and Spiegel was amazed to find that the women who had been to the group meetings survived *twice as long* as the women who faced the disease by themselves. Those who attended the groups lived for thirty-seven additional months on average, while those who did not attend died in nineteen months on average. Furthermore, only three women survived over the ten years of the study and all three had taken part in the group sessions.

A few years after the *Lancet* had published David Spiegel's findings, another similarly striking set of results was published in *The Archives of General Psychiatry*. Another psychiatrist, Fawzy I. Fawzy, had followed a group of patients suffering from melanoma, a potentially fatal skin cancer. Again, half his patients went through group therapy while the other half received the same medical treatment, but no group therapy. The group therapy sessions were designed to help the patients in three different areas: gaining support from other group members, learning how to interrelate with other people to develop active ways of coping, and developing relaxation techniques. After six years, Dr Fawzy discovered to his amazement that patients in his therapy groups were *three times less likely to suffer a recurrence and three times less likely to have died.*

Fawzy also observed that the patients who were most upset at the beginning but who developed an active way of dealing with their stress were significantly more likely to remain disease-free. The group therapy patients also maintained a significant increase in their natural killer cells for up to six months after finishing the therapy. We know that natural killer cells can destroy metastic cancer cells, which is why these patients were better able to fight off any spread of the disease and had such a lower rate of recurrence and death.[2]

Again, this would seem not to have been a chance finding, because Lydia Temoshok, a psychologist specialising in clinical health psychology and behavioural medicine, especially in regard to the mind–body and biobehavioural connections in cancer and HIV/AIDS, had previously reported similar findings in a study that she made with a group of patients with melanoma (skin cancer). Temoshok found that those who tended to suppress negative emotions and please others had thicker lesions, which indicated a less favourable prognosis. By using sophisticated tests of emotional expression, she found that patients who were much more emotionally expressive of both positive and negative emotions had a stronger immune response to their tumours and also had less aggressive cancers.[3]

All these studies revealed gains in life expectancy that could never have been achieved by any medical treatment. So what exactly was it that caused such spectacular results? Dr Spiegel felt it was that:

❍ Patients received the social support of other women with the same illness who could understand their particular suffering.

❍ The group offered a safe place to share emotions such as grief, fear and anger.

❍ Each patient was taught self-hypnosis and relaxation techniques to control pain.

❍ The women were encouraged by the group therapist to be more assertive with doctors and oncologists.

○ The therapist enabled the women to openly discuss and master fears of dying and they were able to explore existential and spiritual issues related to both living and dying.

○ A therapeutic attitude encouraged the women to cherish each day, to lessen social obligations, repair important relationships and realise their creativity.

I know that several of my patients attend support groups and, as one of them told me, 'I have learnt a substantial amount about my condition, and have found comfort in the knowledge that I am not alone with my own personal crisis. It seems that crisis and trauma is mingling amongst us all the time.'

Expressing Emotions

One of the most valuable aspects of support groups is that they allow people to express their emotions. At London's King's College Hospital, Dr Steven Greer and his colleague Tina Morris carried out pioneering work on the relationship between breast cancer and the expression of anger, which was published in the *Lancet* in 1990.[4] They discovered that women who were later diagnosed as having breast cancer differed from women with benign breast disease in how they expressed anger. The women with cancer showed a greater level of anger suppression and then sometimes extreme expressions of anger during their interviews. They tended to hold in anger for as long as possible before venting it, but mostly tended to suppress it. They also had a tendency to avoid emotional conflict and trouble.

In another study Keith Pettingale, Greer and Morris, followed sixty-nine women with early breast cancer over a five-year period.[5] At the start of the study they evaluated how each woman was coping with her diagnosis. After five years they found that those women with what they called a 'fighting spirit' were more than twice as likely to be alive than those women who had seen themselves as helpless and hopeless. Steven Greer defined this fighting spirit as 'being in charge' and 'being determined to beat the disease'. He also believed that having the ability to express emotions such as anger, assertiveness and optimism had a large role to play. These remarkable findings were still relevant fifteen years later and Greer went on to develop a mind–body programme for cancer patients called 'Adjuvant Psychological Therapy'.

The fact that Steven Greer and his colleagues showed that women with cancer tended to 'suppress their anger' and 'avoid conflict and trouble' suggests that expressing emotions such as anger in some way helps the body's defence against the disease. George Solomon and Lydia Temoshok believe that they have found what they call an 'immunosuppression prone' personality in their work with AIDS patients which has much in common with what Temoshok had also observed in her work with cancer patients. They found that compliance, conformity, self-sacrifice, denial of hostility or anger and non-expression of emotion seem to be linked to a poor prognosis in cancer patients, while other personality traits seem to be beneficial.[6]

Personality Traits That Enhance Survival

○ A sense of purpose and meaning in life.

○ A sense of personal responsibility for one's health.

○ An ability to express one's needs and emotions.

○ A sense of humour.

Lynne, one of my long-surviving cancer patients, told me how a friend had sent her a handwritten list of personality traits which Dr Carl Simonton, author of *Getting Well Again*, had described as being commonly held by cancer survivors. They tend to:

○ Be successful in their careers.

○ Enjoy their careers.

○ Be receptive and creative.

○ Be sometimes hostile/able to be hostile.

○ Have a high degree of self-esteem and self-love.

○ Be rarely docile.

○ Be intelligent and self-reliant.

○ Value interaction with others.

○ Appreciate diversity among friends and acquaintances.

Lynne said that her friend had written a hastily scrawled note near the bottom: 'Sounds like you!' But what were the personality traits that had helped move her into what she called 'this mess'? She felt she had been:

○ Hypercritical, expecting perfection of herself (and to a lesser extent of others).

○ Impatient.

○ Quietly judgemental.

○ Honouring and responding to the needs of others, while neglecting her own.

○ Doing what she felt she should rather than what she really wanted to do.

○ Feeling perpetually pressed to accomplish.

I had also allowed a handful of relationships to continue in my life, which were harmful and unpleasant. There was a mutual charade of friendliness for the sake of harmony, but these relationships were toxic. Somewhere along the line I had lost a good part of my true self and became a person whose life was dictated excessively not only by the charade, but also by the thoughts and needs of others. Ultimately an abundance of negative emotions was hidden deep inside. Without knowing it or meaning to, I had stockpiled anger and hurt there.

Lynne found that a book by Joseph Campbell, *The Hero with a Thousand Faces*, was particularly helpful. It tells the story of a hero who ventures into the unknown, moving blindly into a mysterious and dangerous abyss. From his life-threatening adventures he gains two crucial elements, experience and knowledge, survives the event and returns to the community with new energy and vision. 'This was a fine concept,' said Lynne. 'I embraced it and decided to be a hero. It was better than remaining an ignorant fool.'

Dealing with Anger

If you feel that you are the sort of person who has been described by researchers such as Spiegel, Greer, Solomon and Temoshok, what can you do about it? Not everybody wants to go to a cancer support group or to counselling sessions, even if it may improve their prognosis. And how can you turn an emotion like anger, felt by so many of my patients, into assertiveness? As Woody Allen famously said in one of his films, 'I can't express anger. I internalise it and grow a tumour instead.'

Of course it is perfectly natural to be angry when your life has been turned inside out, which is often what happens with a serious illness. These feelings are normal. What is important is what you do *with* them, not that you feel them in the first place. The best way to deal with angry feelings is to recognise them, accept them and find some way to express them appropriately. If you do not deal with your anger, it can get in the way of almost everything you do.

In her book *The Dance of Anger*, psychologist Harriet Goldhor Lerner writes of anger as a messenger worth listening to. It can be a strong indicator of emotional hurt and vulnerability, too much compromise in personal relationships, suppressed emotional issues, over-extension at work or home, or the need to take more responsibility for your life. She believes that standing up for your rights and needs without blaming others is a good way of learning to be assertive, rather than angry, at critical development points. There are other ways, too, which are explored later, but here are some quick tips for dealing with anger:

GUIDELINES FOR RIDDING YOURSELF OF ANGER

○ Try to see the situation from the other person's point of view, and understand why they acted in the way that made you angry. Recognise that other people are under stress too and that some people deal with stressful situations better than others.

○ Express your anger in an appropriate way before it becomes too severe. If you wait until your anger is severe, it will impair your judgement, and you are likely to make other people angry in return.

❍ Get away from the situation for a while. Try to cool off before you go back and deal with what made you angry.

❍ Find safe ways to express your anger. These can include beating a pillow or cushion, yelling out loud in your car or a closed room, or doing some hard and vigorous exercise. Sometimes it helps to vent anger with someone who is 'safe', someone who will not be offended or strike back, like a counsellor or friend.

❍ Talk to someone about *why* you feel angry. Explaining to someone else why you feel angry often helps you to understand why you reacted as you did, allowing you to see your reactions in perspective.

Writing a Journal

Many of my patients have kept a journal of their healing journey, finding it a useful tool for focusing on feelings such as anger and then exploring and learning from them. There is a difference between a diary and a journal. A diary is a day-to-day record of how you spend your time. It focuses on the *outward* events of your life – where you went and when, what you did with whom, what you saw and heard and said. While a diary may include your reflections about anything that has happened, that is not its main purpose. A journal, on the other hand, focuses on your *interior* life – how you feel about some matter that has grabbed your attention. It may involve memories about something that once happened or your thoughts about what you hope will happen. A journal is always personal in nature and it is written for no one but you. It's an expression of who you have been, who you are, and who you are becoming. In a journal you don't try to cover every aspect of your life – you cover what you want to, what you're led to and what means the most to you as you sit down and begin.

A journal is a good place to note the unfolding of your thoughts as they occur. Through writing them down you may be able to identify any feelings you have been blocking and to welcome them, allowing yourself to be who you are and to release stifled emotions. Allow your innermost feelings to be aired in whatever way seems best. Focus on any meetings with others – did you feel comfortable with them? What feelings did they generate in you during the encounter – tension, anger, hurt, joy, love?

If you encounter a block in writing down your thoughts, just sit for a while and reflect on where the reluctance is coming from, or simply write down that you feel unable to express what has happened in words. You can always go back to it later when your insight may be clearer.

After finding that writing about his own secret pain helped him to recover from depression, James Pennebaker, a professor of psychology at the Southern Methodist University in Dallas, demonstrated in a remarkable series of experiments that getting people to write down the thoughts, fears and feelings that most upset them had a beneficial and measurable effect on their health. The volunteers were merely asked to write for twenty minutes a day over a period of four days. Compared to control groups who merely wrote about trivial day-to-day events, the people who wrote about traumas made significantly fewer visits to the doctor, reported fewer symptoms of illness during the following six months and had fewer days off work. Pennebaker also discovered that they showed an improved liver enzyme function and that their T cells were more active for six weeks afterwards.[7]

Changing Negative to Positive

Donald Spence carried out a fascinating piece of research work by analysing interviews with a group of over sixty women before their biopsy results for cervical cancer were known. He discovered that when writing about their feelings, different women were using quite different key words in describing their feelings. *Dark, conflict, tense, cancer, disgusting* and *difficulty* suggested a feeling of hopelessness, whilst words like *wish, yearn, desire, eager, expect* and *longing* suggested a more hopeful attitude. Spence found that the women showing a greater sense of hopelessness were more likely to have a positive biopsy result showing cervical cancer.[8]

Two other researchers, Dr A. H. Schmale and Dr H. Iker, went even further in another study involving 68 women who were about to undergo a biopsy for possible cervical cancer. Amazingly, they were able to predict with a 73 per cent accuracy rate which patients actually had cancer! It was based on just one factor – whether or not the patient felt a sense of hopelessness.[9] This shows how important it is that you remain positive.

Rob was forty-six years old when he was diagnosed with the asbestos-related cancer mesothelioma, which was probably linked to his work over many years as a builder. When he first wrote to me in 1997 he explained that he had only just been diagnosed and had had more than three litres of fluid removed from his right lung, which had been found to contain cancer cells. He had a tumour in his right lung and a pleural thickening of both lungs. Because this kind of cancer does not generally respond to chemotherapy, he had been sent home from hospital without any medical treatment being offered.

I'm not saying that Rob was not frightened, but I could see that he was not going to let it beat him. He was positive, enthusiastic, funny and had wonderful support from his wife, June. Now, over three years later, he is still working flat out, often arriving for his appointments with me in the nick of time because he is so busy. His doctor's monitoring shows that the cancer has not gone away but has stabilised – something that is pretty much unheard of in cases of mesothelioma.

Coincidentally, Clive came to me at the same time with exactly the same problem. He was also the same age and also a builder. Sadly the difference between Rob and Clive was enormous. Clive was angry and unable or unwilling to talk about his illness to anybody. His mood was downbeat and pessimistic and he could see no future ahead. 'I've been watching the harvesting as I've come here to see you today,' he said on his first visit, 'and thinking that it's the last time I'll ever see it.' He died within three months of diagnosis.

Sandra Levy, an associate professor of psychiatry and medicine at the University of Pittsburgh and former director of behavioural medicine in oncology at the Pittsburgh Cancer Institute, has also carried out numerous studies on the link between cancer and emotional states. She followed the progress of thirty-six women who had suffered a recurrence of breast cancer. Seven years later, two-thirds of them had died. However, Levy found that a common factor among the survivors was a sense of joy. This was actually a more accurate predictor of survival than several other factors that are used by doctors to determine prognosis.[10] The women in the study had managed to hold on to a capacity for joy *despite* their illness. This allowed them to maintain optimism and hope, which are known to be so important in the healing process.

The obvious link between the studies of Greer and Levy is that those women who did best were expressive of both positive and negative emotions. It was those who bottled up emotions who fared worst of all. From my own work, I have come to believe that there are ten areas where we are most likely to find negativity creeping into our lives. If we change these negative areas into *positive* areas, we can gain new insights that will benefit our health and happiness.

GUIDELINES FOR CHANGING NEGATIVE TO POSITIVE

○ Think well about yourself and your achievements and take time to reaffirm these on a regular basis. Remember, too, that the basis of being able to love or respect anyone else is to first learn to love and value your own self.

○ Rather than worry or complain about what you don't have, appreciate what you *do* have. I believe that there is a basic law in life that says we don't always get what we want, but we get what we need.

○ Surround yourself with beauty and light, both inside and out.

○ Do not allow other people's criticism to affect you. Have faith in yourself and your abilities. Remember that criticism is often another way of expressing jealousy and often appears in those who lack self-confidence and self-worth. The unhappy and troubled person can also be critical.

○ Accept each new circumstance as an opportunity for growth and self-improvement. We learn from experience, whether good or bad.

○ Every cloud has a silver lining. Even unpleasant events in life have a reason for occurring and come as part of our learning process.

○ Leave yesterday's sadness behind you and look forward to tomorrow with hope and joy. Why worry over a past event that you cannot change? Let it go.

○ Don't fret over what is too late to change. Put it down to experience and remember that yesterday's mistake can be tomorrow's triumph.

O Let go of what you no longer need. Even though you may still want it, let the outworn go so that you can be open and receptive to new circumstances.

Setting Goals

I first learned about the power of goal setting when I was young and inexperienced as a healer. I was working with a lady who was terminally ill and who had been given three to six months to live. She came in to see me one morning and looked terribly ill. Because of my inexperience, my face must have shown what I thought. 'Don't worry, dear,' she said to me. 'I'm not going to die yet. I've got my daughter's wedding to go to next year.'

Although I didn't say it, I thought that was most unlikely, given the fact that the wedding was over fifteen months ahead, but against all medical expectations the lady survived long enough to see her daughter walk down the aisle. She died just two weeks later. To this day I am convinced that she squeezed that extra time out of her prognosis because she was so determined to be at her daughter's wedding.

If you are going to set yourself goals do make sure that you set short, medium, and long-term goals in order to avoid slipping over the side when you've reached your goal. Goal setting is also a very good way for the whole family to get together and assist in the patient's recovery. Family and friends can keep optimism alive by reminding the patient, in bleaker moments, of the goal they are aiming for.

A well-known figure whose goal kept him going is national hunt jockey Bob Champion. In 1979, when he was one of the top five British jockeys, he was diagnosed as having testicular cancer that had spread into the lymph glands in his chest. At the age of just thirty-one, he was given eight months to live without treatment. He recounts in his book *Champion's Story* in forthright, undramatic terms his feelings and experiences throughout the gruelling two-year period that followed.

The initial diagnosis left him shocked and scared: he hated the idea of an operation and the fact that he would probably be left sterile due to the side-effects of the chemotherapy was another cruel blow, for Bob dearly loved children.

The one overriding thought that kept Bob going through the darkest days of his treatment was his obsession with winning the Grand National on Aldaniti. His triumph in the 1981 Grand National, when he *did* ride Aldaniti to victory, is now legend.

Funnily enough, an old schoolfriend of mine was also diagnosed with testicular cancer at the same time as Bob Champion and went through the same gruelling chemotherapy treatment, having been warned that as a side-effect he would not be able to father children. He came to me for regular healing sessions for over a year and not only beat the cancer but went on to have four daughters!

EXERCISE: TO HELP YOU FOCUS ON YOUR GOALS

One of the exercises from my seminar has helped many participants to focus more clearly on their goals. Ask yourself the following questions:

1 What goal would you like to reach in your life?

2 Is there anything you would have to let go of in order to achieve it (belief, attitude, thing, person)?

3 What is the essence of this goal? Is there any other form that will give you the essence of what you want?

4 What is your motivation to achieve it? What would you get out of it?

5 Often inner urges or whispers in your mind are connected to your goal, even though they may not seem to be related. List any inner urges you have had.

6 What specific step, no matter how simple, can you take in the next week towards your goal?

Cilla, one of my patients who in her mid-thirties was diagnosed with breast cancer, found that goal setting can be even simpler – and that it benefited her in another unexpected way. While she was going through surgery, chemotherapy and radiotherapy, she developed an interest in mosaic design.

'I discovered, to my benefit, that it demands all my thought processes and therefore distracts me from my persistent concerns and worries, even if it's just for an hour or so. It doesn't require any particular artistic skills, but just patience and an ability to plan in stages. I have recently completed one piece of work that I had reserved to work upon after my young daughter had gone to bed each night, and so took several months to see through to the end. My only problem now is that I have not prepared a new project to continue distracting myself from reality!'

Completing mosaics became Cilla's goal and helped her through all her treatment.

Facing the Dragon

There is an old fairy tale about a huge dragon that lived in the mountains outside a village. It was so enormous that all the villagers were terrified of it. Sometimes it blew puffs of fire and smoke down at them. When they retreated and ran away, the dragon grew even larger than before. One day a villager decided that he would do something about it and so, armed with a very stout heavy stick, he set off towards the mountains where the dragon lived. But something odd started to happen, because the closer he got to the dragon the smaller it became. When he finally came face to face with the dragon he discovered that it was nothing more than a little fire-lizard.

Toxic emotions such as anger, despair, resentment and hopelessness are rather like that dragon. The more you retreat from them, the bigger they proportionally become in your mind. By confronting them and dealing with them, whether by talking, writing or in some other way, they begin to dissolve away. It is emotions that become stuck or unexpressed that make it difficult for us to have any feelings. If we deny important emotions such as anger, grief or sadness, we start to create a bottleneck and other emotions, including the positive ones like joy, hope and laughter, will find it more difficult to make their way through to our consciousness.

Chapter 4

THE HEALING BENEFITS OF LAUGHTER, HOPE AND OPTIMISM

W hen I first moved to Suffolk, with its wide-open skies and undu-
lating hills, I happened to find the most delightful pub hidden
away in a little-known hamlet. Even though it was in the early 1980s,
time had completely passed it by and it was a throwback to an earlier
part of the century. The brewery had yet to introduce bar meal menus
on plastic laminated cards offering scampi in a basket or soup of the day
straight from a tin. Instead the walls and ceiling were yellowed with
nicotine, the tables and chairs were rickety and creaking, and the floor
was covered with a worn and grubby piece of linoleum.

I fell in love with the pub, not so much because of its décor but because
of the wonderful local people I met there. Being a rural area most of
them were farm workers although a good many had long since retired.

I spent many hours talking to a man known to all his friends as Dorby,
whom I have often said became my guru and from whom I learned a great
deal about optimism, humour, hope and the value of social support – all
of which I came to appreciate as being so valuable in the healing process.

While so many of us are driven to produce and meet deadlines, always
running out of time, stressed and deprived of sleep, Dorby and his friends
had listened for years to that small voice within that encouraged them
to spend more time playing, or praying, or listening to music, or being
with loved ones or friends.

When I first met Dorby he was well into his eighties and had been
drinking beer and smoking his own roll-up cigarettes since he was about
twelve years old. He was a small, rotund figure who was never seen without
a cloth cap and he exuded humour, laughter and kindness. His eyes looked
in different directions and if somebody told him a joke he would laugh

until he had to catch his breath, his ever-present cigarette moving from one side of his mouth to the other. Whatever he owned, which as a retired farm labourer was very little, he would share with others.

Although Dorby could not quite understand my work, he knew I was a healer and was fascinated by it. One evening, after many pints of Greene King beer, we were talking and he came up with a scenario.

'If you had a man who was healthy,' Dorby said in his broad Suffolk accent, 'and you put a stone in his shoe and then he had to walk for a mile, he wouldn't be very happy. He'd complain the whole time about the stone that was hurting him. But if you had someone else who couldn't walk because they had some disease, but you healed them so they could walk again, they'd be happy to walk a mile with a stone in their shoe!'

This encapsulated Dorby's philosophy of cheerfulness, gratitude and optimism – all qualities we need on the healing journey.

The Healing Power of Laughter

Of course Dorby was not the first person to appreciate the link between humour and good health. Four hundred years ago Robert Burton wrote in his book *Anatomy of Melancholy*, 'Humour purges the blood, making the body young, lively, and fit for any manner of employment.' Mirth, he said, is the 'principal engine for battering the walls of melancholy . . . and a sufficient cure in itself'.

Immanuel Kant, in his *Critique of Pure Reason*, wrote that laughter produces 'a feeling of health through the furtherance of the vital bodily processes, the affection that moves the intestines and the diaphragm; in a word, the feeling of health that makes up the gratification felt by us; so that we can thus reach the body through the soul and use the latter as the physician of the former'. More recently, Sigmund Freud believed that mirth was a potent way of counteracting nervous tension and that humour could also be used as effective therapy.

Norman Cousins probably did more to draw serious attention and discussion to the healing power of laughter after he described his remarkable recovery from ankylosing spondylitis in his book *Anatomy of an Illness*. The book caused a significant stir in the medical community because it related an autobiographical and anecdotal account indicating that positive emotional states can cure the body of a serious disease.

Ankylosing spondylitis is a disease that affects the connective tissues of the body, which can lead to considerable difficulty in moving the limbs and can lead to nodules appearing all over the body. Furthermore, it is rare that anybody fully recovers from it. However, Cousins did just that by taking very high doses of vitamin C and by embarking on a programme of watching films that would make him laugh – including classics from the old *Candid Camera* series and old Marx Brothers films. He commented, 'I made the joyous discovery that ten minutes of genuine belly laughter had an anaesthetic effect and would give me at least two hours of pain-free sleep.'

Cousins went on to say that while cancer, in particular, has been associated with intense states of grief, fear or anger, it does not make sense to suppose that emotions can only have a detrimental impact on our health. As we have already seen, positive emotions can contribute strongly to health and well-being. They can be life-giving experiences.

While originally doctors and researchers scoffed at Cousins' story, it has now been demonstrated in numerous studies that laughter and other positive emotions can enhance the immune system. Recent medical research has also shown that laughter improves the transfer of oxygen and nutrients to internal organs, improves the blood flow to the body's extremities and improves cardiovascular function. Perhaps most interestingly we now also know that laughter plays an active part in the body's release of pain-killing chemicals known as beta-endorphins. This gives us a better understanding of why Norman Cousins found that watching Marx Brothers films led to pain reduction. It is also probably the reason for the hysterical laughter of somebody who has been injured in an accident – it's nature's way of getting the brain to release endorphins to relieve a sudden onslaught of pain.

For many years I have noticed that those patients of mine who seem to experience the lowest levels of pain are invariably those who can laugh, sometimes at themselves in times of difficulty or danger.

Cilla, the patient of mine mentioned in the previous chapter, found great therapeutic value in humour and laughter. She says:
'To encourage myself to continue feeling positive and to lift my spirits, I find myself choosing funny films, like Monty Python material, and silly songs, as produced by the Bonzo Dog Doo Dah Band – *My Pink Half of the Drainpipe*. Occasionally, I resort to something very silly indeed: a "designed" daydream in which England wins the World Cup! It may be a once in a century occurrence and I am therefore well aware that I

may not be around for the next time, so to avoid disappointment, I have arranged for such an event to have already taken place. Can you imagine how this nation would react should this ever occur again? Just to think of it does strangely lift one's spirits, and the best thing is that cancer can't control your daydreams, and they still come for free.'

Another of my patients, Rosie, who was badly brain-damaged in a car accident some years ago, also says that humour is essential and she raises her spirits by watching videotapes of *Fawlty Towers*, *Mr Bean*, Ben Elton or *Some Mothers Do 'Ave 'Em*.

Put on a Happy Face

Researchers at Clark University in Worcester, Massachusetts, observed that simply having people adopt the facial expression of a particular mood actually created that mood in the people themselves. Expressions of fear brought on feelings of fear and stress, and so on with sadness, anger or disgust. However, when the researchers asked them to repeat over and over again the letter 'e', which makes the face adopt an expression similar to a smile, feelings of happiness were engendered. This piece of research seems to support the old idea that we should 'spread sunshine all over the place, and put on a happy face'.

Someone who smiles a lot tends to have a more positive effect on other people than a person who is always serious. Not surprisingly, smilers are thought of as warm, outgoing people, whereas those who restrict their smiles are seen as cold and withdrawn. Frowns make you feel worse than ever and if you suffer from headaches it could be because you frown too much. A smile is universally recognised and is probably the most important aspect of body language.

I believe that humour is a very great coping mechanism, and that if we are anxious or angry we can often break out of it by laughing at ourselves. I also believe that people who can laugh at themselves cope with obstacles and problems far more effectively and rebound more quickly than those who simply cannot smile at a misfortune.

One Japanese study suggests that laughter can have a balancing effect on natural killer cells and other white blood cells in people with non-standard levels, raising or normalising cell activity.[1] In the United States researcher Kathleen Dillon and her colleagues carried out an experiment with ten students who first watched a humorous videotape, *Richard*

Pryor Live, and then an ordinary teaching video. Their levels of salivary immunoglobulin A, a type of antibody that seems to defend against viral infections of the upper respiratory tract, were measured before and after watching each video.

After watching the humorous video the antibodies of the participants increased, yet viewing the teaching video had no discernible effect. Furthermore, the researchers found that the students who said that they used humour as a means of coping with stresses in life had consistently higher levels of immunoglobulin A before watching either film.[2] All this suggests that laughter has some kind of normalising effect on both our moods and our immune system.

Laughing Gas

Dr Michael Miller, Director of the Centre for Preventative Cardiology at the University of Maryland, presented evidence that an active sense of humour may influence heart disease to the American Heart Foundation's annual conference in 2000. He had devised a questionnaire to assess whether or not someone has enough *joie de vivre* to protect them from heart disease. The responses of 150 patients who had either suffered heart attacks or been treated for clogged arteries were compared with those of the same age who had no history of heart trouble. Volunteers were asked how they would respond to day-to-day situations such as arriving at a party to find someone else wearing the same outfit or having soup dropped into their laps by a waiter. The results showed heart attack patients were 40 per cent less likely than their healthy counterparts to laugh in these and other tricky situations.

Michael Miller and his colleagues are now looking to see precisely which chemicals the act of laughing might release. One candidate is nitric oxide, known to dilate blood vessels. 'Wouldn't it be ironic if laughing gas turns out to be protective for the heart?' Miller says.

The advantage of humour is that you can safely release a lot of repressed thoughts that you would perhaps not normally get a chance to express. One of my patients, a lady with Parkinson's disease, says that for her laughter is a coping mechanism. 'Sometimes I'm doubled up in laughter at my own helplessness,' she says.

In his book *Love, Medicine and Miracles,* Dr Bernie Siegel writes that humour's most important psychological function is to jolt us out of our habitual frame of mind and promote new perspectives:

*Psychologists have long noted that one of the best measures of
mental health is the ability to laugh at oneself in a gently mocking
way – like the dear old school teacher, a colostomy patient of mine
several years ago, who named her two stomas Harry and Larry.
When she would call me and say Harry was acting up again, her
light heartedness helped both of us deal with the situation.*

In October 2000, the German health magazine *Apotheke Umschau*
reported on the work of Professor Gunther Sickl, a gelotologist – or
laughter expert. He claimed that a one-minute guffaw is as refreshing as
forty-five minutes of exercise. 'Phrases such as laughing yourself sick
should actually be turned around to read laughing yourself well,' he said.

The magazine article went on to say that people who want to stay
healthy now have an alternative to fitness clubs: laughter clubs are
spreading around the world, especially in Germany. They were first
conceived by Indian doctor Manda Kataria from Bombay, who started
the first official laughter club in 1995. It now meets in a park in the city
for a good laugh each morning. Professor Sickl offers people who cannot
make it to a laughter club three pieces of advice:

1 Try to keep at least one funny incident at the front of your
mind. Try to remember the little details about it.

2 Secondly, keep a humour diary and record what has particularly
amused you.

3 Finally, keep things that you find funny and keep them in a
collection.

What Happens When We Laugh

Sometimes I explain to my patients that when we laugh, every organ in
our body is affected in such a way that laughing has been called
'stationary jogging'. This is what happens:

O When you laugh, your breathing quickens as you inhale deeply
and exhale through your vocal chords.

O This exercises the face, neck and shoulders, stomach and
diaphragm.

○ Blood pressure is reduced while blood vessels expand close to the skin's surface and improve the circulation. Often people seem to blush or go red when they are laughing and that is why!

○ Laughter increases the amount of oxygen in the blood, which helps the body to heal itself and resist further infection.

○ Laughter lowers the heart rate, stimulates the appetite and burns up calories.

○ A good laugh will also stimulate beta-endorphins, the body's natural pain-killing tranquillisers, leading some researchers to suggest that laughing can prevent ulcers and digestive disorders.

The Healing Power of Hope

There is a story about two oncologists who are having breakfast together before the start of a conference on cancer treatment. One complains bitterly, 'You know, Bob, I just don't understand it. We used the same drugs, the same dosage, the same schedule and the same entry criteria. Yet I got a 22 per cent response rate and you got a 74 per cent. That's unheard of for metastatic cancer. How do you do it?'

His colleague replies, 'We're both using Etoposide, Platinum, Oncovin and Hydroxyurea. You call yours EPOH. I tell my patients I'm giving them HOPE. As dismal as the statistics are, I emphasise that we have a chance.'

Sadly the story is not true but was made up by a medical oncologist practising in La Jolla, California, to illustrate a point that he wanted to make. Quite obviously, if it had been true, it would have changed everything we know about cancer and its treatment because optimism would be the most powerful anti-cancer agent yet discovered. Still, as we will see, the story is actually not so far from the truth because there are numerous genuine reports of a similar phenomenon. I know from my work that optimism and hope are all-important. So do doctors, but too often they seem reluctant to acknowledge that their attitude towards their patients has any effect.

One of the exceptions, Dr Bernie Siegel, writes in his book *Peace, Love and Healing* of the importance of love and hope:

I consider it my job as a doctor to give my patients both, because that's what they need to be able to live. Since I don't know what the outcome will be for any individual, no matter what the pathology report says, I can in all honesty give everyone hope.

In 1987, the *British Medical Journal* published an extraordinary study showing that if a doctor was positive and hopeful it in turn affected his patients. Entitled 'General practice consultations: is there any point in being positive?', it was written by a Southampton general practioner, Dr K. B. Thomas. His interest in the subject had been aroused, as he explained in the introduction, after he heard a comment from another doctor: 'The reason why Dr Smith is so successful is because he is so positive.'

Dr Thomas selected 200 patients with problems such as sore throat, giddiness, nasal congestion and aches and pains. They were not seriously ill, but he was unable to make a definite diagnosis. He decided to compare the effect of telling them honestly about his uncertainty with the effect of giving them a firm diagnosis and promise of recovery. He also wanted to discover if adding a placebo prescription made any difference to their recovery. Randomly he divided the patients into four groups: A, B, C and D.

○ Group A was given a firm diagnosis and a prescription for a drug they were told would certainly make them feel better.

○ Group B was given a firm diagnosis and told they needed no prescription to get better.

○ Group C was told, 'I cannot be certain what is wrong with you' and given a prescription with the words, 'I'm not sure if the treatment I'll give you will have any effect.'

○ Group D was told, 'I cannot be sure what the matter is with you and therefore I cannot give you anything.'

Two weeks later, 64 per cent of those given a deceptively positive consultation were better, compared to 39 per cent of those who were given honest uncertainty. Giving the patient a prescription made very little difference, probably because the doctor had already maximised the placebo effect by being so positive. The report concluded that the doctor himself may be 'the most effective treatment available'.[3]

The Placebo Effect

Linked to this is the well-known 'placebo effect', which is just another example of the body's ability to heal itself. Dr Jeanne Achterberg, President of the Association for Transpersonal Psychology, explains that the effectiveness of the placebo varies 'depending upon how much the patient expects to benefit'. In other words, those who believe they will get better have a significantly greater recovery rate than those who believe they will not get better, or believe that they will get worse.

In their book *Remarkable Recovery*, Caryle Hirshberg and Marc Ian Barasch surveyed 50 patients who had recovered from cancers that should have been fatal. Belief in a positive outcome was cited by 75 per cent of the patients and 71 per cent felt that a fighting spirit was essential.

GUIDELINES FOR FINDING HOPE

It is not always easy to be hopeful. If, like some of my patients, you need to give yourself hope during a particularly difficult time, here are a few ways that I recommend:

○ Be positive. Tell yourself that you have the choice to look at any hopeless situation and take either a positive or a negative attitude (*see page 53*).

○ Look at what you have left and not at what you have lost.

○ Tap into positive memories. We all have positive memories that we have forgotten. Recall them, especially your past successes and the times you overcame difficult situations. They can empower you.

○ Calm down. Relax. Think. Never make an irreversible decision at a low point in your life. Quick decisions are impulsive and reactive. They will only make a problem worse.

○ Practise reacting positively. Believe that every scar can be turned into a star!

○ Set goals. You can improve your future if you set yourself clear goals (*see page 56*).

The Healing Power of Optimism

If you have a sense of personal power, you tend to be hopeful and optimistic most of the time. If you feel hopeless, you also tend to feel pessimistic. Life inflicts the same setbacks and tragedies on optimists as it does on pessimists. The difference is that optimists weather them better than pessimists do. Optimists bounce back from defeat by understanding the importance of learning from past setbacks and using the experience to move forward. Pessimists find excuses to rationalise their failures and are convinced that it is pointless to even try.

Professor Martin Seligman, a psychologist at the University of Pennsylvania, has studied pessimism and optimism for decades and has observed that pessimists get depressed more often, achieve less at school and have worse physical health than their peers. Author of *Learned Optimism* and one of the world's leading authorities on the subject, Seligman believes we are all optimists by nature and that not only does optimism help prevent disease, but it is also a crucial ally in the healing process. Seligman conducted one study with thirty cancer patients who underwent therapy to boost their optimism and overcome self-defeating beliefs. All of the patients had a type of cancer that had a high chance of recurring. 'The course was designed to make them more optimistic about events in their lives; it didn't focus on cancer,' Seligman explained.

The course succeeded in making the thirty participants more optimistic and the researchers also discovered that the patients who took the course afterwards had more natural killer cells than patients in a control group who had received only the standard medical treatment.

Seligman defines optimism in terms of how people explain to themselves success and failure:

○ Optimists view failure as something that can be changed so that they can succeed next time.

○ Pessimists take the blame for failure, ascribing it to some lasting characteristic that they are helpless to change.

The Power of Belief

It seems important, if not crucial, for both the patient and the doctor to be hopeful and optimistic. If a doctor is seen as powerful and trustworthy, the patient gets better faster; indeed, one study has shown that reassurance and support from the doctor raises the threshold of pain tolerance in hospital patients.[4]

Just as positive support and encouragement from a doctor can promote healing, prejudices or discouraging statements can bring about what has been called a 'nocebo' effect by undermining the patient's confidence and hindering the healing process. A Canadian study showed with dramatic effect that people who see their health poorly die earlier and have more disease than those who see themselves as healthy. Over 3,500 senior citizens were studied for seven years. Their subjective health status was measured at the beginning by the question: 'For your age, would you say, in general, your health is excellent, good, fair, poor or bad?' Their objective health status was assessed by reports from their doctors on medical problems and how often they needed hospital treatment or surgery.

The results showed that those people who rated their health as poor were almost three times more likely to die during the seven years of the study than those who viewed their health as excellent. But, surprisingly, subjective health from the patient was more accurate in predicting who would die than the objective health from the doctor. Those who were viewed as in poor health by the doctors survived at a higher rate as long as *they believed their health to be good*.[5]

In 1979, George Vaillant published the results of a study that had started with over 200 healthy undergraduates of Harvard University in the early 1940s who had completed questionnaires every year or every other year. He found that as the men entered middle age 'positive mental health significantly retards irreversible midlife decline in physical health'. Of the 59 men who were most optimistic, as assessed from their twenties to their forties, only 2 had become chronically ill or died by the age of 53. Of the 48 men who were the most pessimistic, *18* had become chronically ill or had died by that age.[6]

In 1987 Vaillant, Martin Seligman and psychologist Christopher Peterson published another study updating the situation of 99 of those men. Seligman said: 'The men's explanatory style at age 25 predicted their health at 65. Around the age of 45 the health of the pessimists started to deteriorate more quickly.'[7]

Optimism and Health

Optimism and hope have healing powers. For example, 122 men who had had a first heart attack were assessed according to their degree of optimism or pessimism. Eight years later, of the 25 most pessimistic men, 21 had died, yet of the 25 most optimistic, only 6 had died. Again, their mental outlook proved better at predicting their survival than any medical risk factor. In another piece of research, optimistic patients about to have heart bypass surgery had a much faster recovery and fewer medical complications during and after surgery than did the pessimistic patients. This is particularly interesting as 'complications during surgery' are referred to which suggests that even in an unconscious and anaesthetised state optimism or pessimism is still having an influence.[8]

A study of people paralysed by spinal injury showed that those who had more hope were able to achieve greater levels of physical mobility compared to other patients with the same level of injury, but who felt less hopeful.[9]

Finally, optimists really are less likely to suffer an early death than pessimists! An important study carried out by psychiatrists and psychologists from the famous Mayo Clinic administered a personality survey between 1962 and 1965 to 839 people whose average age was 35. Of that group, 124 were classified as optimistic, 197 as pessimistic and 518 as mixed. Thirty-five years on, the researchers reported in the *Mayo Clinic Proceedings* that the most pessimistic participants showed a *91 per cent increase in the risk of premature death*.[10]

I agree with Martin Seligman's belief that we are optimists by nature but that sometimes the sunshine of optimism gets clouded over by events in life that then push us into pessimism. Optimism also has a strange power over other people. The optimist is generally a buoyant person, able to be a bit more tolerant or generous in the moment, which means they tend to bring out the better parts of people or situations without really trying. Optimism leads the optimist to feelings of gratitude and the wish to share their good fortune with others. It also tends to inspire actions that are benign and just plain helpful to others. The person who sends out a positive message very often gets a positive response.

My Pointers to Becoming an Optimist

To provide some guidance towards your goal of optimism, I would offer the following key steps:

Develop a positive mental attitude What distinguishes an optimist from a pessimist is the way in which they explain both good and bad events. Facts are facts, but you have a choice about how you interpret them and once you can begin to see that, a whole new world of freedom lies ahead of you. The happiest people are generally those who accept that life perhaps isn't perfect, but nobody is responsible for their happiness except themselves and they don't take it personally when things are unsatisfactory. Comparing life as you think it should be with life as it is and then blaming yourself or others when things don't fit in with your ideal is quite a good way of becoming pessimistic. So have a look at the situation, whatever it is, and see if you can't find another way of interpreting it. You can look at one failure as a springboard from which you can bounce back, rather than a steamroller that's flattened your ego. However bad a situation may be, there is always a creative way of reacting to it if you only look.

Set positive goals As we discovered in the previous chapter, setting goals is another powerful means for developing a positive attitude and lifting self-esteem (*see page 56*). Goal setting can be used to create a 'success cycle' and is a very good way for a family to band together and help in the patient's recovery. When you set goals, do not use any negative words in your goal statement. Be specific, because the clearer your goal is, the more likely you are to reach it. Remember to set up short-term goals that can be used to help you achieve your long-term goals. Ask yourself each morning and evening, 'What must I do today to achieve my long-term goal?'

Become aware of self-talk We are always talking to ourselves inside our heads and it affects our unconscious minds. Sometimes the pessimist's thoughts are a stream of constant self-doubt or self-criticism. Try listening to what you are telling yourself because once you hear it you can start contradicting it. It may help you to draw up two lists of beliefs that you have about yourself. On the first, list all your negative beliefs and on the second, list all your positive beliefs. Have an objective look at the negative ones. Are they really founded in fact? They may seem to be only because you have been listening too well to them. Try changing your negative beliefs, but be realistic about it. If you have been telling yourself for years that you are no good at making friends, it may well appear to be true. But consider the possibility that the reason you found it difficult is not because there is something terribly wrong with you, but simply that you have been acting on that belief as if it were an instruction. You could change it to: *'I'm willing to make more friends'*, cross it off the negative list and add it to the positive list. When you have gone through all the negatives, having replaced them with positives wherever you can, screw up the negative list and throw it away or burn it. Now put the list of positives somewhere you can see it and focus on it.

Use positive affirmations Affirmations are another form of self-talk that you can use to change the way you think. They are positive sentences or phrases similar to songs you hear on the radio and then find going round inside your head and can imprint your subconscious mind to create a healthy, positive self-image, can break the circuit of negative thinking and call a halt to the production of stress hormones. Most importantly, affirmations can help you to release feelings of guilt, anger or even grief from past events that may have contributed to your illness. More on affirmations in the next chapter.

Use positive imagery For many years I have asked my seminar participants to imagine they are holding a lemon which they then start to peel. Having taken some moments to do this, they then raise the freshly peeled imaginary lemon to their mouth and bite into it. The response is always the same – there is a great reaction as people's mouths start watering and they have the same experience as they would with a real lemon! I use this simple exercise as a clear demonstration that thoughts really can affect the body. Some of the most promising research on the power of imagery involves visualising white blood cells attacking cancer cells. This was first described by Carl and Stephanie Simonton in their groundbreaking book *Getting Well Again*, which was published in the 1970s. Dr Stephanie Simonton has recently revealed as yet unpublished data showing a 47 per cent increase in the responsiveness of T lymphocytes in cancer patients who had practised guided imagery. You have to be able to picture your life the way you want it to be before it happens. In terms of ideal health, you must be able to see yourself in that state if you really want to experience it.

Laugh As I have explained, laughter enhances the immune system, improves cardiovascular functioning and helps to release pain-killing endorphins into the body. Wise people cultivate humour as a way of coping with life because, let's face it, a lot of life is absurd. Often we find ourselves in apparently impossible situations, but if we can laugh about them, somehow they become enjoyable, or at least tolerable. So often people say, 'You'll look back on this and laugh.' Why wait? See the humour in the situation and have a good laugh straight-away!

Angela is one of my patients who found these key steps for optimism absolutely invaluable. For almost twenty years she had suffered from head pains and in the four years before I began to work with her, the pain had worsened to such an extent that, as she said, 'It seems to control my life and prevent me from doing many things I would like to do.' Angela and her husband had not even been able to enjoy a meal out in almost twenty years because of the level of pain she was in. She was more than willing to learn many of the techniques that I felt would be of benefit and within a few sessions her long-standing head pains had all but gone.

Subsequently, Angela was able to reclaim much of her life and she and her husband had begun to enjoy many pleasurable pastimes that others take for granted. Then she was diagnosed with systemic lupus, a chronic disorder of the immune system. The news, she said, was 'like being hit with a sledgehammer'. Fortunately, all that she had learned while we worked together to heal her pain now became of even greater value.

'For two weeks I felt very low, trying to accept what was happening to me and trying to think of a way to fight this illness. Suddenly a voice in my head asked me if I was going to let everything I'd learned over the previous two years fly out of the window. I was not! I gave myself a good talking to, took all the negative thoughts out of my head and replaced them with positive ones, and told myself that this was another challenge that I was going to fight. Fortunately, I have now learned so much about how to relax, not to get stressed-out over silly things and not to worry unnecessarily. When I think of how I used to be, I cannot believe this is really me saying these things. I have changed so much and other people have noticed.'

This was a good basis that led to Angela being able to deal effectively with the various symptoms of the systemic lupus.

The Healing Power of Social Support

Just as laughter, optimism and hope can positively influence our health and well-being, so too can social support. Quite how or why social interaction influences our health is still not properly understood, but while traditionally medicine has focused its attention on the sick person, there is now mounting evidence that health and disease are reflections of social connectedness or lack of it.

In 1988, Dr James House published research that was to influence the way many health professionals looked at illness. He reviewed 6 studies of over 22,000 men and women from different communities around the world and discovered that people without well-established support systems had significantly shorter life expectancies. Those with very few friends and supportive relationships had a death rate *2 to 4 times higher* than those with considerable networks of support.[11] Social relationships seemed to rival the well-established health risk factors such as cigarette smoking, blood pressure, obesity and lack of physical activity. While smoking increases mortality risk by a factor of just 1.6, social isolation does so by a factor of 2.0, making it a greater health risk.

The evidence is clear that this factor is not confined to serious or life-threatening disease, but also your chances of getting a cold. In one study, 276 volunteers answered a questionnaire about their social ties – whether they were married, had children, worked, had friends, were a member of the local church, etc. They then had drops containing live cold virus sprayed into their nostrils. It was found that the volunteers with many different *types* of social tie were much less likely to catch a cold than the less gregarious, and if they did, the cold was likely to be less severe.[12]

It wasn't the number of friends the volunteers had that was important, but the number of different social groups to which they belonged. Those with the fewest (one to three) different types of social tie were four times more likely to get a cold than those with the most (six or more) types of social tie. Other factors found to *increase* their chances of getting a cold were smoking, alcohol abstinence, poor sleep, a low intake of vitamin C and being introverted.

People Need People

People need people for their very health and survival. We now know that married people tend to have stronger immune systems than those who are not married and that happily married people have more robust immune responses than the unhappily married. Harmonious relationships, including your relationship with yourself, usually result in better health. However, we are so often moving around. We move to take a new job or to seek education and many people have jobs that push them towards a nomadic lifestyle. Even people like Dorby, who lived in the same small village all his life, find that they frequently have new neighbours. Figures show that marriages are now shorter than ever. Consequently many people feel rootless, with very little feeling of home or community, and this feeling of being cut off from people and having no one to turn to creates a medical risk.

In 1995 the respected medical journal *Cancer* published the findings of a group of Canadian researchers led by epidemiologist Elizabeth Maunsell. They had followed the progress of 224 women with cancer that was either confined to the breast or had only spread to local lymph nodes. The patients were all asked whether or not they had talked to or confided in a person, or people, during the three months after their surgery.

The findings of the study were that the seven-year survival rate among women who had not talked was 56 per cent. Those who had shared their feelings with just one other person had a 66 per cent survival rate, while those who had confided in two or more people saw their survival rate go up to 76 per cent.[13] Although we have these extraordinary statistics we still do not really know *why* talking and expressing feelings should have such a striking effect on survival but again, if a new chemotherapy drug was discovered to have a 20 per cent increase in survival rates of breast cancer patients imagine the attention it would get from the medical profession and the media!

Dr Karen Weihs, an assistant professor of psychiatry at the George Washington University Medical School, is due to publish a report in 2001 which will again show that survival rates of women with breast cancer were dramatically higher among those with a wide circle of supportive friends. She asked women diagnosed with the disease to list those outside their home they could rely on for help or support in times of trouble. The lists varied between two and ten, with an average of six.

Dr Weihs found that survival odds grew as the number of close friends went above six. She believes that feelings of security may calm women and lower their production of stress hormones. As the hormone levels drop, immune function improves and the body is able to fight the cancer more effectively, thus lowering both the risk of death and the chance of the cancer recurring.

This remarkable phenomenon of the benefit of counselling or a friend in whom you can confide is not specific just to cancer patients. In the early 1980s a report was published showing very similar survival figures over a five-year period for patients suffering from high blood pressure. Four hundred patients each underwent a ten-minute counselling session with a family member and then with a group of patients and their families. At the end of the five-year period those in the support group had a death rate *57 per cent lower* than those in the control group, which again would seem to underline the importance of family members or friends giving support and encouragement.[14]

I know that having friends in whom they can confide has helped many of my patients to get better. One of them told me:

There are benefits to an illness. The value and impact of friends is overwhelming. When they knew I had a problem I was inundated with 'Get well' mail and phone calls from all over the world (you know that we lived in several different countries). I had never known before how much compassion friends are able to show and transmit. Even less had I realised how comforting and stimulating those communications of empathy are. And it has never stopped. Sometimes I feel embarrassed.

Many reports have illustrated just how important were the connections between health and social ties. One of these was published in the *British Medical Journal* in 1993. Each man living in the Swedish city of Gothenburg and born in 1933 was offered the chance of having a free medical examination. In all, 752 men took up the offer. Seven years later they were contacted again. In that time forty-one of them had died. Those who had originally said they were under intense emotional stress had a death rate three times higher than those who said they were living a relaxed and happy life. The stress factors cited by the men included

serious financial problems, divorce, redundancy or being sued by somebody else. Having experienced three of these difficulties within a year
before the medical check-up was a stronger predictor of dying during
the following seven years than medical indicators such as high blood
pressure or high cholesterol levels. Among the men who said they had
a good network of intimacy with their wife and close friends, *there was
no relationship at all* between high stress levels and death rate.[15]

In America, Dr Phyllis Moen carried out a remarkable thirty-year
study by following the progress of 427 married women, ranging in age
from twenty-five to fifty, between 1956 and 1986. As with the other
researchers, she found that women who took on multiple roles or were
members of volunteer organisations had fewer major illnesses, better
mental health and greater longevity than other women in the study. She
felt that the women volunteers got out into the world to help strangers
and to connect with members of their community and were more 'socially
integrated' and therefore less lonely and isolated. Helping others creates
social bonds. However, the fact that they engaged in multiple roles
showed they did not feel constrained by wife and mother roles. They
were committed wives and mothers, but they went beyond the 1950s
model of the perfect woman by embracing other sides of themselves.[16]

The Healing Power of Love

Before we can really feel in touch with others, we must learn to feel
really connected to ourselves. Being completely alone, without any
connections to other people, can also lead us to feel disconnected to
ourselves. We seek out relationships for many different reasons, but in
all of them we are asking for the same thing: we want to be recognised
and loved for our own uniqueness and at the same time we want love
and to feel connected to another. For those who manage it, or at least
find some semblance of this balance, there is the reward of better physical,
psychological and spiritual health.

Although there have been some studies that have set out to try to measure
the effects of love, there have been some which show graphically the effects
of not being loved. One of the most impressive was unwittingly carried
out in Germany just after the Second World War. In this study researchers
looked at children growing up in two orphanages that were quite close to
each other. Due to rationing all the children were getting identical amounts

of food. In the Bienenhaus orphanage the children suffered under the tyranny of the stern and forbidding Fräulein Schwarz.

The children in the Bienenhaus orphanage put on less weight and grew less quickly than children in the nearby Volgenest orphanage cared for by the affectionate and warm-hearted Fräulein Grün. Then, part way through the study, the grim Fräulein Schwarz replaced the affectionate Fräulein Grün at the Volgenest orphanage. Despite the fact that the children under Fräulein Schwarz's care now received extra food, they did not thrive. In fact the average rate at which the children in the two orphanages were growing was reversed.[17]

Sigmund Freud said many years ago, 'In the final analysis, we must love in order not to fall ill.' I am convinced that this is the root of many of our health problems and it is now being borne out by research. Dr David McClelland, a professor of psychology and social relations at Harvard University, is particularly interested in the effects of love on the immune function and neurobiologist Rita Levi-Montalcini won the Nobel Prize for Medicine for her discovery of what is known as nerve growth factor (NGF) which, she showed, affects cells in both the immune and central nervous systems. This helps to explain how the emotional state of an individual could be related to immune function.

Although McClelland, Levi-Montalcini and other researchers like them may not yet know how or why our emotions so demonstrably affect our immune systems, it is clear that they are somehow linked. David McClelland reported that when college students were shown a film of Mother Theresa helping the sick and dying poor of Calcutta, their immune functioning immediately increased and remained heightened one hour later.[18] It would appear therefore that even *watching* a person engaged in a selfless or loving act may affect the observer.

Looking for Love

The problem is that most people are looking for love to come from outside them, yet our ability to love can only come from within. Many people who feel unloved, try to earn love from others by pleasing them. Many of my cancer patients are 'too good to be true'. Their helpful and self-effacing behaviour is saying, 'Please love and accept me.' But the best way to put more love into our lives is to start giving love, and the best place to start is by learning to love ourselves.

Very often our feelings of being unloved and unlovable go back to early childhood. Some people live out their lives looking for the love they didn't get as children. I once saw a wonderful piece of graffiti written on a wall: 'It's never too late to have a happy childhood.' Of course you can't go back to your parents and do it all over again, but you can start giving yourself the love now that you didn't get then.

Some of my healing work is done not individually, but with groups of up to fifty participants at a time in what I call 'healing circles'. Everybody sits joining hands, linked in a circle while I go around the outside of the circle giving healing to each person for a minute or so. As long as participants are joined together in this way I feel that it not only helps to pass the energy around the circle but also that I am working, on an energy level, with a unit rather than fifty different individuals. Since each circle tends to last for about fifty minutes, I feel that it has the same effect as working with each participant for that total length of time. The results from my healing circles have been as good as those from individual sessions. Obviously people join circles for different reasons and have different healing needs: some come because of a physical need, some for emotional healing, some to take the time to think of others who need help or healing. From all the letters I receive after the healing circles it is clear that for many participants their healing starts on an emotional level, releasing blocks to physical health. The following letter is a good example:

> I recently attended one of your healing circles in Exeter. I found the experience deeply moving and thought that you might like to hear about it. I came to see you for two reasons. The first is because I have been trying for a child for over seven years. The second was because I have also had ME for the last three of those years, and although it was better than it had been, I felt very trapped in a cycle of stress and illness.
>
> Sitting in the circles I had no idea of what to expect. I am quite alternative and 'green' but not a very 'esoteric' person, which made what happened all the more surprising to me. I tried just to let go onto the beautiful music and this is where I went . . .
> First, I was sitting on my sofa at home. I became smaller and smaller until I turned into a white bird – a gull maybe. I flew out of the window and into the sky. At this point I thought maybe I would have

a feeling of freedom and lightness – maybe this is what I needed – but no. I flew directly off up the A38 towards the east. I felt in control but not of where I was going. I just followed. It soon became very clear I was flying to London, over all the familiar landmarks that I knew so well. As I reached London the journey became more and more detailed. Across the streets of west London, past Euston, King's Cross, up to Islington and on to Hackney – the route I have always taken. And then I was there, circling above my parents' house, the house I grew up in. I could see myself aged seven or eight. I was standing in the cold bleak hall by myself. I knew I had to fly down to contact this child but was prevented from doing so by a wall of pain so vast that I thought it would break my heart. I don't think I have ever cried so deeply (and I have cried a lot before). My heart just hurt so much. Someone then came and touched me (one of the healers who was helping you). I immediately felt a wave of calmness wash over me and in this I was able to fly down and meet and then become this child.

(At this point it might be helpful to know that, as a child, I received almost no physical or emotional love from either parent.)

Standing in the hall (as a child) I felt very unhappy, desolate and not knowing what to do. The words 'Why don't you love me?" went round and round my head.

(As an adult, I have known for a long time about this lack of love and have done lots of work about getting angry with my parents but I have never remembered how I actually felt as a child – just what happened.)

I wandered around the cold house wondering what I should do. Then it seemed that I was the bird again. And I could see that it really wasn't the child's fault that its parents didn't love it. That the child was a beautiful and lovely child that deserved to be loved. That it hurt and it was bad luck that the parents couldn't love it. It wasn't the child's fault – how could it be? And then I took the child and together, as two birds, we flew back over the dirty streets of London, on and on and on until we reached Devon. As we reached the sofa, we turned back into people – it felt very strange – like a big me and a little me. (At this point you put your hands on my shoulders.) I cuddled the little me and gradually she sort of disappeared into the big me.

And suddenly as I write this, I realise for the first time in my life that this is probably what people mean when they talk about 'Loving yourself' – I have never really got it before.

GUIDELINES FOR PUTTING MORE LOVE INTO YOUR LIFE

Here are some of my suggestions:

❍ Be kind to yourself. Encourage and praise yourself and don't be harsh on yourself if you don't come up to your own expectations.

❍ Talk to someone. Human beings are group animals and talking things through with other people can be helpful in several ways. It can take some of the edges off a problem and instead of going round and round in circles, you can start to see new solutions and possibilities.

❍ Remember love. List at least three times in the past when you felt a surge of loving feelings as you thought of or talked to someone, or gave them love.

❍ Think of three people who could use your love. Recall those loving feelings you had in the above list. Send that love out to these three people.

❍ Remember unexpected love. Think of three times someone gave you love that was unexpected.

❍ Express love. Think of some way you could surprise and delight someone tomorrow with an expression of your love.

The Healing Power of Forgiveness

So many people remain locked in the past by continually reliving the events that caused them pain. But your past is not happening to you *now*, unless you are recreating it for yourself. Accept that things happened once and no amount of brooding is going to alter that.

If you have suffered a great deal of emotional pain and hurt in the past, you may well be carrying around a heavy burden of anger and resentment against those who hurt you. Sometimes these feelings may have turned into anger and hatred against yourself. Self-hatred, for example, is a common cause and symptom of depression. Let it go. Remember that the resentment you feel is producing harmful chemicals in your body and is probably affecting your view of the world as a whole. It won't alter the past one little bit, but it will affect the present. Make a decision to release yourself from the past.

Forgiveness is crucial to this process. It renews life by finishing unfinished business. If you have been through a broken or lost relationship and you are holding feelings of anger, resentment or bitterness, you are harming only yourself. If you can, forgive the people who have hurt you. They were probably unhappy and confused themselves. By forgiving others, you are helping to heal yourself and you are also creating space in your life for more positive helpful people to come in.

If forgiveness is difficult for you to accept, simply think of releasing yourself and breaking the links that tie you to those who hurt you. You can imagine the people you are angry with, tell them that you forgive them and let them go. Do not imagine yourself hurting them but let them walk away to a distant place where they will be happy and out of your life. You may not initially *feel* forgiving, but what is important is your *willingness* to forgive.

Forgiving Yourself

You may also need to forgive yourself. Whether you have actually done something that you really regret – and there are very few people who have not – or whether you suffer from that overall sense of guilt that so many people seem to be burdened with, feeling guilty will not put anything right. Remember there is still a child within you who is growing and learning and is bound to make some mistakes. Allow yourself to be imperfect, let the mistakes go, forgive yourself and love yourself. You

cannot always control the things that affect you, but you *can* control
the effect they have on you.

Lillian was a lawyer working for the Norwegian Department of Justice
before a whiplash injury caused by a car accident confined her to bed
for several months. Her movement was further restricted by rheumatoid
arthritis. By the time she heard about me, she had already tried a
range of treatments to improve her condition, none of which had had
much effect. Lillian enrolled for one of my seminars and, during a
healing circle on the second day, experienced a tremendous reaction:
  'Matthew went around the circle and touched everybody for a short
while. When he touched me, a very strong wave of energy washed
through me and I felt a deep peace and gratitude. I had had no expectations, so I was quite bewildered about my reaction.'
  Lillian's husband collected her after the seminar and they started the
long drive home. Lillian cried for almost three hours during that
journey, releasing long-buried memories of her mother, who had died
of a brain tumour when Lillian was eighteen years old. Afterwards, she
told me, she felt very much at peace.
  During the three days after the seminar Lillian was able to step out
of herself and see her life from a distance, recognising previously undis-
covered patterns and connections. When she woke up on the third
day, she was free of pain for the first time in several years and felt a
tremendous joy of life. She could move in such a way that the injured
area between her shoulders was more relaxed, and her circulation was
greatly improved. The most important aspect of the transformation she
underwent at this time was the evaporation of fear, especially of death.
Lillian said she had previously been one of those people who are afraid
of everything – of the dark, of flying, of illness. For the first time in her
life she felt safe and enveloped by love.
  The extraordinary feelings Lillian experienced gradually subsided in
the following weeks and months. Initially this return to normality
distressed her and she wondered what she had done wrong. Then she
realised that she had to be the one to take herself forward and tackle
the life that was waiting for her. The healing had been the tools, but
the means lay in her own heart and mind.
  'One of the most important things Matthew says is that you must
have the willingness to confront yourself. To me this is about taking

hold of the things you have suppressed and stored away. It can be a tough process sometimes. I can see I have only just started this work, but what has been of great help to me is that I have learned how important forgiveness is.'

Time and again I have seen workshop participants going through the often-cathartic experience of forgiveness, which can lead them to reclaiming their life. To help them, I use the following exercise. You might like to have somebody read it to you or to make your own recording of it.

EXERCISE: THE BRIDGE TO FORGIVENESS

Reflect for a moment on what the word 'forgiveness' might mean. What is forgiveness? What might it mean to bring forgiveness into your life or into your heart?

Begin by slowly bringing into your mind the image of someone for whom you hold resentment. It might be somebody from your childhood, an ex-partner or a close friend. Perhaps you felt let down, abandoned, abused, betrayed, humiliated, rejected or misunderstood.

Take a few deep breaths and, as you let them out, allow yourself to become more relaxed and peaceful inside. Imagine that you are being surrounded, filled and protected by a very clear white light. This light is here to heal you from any past memory or hurt. Become aware of all the love you have within yourself. It might be by recalling the love you have for a child, your partner, a pet animal or a piece of music. Ask that this loving awareness now guide you as you expand beyond previously limiting experiences, which can now be released from your memory in order to make way for understanding and freedom.

Remember an upset that you have experienced in a relationship. It might be a disturbance that occurred with someone you valued and cared for, or whose approval and respect was important for you. Bring a specific incident to mind, with as much detail as possible, so that you can imagine it unfolding now. What was being said? Or not said? What were the attitudes, gestures, expressions or facial features? What was the true source of the upset or disagreement? What was your point of view? How did you justify your position to yourself and the other person?

Let that scene fade away. Take in a couple of deep breaths again and, as you let them out, let your shoulders drop. Allow your body to now release any tension it may have been holding.

Imagine now that you are standing on one side of a river. It might be a small stream, a wide estuary or anything in between. Reaching from one side of the river to the other is a bridge. At the far side stands the person with whom you experienced disappointment or hurt feelings. Notice the structure of the bridge. Is it made of ropes, steel girders or perhaps stone? Does it look very solid? Or is it flexible to allow for the movement of wind or heat? How does the bridge span the water? Is it high above it, or close to it? Is the bridge suspended or supported by columns? What are the qualities within you symbolised by the bridge?

Steel girders might be your integrity. Ropes might be your flexibility. Look at the water you are crossing. What challenge does it symbolise to you in your relationships with others? Fast-moving water might be emotions that sometimes get you into difficulties, a wide river the distance at which you sometimes keep yourself from others.

Imagine now that you are stepping onto the bridge and notice how firm it feels beneath your feet. Even if the wind seems to move the bridge a little bit, you are confident that it will support you as you cross over it. See yourself walking along it until you arrive at the midway point. Feel the excitement as you watch the water flowing beneath you and, as you look towards the other person, notice their qualities of warmth and contentment.

As you continue to cross the second half of the bridge, you feel lighter and freer as you come closer to the person on the other side. Now greet that person. Smile and reach out to shake hands or share a hug. The loving that you now extend towards the other person is being expanded within you as their loving comes back to you. For a moment, invite them into your heart. Be aware of any fear or anger that may arise to limit or prevent that entrance. Silently, in your heart, say, 'I forgive you.' For a moment, let go of those barriers of resentment, so that your heart can feel the possibility of forgiveness.

Say, 'I forgive you for whatever pain you may have caused me in the past, intentionally or otherwise, through your words or actions. I forgive you for whatever you did, or whatever you didn't do. I forgive you. I forgive you for your anger, your fear, your confusion.'

Allow that person to be there with you in the stillness and warmth of your heart. Let them be forgiven. Having finished so much business, let that person go on their way – touched by the possibility of your forgiveness. Giving yourself whatever time you need, allow that person to depart, noticing any feelings as they leave.

Claire came to one of my seminars because she felt that she needed help with a personal issue that went back twenty years. At the age of eighteen she had had an abortion and immediately afterwards went back to work and continued her life. It was only many years later that she began to experience terrible guilt and grief. She felt that she somehow needed the unborn child to forgive her for the abortion, but as the following meditation progressed, a different scenario emerged.

When this meditation had finished, Claire was surprised and somewhat taken aback by her emotional outpouring. More than anything, she was very surprised to find that the person on the other side of the bridge was not the unborn child, but herself. As she forgave herself, she realised that she had been young and in trouble when she had had her abortion. Now she was no longer trying to escape a lingering unacknowledged sense of loss.

The Best Advice

A recurrent theme throughout most of Aldous Huxley's life was that 'One never loves enough.' In a lecture shortly before he died, he said, 'It is a little embarrassing that, after 45 years of research and study, the best advice I can give to people is to be a little kinder to each other.'

That is probably the best advice I, too, could probably give – with an addendum:

Be a little kinder to each other – and to yourself.

Chapter 5

CHANGING
BEHAVIOURAL PATTERNS

Our attitudes are so important on the healing journey and many of these are established quite early in life. Without meaning to, the adults around us pass on what they themselves once learned. Then, as adults ourselves, we tend to simply rerun the equivalent of these old hard-drive computer programmes. Some are invaluable to us while others are not. All the same, we tend to recreate the emotional environment we knew, regardless of how limiting or destructive it might be. We need to explore the process of loosening the chains.

I have treated Lynne over a period of years during her battle with cancer. There have been several periods of remission, some of them quite lengthy, punctuated by recurrences. I first met her when I was lecturing in Hong Kong and she and her husband Geoff were living there. They later returned home to the United States but Lynne, always motivated and positive, has been to Britain numerous times to visit me for healing sessions. It was after one of those sessions that she told me a wonderful story that later became the title of a book about her experiences, *The Elephant's Rope and the Untethered Spirit.*

Lynne described a visit to India during which she met a beautiful elephant and her master selling rides near the old Amber Palace in Jaipur. While resting between work periods, the elephant seemed to be prevented from roaming by a very thin rope tied around one of her back legs and then to a heavy piece of undergrowth. The master would routinely sit down and smoke with his friends fifty yards away, a distance which, it seemed, would have given him very little influence over the elephant's mobility. With a very slight pull this large animal could have easily escaped or at least chosen to wander where she pleased. Lynne was curious about it and asked the master why his elephant didn't run off.

'When she was a baby,' he explained, 'a chain was put around her leg and then around a tree. She tried to break it but she couldn't. After a while she didn't try. I put the thin rope on her now because she doesn't know that she could break it. Her idea about it is from when she was small.'

Lynne told me that years later the story came back to her as a metaphor in her fight against cancer. 'Without knowing it, I, too, had been bound by an assortment of emotional, intellectual and psychological ropes – chains that had powerfully transformed themselves into limiting, though comfortably familiar, perspectives, attitudes and patterns. They were all a part of me, so extensively embedded that I didn't know that they might or could be separated out.'

Imprinting

In the early 1930s Konrad Lorenz, an Austrian zoologist who in 1973 won a Nobel Prize for Medicine, spent a great deal of time observing birds such as chickens, ducks and geese both in the wild and in farmyards. In his classic studies he described how, under certain conditions, newly hatched goslings and ducklings will follow and become socially bonded to the first moving object they encounter. Lorenz used the word 'imprinting' to describe the process by which this social bond was formed. The latest findings have led scientists to the unexpected conclusion that imprinting occurs in many species, including man.

Very early on in life the world shapes our development. Each experience, no matter how small, leaves its mark on us by stimulating more brain cell connections. With each new experience some connections are weakened while others are strengthened in a constant process of wiring. How our individual brains take shape depends on which connections are reinforced. Much of who we become is the result of our brains absorbing what's going on around us. Often we are unaware of this process but occasionally something is so significant that it alters our brain and becomes a memory.

Emotional memories register with particular potency. The problem for us in everyday life is that if a particular feature of an event seems similar to an emotionally charged memory from the past, the emotional mind responds by triggering the feelings that went with the remembered event.

Dave suffered from Parkinson's disease and found that memory provided him with an unexpectedly helpful tool. Parkinson's disease is a neurological disorder in which cells in the part of the brain that controls movement are lost, sometimes causing severe difficulty in performing movements. Everything, from walking, talking, swallowing and writing to even smiling can be affected. I was trying to help Dave to improve his walking. He would have great difficulty in starting to walk, and often had to be 'launched' by his wife. Once walking, he then had difficulty in stopping – unless he came to a doorway which, for some reason he couldn't understand, caused him to freeze on the spot so that he could not move forward.

One day as he was making a great effort to leave my healing room, some loose change fell out of one of his pockets and the coins rolled out through the doorway into my waiting room. Without thinking, probably distracted by the coins, Dave leant over to pick them up, passing through the doorway as he did so. He had solved his biggest difficulty. From that point, he always carried a folded handkerchief with him that he would throw through any doorway ahead of him. So long as he could focus on it, he had no problems with freezing to the spot!

The imprint of a horrific experience can affect people for the rest of the lives, as a study of Holocaust survivors found. Almost fifty years after they had lived through near-starvation, the killing of family and friends, and the constant terror of the Nazi concentration camps, one-third said they still felt fearful. Nearly three-quarters said they still felt anxious at reminders of their experience such as the barking of a dog, a knock at the door, the sight of a uniform or smoke rising from a chimney. After almost half a century, 60 per cent said they thought about the Holocaust almost every day and 80 per cent said they still had nightmares about it.

Messages that Harm or Heal

Too often we really don't take seriously enough the power that words and images have in our lives. Instead of empowering ourselves with positive thoughts, images and messages, we listen to authoritarian figures – whether they are parents, teachers, doctors or media.

Cardiologist Bernard Lown wrote the introduction to Norman Cousins' book *The Healing Heart* and told a story about a doctor who was making hospital rounds with his students. The doctor referred to a patient's problem, tricuspid stenosis, by its initials. 'Here is a classic case of TS,' he announced, leaving Lown and the other students in the room by themselves with the patient as he departed. Lown immediately noticed that the woman was very distressed; her pulse rate soared and her lungs began to fill with fluid. When he asked her why she was so upset, she explained to him that it was because the eminent doctor had said she was a 'Terminal Situation'. Whatever reassurances the young doctor gave her made no difference. Because the eminent doctor had said she was 'TS' she could not be persuaded that her problem was actually quite minor. Shortly afterwards she went into heart failure and died.

Very often parents unwittingly cause similar damage to their children. A command or imprint can go deep into the mind and leaves its mark there long after the initial situation has been forgotten.

Gerald, a charming man in his sixties, first came to me suffering from asthma which was sufficiently bad that he was being hospitalised after severe attacks two or three times a year. On his first two visits to me he came by himself and we talked briefly about his family, his work and his hobbies. On his third visit he brought his wife along to meet me for the first time. We sat in my room and I asked him if his asthma had responded to the first two healing sessions. He replied that he had hardly had to use his inhaler and that his breathing was now far easier even if he physically exerted himself more. I then noticed his wife giving him a rather strange look as if to encourage him in some way.

'Gerald,' she said, 'have you told Mr Manning why you are really here?'

There was a silence for what seemed ages but was probably no more than a few moments as Gerald shuffled uncomfortably and looked down at his feet. If he is not here for treatment for asthma, I thought, what is his real problem and why has he not told me? As I guessed, he had been too embarrassed to tell me about it until persuaded by his wife.

At the age of eight, Gerald had been sent off to boarding school. This had made him feel unloved and rejected and he quickly grew to hate the Spartan regime of his new school. He had a disabling stutter and, because he was very shortsighted, he wore thick-lensed spectacles. Almost from the start he was bullied unmercifully by the other boys. To cap it all there was a particular teacher who would also make fun of him and castigate him in front of all the other boys. 'You stupid idiot! Why can't you do it like the other boys? Only you could be so stupid!' the teacher would scream at him. Gerald learnt to keep his head down and instead of getting involved with school activities found solace in books.

When he eventually left this school, Gerald discovered to his horror that the bullying teacher had gone with him – not physically, but as a voice inside his head. From now on if he made any kind of mistake he would hear the teacher shouting at him, belittling him and poking fun at him in front of his classmates. Worse still, if he felt that he had really let himself or others down he would start punching himself.

Although I now understood why Gerald had been reluctant to share his story with me, I found it extraordinary that nobody had been able to help him deal with these problems. Gerald was suffering from imprinting. Because of the very powerful way that words had been planted in the back of his mind their effect had remained throughout the rest of his life.

On one of his last visits to me, Gerald told me that he had almost beaten his problem. 'There was one thing, though, last week that made me angry with myself,' he told me. 'When I'm driving I have always had an obsession with watching the mileometer as it turns over major mileages. Last week I saw that it was reading 39,996 miles and because I knew the road well, I had worked out when to look down to see it turning over to 40,000 miles. When I got close to it there were roadworks and I was so busy negotiating the contra-flow system for the traffic that I forgot to watch it turn. The next time I looked down it said 40,002 and I was so annoyed.'

I smiled, because I have the same habit and would have been as annoyed as Gerald!

Of course we have all been given commands by authoritarian figures while we have been nervous and they have not controlled or spoiled our lives. The fertile soil of low self-esteem, guilt and perhaps a basic inherent belief in the authoritarian statement even before it is spoken, may be necessary. However, even if we have suffered in this way, we can 'update' the unconscious mind. Reassuring it about the fears it has held, even for many years, can alter these imprints.

The Computer Brain

Your brain can be seen as a computer into which all kinds of information has been programmed from your birth onwards, by parents, teachers, society and the media. But because it is *your* brain inside *your* head it feels like you, and what it thinks feels real and truthful to you. So, if your computer brain tells you that you are a worthless person, you'll agree with it. But once you begin to realise what is going on you can start to change the computer programme. It may be vital for your health.

A study reported in the *Lancet* in 1993 demonstrated how people who, in early life, became imprinted with the idea that they were predisposed to life-threatening illnesses actually died sooner than those who did not listen to self-talk. Dr David Phillips and his colleagues followed Chinese Americans who were born during certain years that they believed predisposed them to fatal diseases. They actually died four years sooner, on average, than Chinese Americans born during other years, and at least four years sooner than white Americans who actually had the same diseases as the Chinese Americans but held positive beliefs about the outcomes of those illnesses.[1] The findings were based on a very large sampling – 28,169 Chinese Americans and 412,632 white Americans. 'Our findings and those of others suggest that mental attitude is associated with health,' said Dr Phillips.

Change Your Message

Next time you find yourself thinking something negative about yourself, replace that thought with something positive. It may sound simple but it really does work. Every time you choose to think a positive thought you are re-educating your computer brain.

An imaginary example might be a young woman who is unhappy because she has no partner. Although that should not be a problem, her mother or friends who feel that women are only worth something if they have a man in their lives may have fed her a programme. As long as she continues thinking that way she will go on feeling worthless and probably depressed too. Once she can recognise her belief simply as an old tape that has got stuck, she can replace it with something more positive. It is important, though, to be realistic. If she tries thinking, 'Next week I'm going to meet the man of my dreams,' she is liable to be disappointed. But 'I am worthwhile, whether I am alone or not' will break the circuit of negative thinking that she has got into and will call a halt to the production of stress hormones caused by anxiety. Then, having learned to value herself and lose her anxiety, the right partner may appear in her life just when she least expects it. This sort of thing often happens.

Just changing a word may be enough to change your entire view. The acting profession has the highest rate of unemployment, at around 70 per cent, yet it has one of the lowest incidences of illness. Could the reason for this lie in the fact that an out of work actor never says he is 'redundant'? He will always say that he is 'resting'. There is a world of difference in the two messages.

Try listening to your own messages. If they are not benefiting you, you can learn to change them with some positive affirmations.

Affirmations

Affirmations are simple statements repeated to yourself. They are conscious motivators of your behaviour and they say 'yes' to your potential. Repetition of positive affirmations drives them deep into your personality so they bring about the changes you want. They are probably the easiest and simplest technique we know to influence the conscious mind.

Affirmations have been used for centuries throughout the world in such spiritual and magical practices as prayers and mantras to replace negative thoughts with more positive ones. You can say them while driving your car, while waiting for your appointment with the doctor, or lying in bed before you go to sleep. You simply choose a statement that represents what you want to have happen to you and repeat it to yourself over and over again. Let me show you how to make them work effectively for you.

There are four main types of affirmation:

An affirmation of thought is basically an affirmation of consciousness and through it the inner you affirms a part of its self-image.

Thought helps to create and is an integral part of your reality. Thought coupled with action creates your destiny. To make affirmations work, you must have within you hope and positive expectancy. The thought form has to become a natural habit within you that says, 'There is a way, and I will find it.' It might be weak at first and may not change your circumstances, but if you persevere and are patient, eventually that positive affirmation will come about.

An affirmation of word is used almost like a prayer or mantra. By repeating the affirmation over and over again, it becomes embedded in your subconscious mind and will eventually become part of your reality. It is important that your affirmation has an emotional energy behind it that means something for you. The feelings will count for so much more when you are affirming for what you want. Setting aside a certain time of your day when you are by yourself will establish a powerful rhythm to enhance your affirmations.

An affirmation of feeling comes about because as you become more aware of the feelings that things arouse in you, you will notice that everything around you has an energy imprint that describes its intrinsic quality. The feelings you generate will pull you into areas of the physical world that match those feelings. As you develop affirmations of feelings, you will want to work on expanding your ability consciously to receive and trust sensory information from those feelings. Feelings never lie and a person cannot hide what they feel. A good affirmation to use for expanding your feelings could be, *'Today I express love and openness to each person I meet, because I know that I am also truly lovable.'*

An affirmation of action is when you are looking to create actions to support your affirmation. It might be rewarding yourself for something well done, rewarding someone else or creating a discipline in your life to support whatever it is that you are aiming for.

An affirmation works by filling your mind with thoughts that support your goal. The words suggest to your mind what it should be thinking and it effortlessly picks up the implications and message of your affirmation. There are several key points to bear in mind when making affirmations.

GUIDELINES FOR MAKING AFFIRMATIONS

O Use the present or past tense. Don't use the future tense because you want your mind to know that it has already happened.

O Be *positive*. Use the most positive terms you can. Never use negatives in affirmations.

O Keep affirmations short and specific. They should be like a mantra – short and simple, easy to say, and easy to repeat. It may help you to remember them if you write them down.

O Repetition, repetition, repetition. Repetition is necessary for the positive affirmation to replace any negative thoughts that are already in your mind.

O Make time. Always have a particular time of day set aside for your meditations or affirmations. It helps to set up a pattern for you so that you do them on a daily basis.

Examples of Affirmations

As a guide, the following simple affirmations, taken from my self-help recordings, have helped thousands of people:

O My deep desire for all that is positive and healthy keeps me on the path of a more fulfilling and happy life.

O My life is filled with confidence and vitality. This vitality is now being released into every cell of my physical body.

O Every part of my body is responding to my positive direction. I'm feeling healthy. I'm being filled with strength and upliftment.

O I feel great enthusiasm for my new life of personal achievements. The love I release from within gives me greater strength in my everyday life.

○ I know that a positive approach to life will also inspire me with greater energy.

○ I know that positive thinking and pleasant emotions increase my vitality and improve my health.

○ Even now as I rest, healing energies are flowing through my body.

Negative Labels

Dr Brian Roet has helped many of my patients by using similar techniques. He has looked at how people hold themselves back by giving themselves 'negative labels' in order to deal with situations for which they do not want to take responsibility.

Labelling, rather like imprinting, follows a pattern of internal dialogue that can be protective, comforting, punishing or excusing. The internal voice is usually in the form of:

○ 'But I'm not worthy of receiving. . .'

○ 'I'm not capable of. . .'

○ 'But I don't have the confidence to. . .'

○ 'But I'm just a failure/sufferer/loser. . .'

GUIDELINES FOR REMOVING A NEGATIVE LABEL

○ Realise that you are wearing a label. You can do this by noticing how you avoid certain situations or feel limited in relationships.

○ Look at ways the label is kept in place by self-talk or by explanations of failures to do, say or succeed in things.

○ Ask family or friends if they notice the label you think you are wearing.

○ Look at the benefits – and restrictions – that it brings you.

○ Think back to when it was first applied, by whom and for what reason.

○ Remember the times when you acted contrary to the label.

○ Catch yourself applying the label. Try to act differently to avoid the stereotyped self-description.

○ Either gradually replace the label with a more positive one or be flexible and have no label at all.

Cognitive Therapy

Cognitive behavioural therapy is a tried and tested method that helps us to identify our negative thoughts, question their veracity and validity, and replace them with new thoughts that are kinder to ourselves and more accurate.

Aaron Beck, a Freudian analyst, first coined the phrase 'cognitive behavioural therapy' after listening to one of his patients describing a sexual encounter. He noticed that as she was speaking she was becoming more and more anxious. Beck assumed this was because she was talking about sex, but when he probed more deeply it was clear something else was going on. She told Beck that while she was talking to him she kept thinking, 'He doesn't like me – he's bored with me.' It was these thoughts that were making her anxious.

A cognitive therapist challenges negative lines of thinking and encourages a person to come up with more reasonable and positive interpretations. Patients are also encouraged to rate their anxieties on a scale of one to ten and to control them with relaxation techniques.

Cognitive therapy is not only very simple but has also been shown to be highly effective at treating a great range of mental disorders from anxiety to sex offences. A study reported in the *British Medical Journal* reported on 188 women who were seriously depressed after giving birth in two Manchester hospitals. Although they were all desperately unhappy, only half of them agreed to take part in the trial. Those women who refused to take part did so because they did not want to be prescribed drugs. The women were then randomly allocated a placebo, Prozac, or cognitive behavioural therapy. The researchers found that the women who received treatment did much better than those who only got a placebo and the cognitive behavioural therapy was as effective as the Prozac.[2]

Of course the biggest problem with a drug-only approach, such as the prescribing of Prozac, is that there tends to be a high relapse rate when people stop taking it, almost certainly because the drug is masking the effects of the problem and not actually dealing with it. Taking pills can also have a negative effect on the quality of your life, making you feel like a zombie. More importantly it can also stop you from learning from the messages that stress and illness can bring. It is like turning off a fire alarm because you don't like the sound of the bell.

In another study, doctors randomly gave patients drugs, drugs plus cognitive behavioural therapy or cognitive behavioural therapy alone. Two years later 78 per cent of the patients given drugs alone had had a relapse or recurrence of their illness. Patients receiving cognitive therapy and drugs, or cognitive therapy alone, did far better, with a relapse rate of only 21 per cent and 23 per cent respectively.[3]

Devising Your Own Treatment

Although cognitive behavioural therapy normally consists of between six and twenty one-hour sessions with a psychiatrist, a psychologist or another trained health professional, you can also devise your treatment. In order to do this you will need to work through several stages:

O Express your feelings.

O Avoid negative thinking.

O Deal with false beliefs.

O Regain control of your life.

O Make sense of your experience.

Quite often a form of cognitive therapy starts for people after they have been to one of my healing circles or seminars. Linda, who had been to two of my circles, provides a very good example.

'I had been overweight (I still dislike using the word "fat") ever since I was a child and had tried every diet and slimming class in the book.

What none of them actually does is address the underlying reason(s) for overeating. It is just a symptom and in my case, as in most, I feel, it is a lack of self-esteem and self-worth,' she wrote.

'I was obsessed with, and addicted to, eating. For the few moments that the food was in my mouth everything was all right again. Of course, when you stop eating you feel guilty, but you also start thinking about when you can eat again just for those few moments of relief. I was never bulimic, but feel that I came close to it and can well understand how it can happen.

'After the healing circles my obsession/addiction to food just disappeared altogether (and also my need to buy magazines). It was as if someone had clicked my on/off switch to off and it was such a relief. I still, somehow, retain the memory of it and what it felt like. Perhaps that never leaves you – I don't know.

'During the next couple of years I lost 4½ stone by *not* dieting, which other people never believed. I had reached an all-time low (or should I say high) of 16 ½ stone, was in an unhappy marriage with a husband who drank and verbally abused me when he was drunk, and in a job which bored me – as a petrol pump attendant in a self-service filling station.

'I then went to one of your seminars and you told us about a lady's experience of turning into a bird and flying back to her childhood home and all the feelings she had experienced as a child, during one of your healing circles. This affected me deeply. Tears were rolling down my face and I realised that as a child (and for most of my adult life) I had always *felt* so ugly. Looking at photographs of myself as a child I am amazed at how pretty I was – masses of dark curly hair and big blue eyes when I was a tot. I truly believe that I overate so that my outward image mirrored my inward one . . . ugly! This was quite a revelation – to realise that this was how I had felt about myself for most of my life.

'Since then I have tried to rectify the situation. I do now feel that, yes, I *am* a beautiful person, with faults and weaknesses of course. That's OK as long as I believe that I'm beautiful inside and not ugly. I still have moments of self-doubt and feel like my awkward, lonely, ugly child did, but they quickly pass. I am now living with a new partner who is a gentle, kind, loving man whose inner strength and encouragement has helped me immensely to believe in myself and my inner beauty.'

Linda had been successful in working out her own cognitive behaviour therapy by first expressing her feelings about lack of self-esteem and self-worth. She had then learned to change the imprinting that had somehow become lodged in her mind from the time she was a small child and she dealt with her false beliefs about herself. I found it interesting that she was married to a man that drank heavily and would then verbally abuse her. It was as if his behaviour reinforced her already incredibly low image of herself. Finally, she had regained control of her life by learning to value herself and by seeing herself as beautiful. Maybe that gave her the courage to leave the bullying husband and gave her the opportunity to find a man who cherished and supported her.

Asking Better Questions of Yourself

One of the best tools for improving the quality of self-talk, which is the basis of cognitive behavioural therapy, is learning to question yourself differently. For example, instead of 'Why does this always happen to me?' a better self-question would be 'What can I do to differently to improve this situation?' Try asking a few of the following questions regularly to remind yourself of how positive and engaged with life you can be:

1 What am I most happy about in my life now? Why does it make me happy?

2 What am I most grateful about in my life?

3 What am I committed to in my life right now? Why am I committed to it?

4 Who do I love? Have I let them know how I feel? Who loves me?

5 What am I looking forward to? How can I prepare for it?

Changing Negative Thoughts

We have already looked at how you can change negatives to positives (*see page 53*) and this is also part of cognitive therapy. Remember that whatever negative thought comes into your mind can be examined and turned into a more positive reaction. If you consider your situation as if it involved someone else you would be likely to take a more realistic view. Write down your negative thoughts and then consider how you can turn them round.

> Like many of my patients, Julie had had a mastectomy after being diagnosed with breast cancer. This had led her to feel that she was no longer a complete woman. However she managed to change this to: 'I may not be a complete woman, but I am a complete person.'

Challenging False Beliefs

Another part of cognitive therapy is to deal with false beliefs by challenging the thoughts and fears that most worry you. Ask yourself:

1 Does this belief make me more stressed?

2 Where did this belief come from?

3 Is it actually logical?

4 Is it true?

If you think that your husband is put off by your mastectomy, then ask him what he really thinks. The worst thing that can happen is that your fears will be justified. On the other hand he may have been looking for a way to reassure you about it but didn't know the right words to use.

Regaining Control of Your Life

Many of my patients, especially if they are undergoing extensive treatment, perhaps on a daily basis, feel that they have lost control of their life. Some of them feel hard pressed to keep up with what they *should* be doing. How many times each day do you hear someone say, 'I should do this' or 'You shouldn't do that'? Every day we hear people refer to hundreds of 'shoulds' with no real basis or authority. The inference when we say or think 'I should' or 'I shouldn't' is that someone, at some time, directed us to behave in a certain way.

There is a danger in trying to motivate yourself with shoulds and shouldn'ts because you can make yourself feel as though you have to be chastised and punished before you can be expected to do anything, and then you feel guilty if you fail to do what you think you should.

Regain control of your life by avoiding what are known as absolute words – 'always', 'must', 'should', 'totally', 'never', 'incredibly' – and replacing them with 'might', 'could', 'sometimes', 'seldom', 'very' and 'often'.

Some of my patients have also felt that they have regained some control by scheduling some activity or challenge into their day. Try making a daily activity plan and list all the things you aim to do. List all the things you have ever enjoyed doing or thought that you might enjoy, even if they are as small as baking a cake or planting some bulbs. There may be something that you have long thought you would enjoy – maybe learning a language or taking up painting. It is not important if you don't get through everything on the list, because the purpose of the exercise is to reinstate some objectives (*see also Setting Goals, page 56*).

Moving On . . .

Many doctors say that the people who cope best after illness are those who return to normal life and only occasionally think about their illness. Some people seem to find this easier than others. Sometimes I treat a person whose entire life, by their choice, revolves around their illness, whereas others want to forget about it as quickly as possible and get on with life.

Whatever your current situation, as you cast off your imprinting and uncover the hidden parts of yourself, you start to discover who you are. With courage your life can start to change overnight.

Chapter 6

STRESS AND YOUR HEALTH

Lorry driver Jim Walker, aged fifty-seven, could have been forgiven for thinking twice when confronted by the sight of a crash victim trapped in a petrol-soaked car wreck early in 2001. Just a few years previously he had had a major operation to unblock an artery in his leg and could not even walk. His own health problems did not enter his mind as he leapt from the cab of his lorry after he saw Lorraine Barker's car smash into a motorway barrier, then career right across the motorway and up an embankment, ending up wedged on its side between trees fifty yards from the road.

Summoning reserves of strength that he didn't know he had, Jim single-handedly pushed the car, still on its side, clear of the trees and heaved it back on to its wheels. He then realised that the young woman driver was still trapped. Terrified that the car would catch fire, Jim set about freeing her. He grabbed the twisted gear stick that was pinning her down and bent it straight before dragging her clear.

'I didn't realise my own strength. I don't know where it came from. To look at me you wouldn't believe it,' Jim said afterwards.

Occasionally you hear of stories like this where, in what seems to be a situation of grave danger, somebody summons the most enormous strength to avert a disaster. We all potentially have the same ability as Jim. It is a throwback to prehistoric times when in the face of danger we had to make a very rapid decision to fight or run away. Today we generally do not have that same need, but the mechanism is still within us and it has become known as 'stress'.

Until 1935 the word 'stress' had only been used by engineers calculating the load-bearing capabilities of structures. It was a term taken from physics, referring to any strain or force strong enough to deform something. Then Hans Selye, a young Canadian doctor who had been doing research work at McGill University in Montreal, published in the journal *Nature* what were then regarded as revolutionary results of his work with human stress. As a medical student in the 1920s he had noticed that whatever illness a patient had, they all *looked* sick. It seemed to him that there was a common pattern of physiological reactions to extreme change. Selye called this the General Adaption Syndrome and through the use of animal studies he identified three basic stages of response to any prolonged negative stimuli:

1 First there was an alarm reaction during which the body mobilised the necessary resources to deal with the perceived threat or attack.

2 The second phase was a phase of resistance during which many of the physiological changes associated with the alarm reaction were reversed, and the body's defences *increased* resistance to the stressor. This 'adaption period', as Selye called it, did not last indefinitely.

3 The third stage, exhaustion, occurred if the stressor was continued. The ability to adapt would fail and the animal would become very prone to sickness and death.

Selye then extended his work to include humans, studying everything from emotional upsets to flu. His colleagues were highly sceptical of his findings, unable to accept that so many different kinds of stimuli could cause the same physiological reaction. But we now know that stress of all kinds can have serious consequences, not just to our quality of life but also to health and sometimes life itself.

Eustress and Distress

According to Hans Selye, stress in itself should not be viewed as a negative phenomenon. It is not the stressor that determines the response but rather the individual's internal reaction to it. This internal reaction is highly individualised and what one person may experience as stress, the next person might see quite differently.

Selye concluded that there were actually two forms of stress because not everyone who is stressed becomes ill. In the early studies of the effects of life events that caused high levels of stress, about 30 per cent of the people observed did not get ill. Partly to account for these findings, Selye came up with the word *distress* (from the Latin *dis*, meaning 'bad'), and *eustress* (from the Greek *eu*, meaning 'good'). Distress is the stress of losing, when we feel insecure, inadequate, despairing, disappointed or helpless, while eustress is the stress of winning or achievement and it brings about positive feelings. Although both kinds have pretty much the same physiological effect, eustress is less harmful than distress.

When eustress is properly handled it provides the motivation to overcome the obstacles preventing us from reaching our hopes and goals. However, when it is allowed to run out of control it can lead to poor performance, illness and possibly eventual death, and this is distress.

When we refer to stress, we generally mean Selye's distress. We often say we are 'stressed' if we are feeling angry, worried, frustrated or depressed, or if we have too many pressures, responsibilities or work-related demands. We also use the word 'stress' to refer to a wide range of physical problems and symptoms that occur within our bodies. So whenever we say that we are suffering from 'stress', what we really mean is that we are having problems or conflicts – emotional, physical, financial, and so on – that are painful or troubling to us. By the same token, if someone says, 'I don't have any stress,' they have merely forgotten that 'stress' is just a word. If you ask instead if they ever have *problems* in their lives, most people will admit that they often do.

You should regard the symptoms of stress as an early warning sign that is there to make you aware of situations that could threaten your well-being.

Fight or Flight

The well-known 'fight or flight syndrome' is the physical reaction to stress when hormones and chemicals are released into the body to help us either fight or run away from a potentially stressful event. It is estimated that we experience fifty brief fight-or-flight episodes every day. They can start when the alarm clock goes off in the morning and you get anxious as you think about the day ahead. The system is a throwback to prehistoric times when it was a means of survival and therefore crucially important. But our nervous systems are not very good at telling the difference between physical threats, when we *really* need to fight or flee, and psychological threats, when we need to think and speak clearly.

When we perceive a situation as stressful there are quite dramatic changes in the body. The hypothalamus, a very small part of the brain, immediately sends a signal to our adrenal glands to release the hormone adrenaline. This in turn stimulates our heart and breathing rates, redirects the blood to our brain, heart and muscles, and raises blood pressure. The liver pours glucose into the blood, the blood sugar level rises, fatty acids are released from the liver, skin and gut, the stomach produces more acid and the spleen pushes out more red blood cells. There is an increase in fibrinogen and blood platelets that are designed to stop bleeding and an increased production of white blood cells to help repair body tissues.

All of these reactions were obviously useful to prehistoric man but have more limited benefit now. In order to see how the original advantage of our stress response can become a serious health disadvantage to us now, let's look at our physical response in a little more detail.

OUR RESPONSES TO STRESS

Release of cortisone from the adrenal glands

Original advantage This provided an immediate protection against allergic reactions, such as asthma or closing of the eyes, after an encounter with an attacker.

Today's disadvantage A release of cortisone, when excessive and prolonged, will eventually cause the adrenal glands to enlarge and the lymphatic system to shrivel away or degenerate, possibly leading to disease. It is also known that cortisone will prevent helper T cell proliferation, thus depressing the immune system. Very high levels of cortisone will also dramatically reduce the stomach's resistance to its own acid, leading to gastric and duodenal ulcers.

Release of thyroid hormones into the bloodstream

Original advantage Hormones produced by the thyroid gland accelerate the body's metabolism, which meant that the body burned up its fuel more rapidly and provided more energy for physical exertion such as running.

Today's disadvantage Prolonged release of the thyroid gland hormones leads to a feeling of jumpiness, weight loss if your food intake remains the same, insomnia and eventually exhaustion.

Release of endorphins from the hypothalamus

Original advantage Endorphins are the body's own morphine, which is why soldiers in the midst of fighting often don't feel the most serious of injuries although they will feel pain from a far less serious injury sustained during peacetime. During the stress of labour endorphins are released to help mother and foetus withstand pain.

Today's disadvantage High levels of unrelenting stress can actually deplete endorphin levels in the body, which has been found to aggravate migraines, backaches and even arthritic pain, although not the actual disease itself.

Reduction of sex hormones

Original advantage Obviously this reduced fertility so that in a time of drought or overcrowding there would be fewer mouths to feed. If hunters or soldiers were away from their partners for a long time, a decreased libido made both partners' lives easier and allowed energy to be focused on the task at hand.

Today's disadvantage Decreased libido can lead to anxiety and problems in relationships. A hormone known as prolactin can also be released by the pituitary gland when we are under extreme emotional or physical stress and this can prevent ovulation.

The shutdown of the entire digestive tract

Original advantage This meant that extraordinary feats of strength could be achieved as blood was diverted to the muscles, the heart and lungs. The mouth went dry because even those fluids were going to be needed elsewhere. The stomach and intestines would virtually stop all their movements, and the bladder and rectum tended to empty in order to reduce any load before battle.

Today's disadvantage If you are under a great deal of stress your mouth can dry up and you need to keep running to the loo! People who eat on the run and under stress can do damage to themselves by quickly forcing food into an inactive stomach. Bloating, nausea or cramps can follow.

Release of sugar into the blood, together with an increase in insulin levels in order to metabolise it

Original advantage It provided a quick burst of energy supply for the sprint.

Today's disadvantage If there are excessive demands on the pancreas to produce more insulin, it can aggravate, or even start, diabetes. If you are under stress and you start eating sweet sugary foods for comfort it becomes even more damaging, as the bloodstream already has high levels of sugar in it as part of its natural reaction to stress.

Increase of cholesterol in the blood, mostly from the liver

Original advantage Cholesterol would take over where the blood sugar left off in supplying energy to the muscles.

Today's disadvantage High cholesterol levels can cause some gall-stones or hardening of the arteries, leading to a heart attack or a stroke. It is important that you don't add more cholesterol to your blood supply if you are under stress. Many convenience foods and fast-food diets are high in cholesterol.

The racing heart

Original advantage The faster the heart worked, the more blood was pumped to the muscles and lungs, which carried more fuel and oxygen during hunting or fighting.

Today's disadvantage It leads to high blood pressure, which, if left unattended, can cause strokes, a burst aneurysm or a fatal heart attack. If you already have high levels of cholesterol in your blood, leading to deposits in the arteries, your heart may be only just keeping up with everyday demands.

Thickening of the blood

Original advantage This is caused by an increased production of red and white blood cells from the bone marrow and the squeezing of the spleen to inject its stored thick paste of blood cells and clotting factors into the bloodstream. This resulted in a greater capacity to carry oxygen, fight infections and stop a bleeding wound.

Today's disadvantage Again, strokes, heart attacks or embolisms are more likely to occur if your blood has thickened as a result of prolonged stress. Drinking fluids helps to dilute your blood.

The skin goes pale and sweaty

Original advantage As the blood was drawn away from the skin towards the muscles, heart and lungs, it also helped to reduce blood loss from any lacerations. The sweating skin was an advantage in providing coolness for the overheated muscles just beneath the skin.

Today's disadvantage It can cause embarrassing sweating and you are less likely to pass a lie-detector test because sweating decreases the skin's resistance to electricity!

The five senses become acute

Original advantage This brought the body to its peak of function, and mental performance was also increased. Dilation of the pupils of the eyes allowed better night vision and better peripheral vision when in battle.

Today's disadvantage You are far more likely to make mistakes if you are under prolonged and excessive stress. It appears that the senses almost 'burn out' after unrelenting stress, actually becoming less efficient. You can become much less observant of details around you, pay little attention to smells or tastes, not hear conversations around you and ignore touch. You don't function as efficiently.

Stress and Cancer

The complex relationship between physical and psychological health is still not completely understood. Although stress factors alter the way the immune system functions, they have not yet provided scientific evidence of a direct cause-and-effect relationship between these immune system changes and the development of cancer.

Yet if I ask my patients why they think they became ill, stress is the most common answer. Janet, for example, was diagnosed with ovarian cancer just months after her husband had died unexpectedly from a brain tumour and her daughter had been diagnosed with breast cancer. Ron was diagnosed with throat cancer six months after he had lost the battle to keep his business afloat and had gone into bankruptcy. Dr Donna Stewart, Professor of Women's Health at the University of Toronto in Canada, and one of the authors of a survey published in *Psycho-Oncology* in 2001[1] feels that blaming stress is one way that people find to make a frightening situation more understandable and controllable.

Although there is scant evidence that stress can cause cancer, there is some evidence that breast cancer patients who feel high levels of stress concerning their diagnosis and treatment show evidence of a weakened immune system compared to patients experiencing less stress. Researchers, led by Barbara Andersen, Professor of Psychology and Obstetrics and Gynaecology at Ohio State University, found that highly stressed women had lower levels of natural killer cells than women who reported less stress.[2]

The effects of the study were actually so clear that they could make a woman susceptible to illness caused by the chemotherapy and radio-therapy that often comes after surgery. Natural killer cells are supposed to attack tumours, so the types of change made to the immune system by stress were the very kind that would influence the spread and growth of tumours. The findings confirmed the age-old belief that a person's attitude to cancer can affect their survival and recovery.

Other scientists were quick to replicate Barbara Andersen's initial find-ings. In 2000, the *Journal of the National Cancer Institute* published a report by Dr Sandra Sephton.[3] She and her colleagues found that abnormal fluctuations in the major stress hormone cortisol are linked to a decreased survival time of women with advanced breast cancer. Women with normal cortisol patterns survived more than a year longer than women with abnormal cortisol patterns. Sandra Sephton noted that the abnormal cortisol patterns have been seen in healthy people under stress, those who are depressed and those who have experienced severe psychological trauma.

Stress and Other Diseases

Although stress has not been proven to cause cancer, it has been shown to be a factor in other types of disease. David Mohr, a Clinical Professor of Neurology at the University of California in San Francisco, now seems to have confirmed that stress is indeed related to disease activity in multiple sclerosis. He and his colleagues followed 48 patients, both men and women ranging in age from 23 to 69 years old, for anything from 12 to 68 weeks. The patients rated the amount of psychological stress and stressful events that occurred during the month. All of them underwent a magnetic resonance imaging (MRI) scan once a month. Mohr and his colleagues assessed stressful life events, depression and anxiety in all the group members. They found that both major stressful events and day-to-day stresses were clearly linked to the development of new brain lesions in the following two months.[4]

Penny is a patient of mine who suffers from multiple sclerosis. In her late thirties, she had suffered from it for about fifteen years, although fortunately she did not have too many symptoms. She would tire easily, occasionally experience minor problems with her balance and sometimes have difficulty walking long distances. Out of the blue, her husband told her that he was leaving for another woman. Penny, devastated, was left to look after three young children single-handedly. Within months of her husband's departure her symptoms had escalated to a point where she was unable to walk unaided and needed a wheelchair. Virtually all of my patients with multiple sclerosis tell me that emotional stress is the major cause of deterioration in their condition.

We should also not forget that children can suffer from stress and are often less able to deal with it than adults. A Californian study of 236 children who had not yet started school found that the children who responded to stress with raised blood pressure became ill more often.

The same researchers found that kindergarten children who were stressed at having to go to school experienced changes in their ability to make antibodies.[5]

Stress can affect immune system functioning to the point that it can accelerate the metastatic spread of cancer; it can increase vulnerability to viral infections; accelerate the onset of Type I diabetes and the course of Type II diabetes; aggravate plaque formation which can in turn lead to atherosclerosis and blood clotting leading to heart attack; and trigger or worsen an asthma attack.[6]

Dr Robert Genco, chairman of the Oral Biology Department at The State University of New York, published one of the more remarkable studies on the effect of stress on the body in 1999 in the *Journal of Periodontology*. He reported that high levels of financial stress and poor coping abilities double your chances of developing gum disease. Genco studied more than 1,400 people between the ages of 25 and 74 and put them through psychological tests to identify and weigh the causes of stress in the participants' daily lives and to measure their ability to cope with stress. They were asked about children, spouses, single life, work stress and financial strain. After accounting for other risk factors – such as age, gender, smoking, poor dental care and diabetes – those who reported high levels of strain and difficulty coping had higher levels of gum attachment loss and alveolar bone loss than those with low levels of financial strain.[7]

Psychologist Janice Kiecolt-Glaser, a Professor of Psychiatry and Psychology in the Ohio State University College of Medicine, and her husband Ronald Glaser, who is Professor of Medical Microbiology and Immunology, have probably produced the largest body of evidence for the effects of stress on immunity in everyday life. Between them, they have published over 350 articles in the area of stress and immune function. Over many years they have studied medical students at exam time, recently divorced couples, carers of those who suffer from Alzheimer's disease and married couples discussing their differences.

In one study they were able to show that how we relate and speak to each other really does affect our bodies. They monitored ninety male–female couples and took blood samples from them before and after they tried to sort out a disagreement. They found that those couples that had the most hostility and negativity during discussions showed a drop on eight immune functions for the next twenty-four hours. 'The more hostile you are during a marital argument, the harder it is on your immune system,' says Janice Kiecolt-Glaser.

In another study they compared the immune responses of married women who were evaluated for the quality of their relationships with their husbands. The same study also compared these married women to women who had been recently separated or divorced. Within the married group, those with high-quality relationships had better immune responses to antigens than those with low-quality relationships. Generally, the married women had higher overall immune responses and, specifically, natural killer cell responses than those who were separated or divorced; within the separated or divorced group, those with a high level of attachment to the estranged spouse had poorer immune response than those with a low level of attachment. The researchers concluded that people who have undergone the stress and trauma of divorce must find a way to express and come to terms with their inner pain or they risk immune system depression and physical illness.[8]

Ronald Glaser and Janice Kiecolt-Glaser have also found that exam stress is associated with a decrease in immunity.[9]

Personality Types and Stress

In the 1950s, a San Francisco cardiologist called Meyer Friedman had an upholsterer come into his office to re-cover the chairs. He asked the doctor what kinds of patient he treated because he noticed that the fabric on the chairs was only being worn out across the front edges and that nobody had been sitting back and relaxing in the chairs. This question was to lead Friedman and his colleague Ray Rosenman to carry out what is now regarded as a classic work that showed that people with coronary artery disease tend to be more hostile, excessively devoted to work, competitive and had a hard-driving nature. They described them as Type As. Type Bs were people who do not behave in this way. Type As would deliberately live a high-stress life that took a heavy toll on their health. Friedman and Rosenman followed 3,154 initially well men for eight and a half years and found that those who were Type A were twice as likely to get coronary artery disease as the men who were Type B.[10] The following lists show the characteristics of the two types.

TYPE A AND TYPE B PERSONALITIES

Type A

They are aggressive and can be hostile if challenged. They are always trying to achieve more in less time and their activities tend to be socially praised and materially rewarded. They tend to show excessive devotion to work.

They are competitive to a point where winning is all-important.

Their speech is clipped and almost telegraphic, punctuated with frequent sighs and a nervous laugh.

They will try to do everything at the same time.

Their humour is usually at the expense of others.

Their conversations will centre on themselves and there is a great use of the words 'me', 'my', 'mine' and 'I'.

They will get annoyed at other people's slowness or indecision, will finish other people's sentences when they are too slow and will honk their horns at other drivers but don't like others doing it to them!

Type B

They are much more placid and easy going and are not aware of any time urgency.

They play a game for fun and not necessarily to win.

They speak more slowly and in a more monotone voice. They are more apt to ramble and can easily be interrupted. They speak softly and don't raise their voices. They will smile with a round mouth and have a deep belly laugh.

They do not try to do several things at once.

They will laugh at themselves.

They aim for things that are worth *being*, not *having*.

They are far less impatient.

They will more often take part in stressful activities of their own making and/or act to increase the stressfulness of their environment.	They value leisure time and use it efficiently.
They are impatient, doing everything quickly and denying fatigue.	They are usually more efficient and are good at delegating.
	They are just as successful as Type As!

In the United States, The National Heart Lung and Blood Institute critically reviewed the evidence for Type A and B personalities and concluded that the Type A pattern is a risk factor in coronary disease 'over and above that imposed by age, systolic blood pressure, serum cholesterol, and smoking and appears to be of the same magnitude as the relative risk associated with any of these factors'.

There are obviously very many people who might fall into the Type A personality, yet do not go on to suffer from heart disease and this is what has been interesting researchers more recently. It is now suspected that *hostility* is the destructive component. Hostility has been linked to blood pressure reactivity, severity of coronary artery disease and death from all causes, including coronary heart disease. This is almost certainly because outbursts of hostility release catecholamines, a group of hormones including adrenaline, noradrenaline and dopamine, which may help to damage the arteries and increase the deposition of plaque on arterial walls.

Over time, repeated traumatic emotional outbursts of hostility or anger can also damage the heart tissue fibres, which can in turn interfere with cardiac circuitry. Sudden increases of adrenaline will also constrict thousands of minute coronary vessels, making the heart compensate by pumping in high-pressure bursts. A combination of this high pressure together with the sudden release of hormones and neurochemicals throughout the bloodstream damages both the heart muscle and the vessels themselves.

How Stress Affects Men and Women

'Job-related stress may increase the risk of cardiovascular disease, but it seems to have a greater impact on a man's arteries than a woman's,' Cheryl Nordstrom of the University of Southern California, told the 1999 American Heart Association's conference. Men who report the most stress have almost five times the risk of hardening of the carotid arteries, the principal arteries of the neck, which can increase the risk of stroke and may indicate that an individual also has a greater risk of heart disease, compared with men with the lowest stress level, even after taking into account high blood pressure, lack of exercise, smoking or other heart disease factors.

Nordstrom and her colleagues found that – unlike in men – there was no link between women's stress level and hardening of the carotid arteries.[11] This may be because women have better social support and because up until the menopause oestrogens may have a protective effect.

It has been known for some time that overcommitment to work is associated with a higher risk of heart disease, but the reason was never properly understood. Then researchers in Holland, led by Dr Eco de Geus of Vrije University in Amsterdam, discovered that overcommitted workers showed changes in metabolism and blood clotting. In particular, workers who were overcommitted to their jobs tended to have a disorder in the body's clot-dissolving system that can lead to a build-up of fatty deposits in the arteries and, eventually, heart disease.[12]

Becoming 'Stress-Hardy'

In addition to the above factors, it seems that some individuals appear to be much more 'stress-hardy' than others. They resist the impact of stress better. Studies into what makes people stress-hardy show that they tend to be people who demonstrate three characteristic attitudes:

1 Commitment, defined as having an attitude of curiosity and involvement in whatever is happening.

2 Control, defined as a belief that we can influence events, coupled with the willingness to act on that belief rather than be a victim of circumstances.

3 A sense of challenge in the face of obstacles and changes that we all experience.

Whether or not stress caused your illness to occur, illness is itself quite stressful for most individuals and their families. If you are ill, it is reasonable to assume that stress may have played a role in causing your illness to occur, but even if it didn't, you and your family can still benefit from learning how to deal with stress more effectively. Stress is merely a word that human beings use to stand for hundreds of specific problems in their lives.

Three Strategies for Dealing with Stress

The band-aid approach Using alcohol, drugs (prescription or illegal), cigarettes, food, sex or anything else to temporarily relieve the symptoms of 'stress'. While these coping strategies may 'work' in the short term, they can have harmful long-term effects that make them undesirable.

The stress management approach Using diet, exercise, meditation, biofeedback or other relaxation exercises to cope with your 'stress'. While these coping strategies have definite advantages over band-aid methods, they still tend to focus mainly on just the symptoms of your problems.

The ideal approach Making stress disappear quickly and naturally by modifying or correcting its underlying causes. While this is by far the best way to deal with problems in life, most people fail to use this approach because they incorrectly understand what causes their stress to occur.

In the next chapters I will describe different strategies for coping with stress. The more you learn to recognise and deal with stress, the less tension and fewer physical ailments you are likely to experience.

Chapter 7

COPING WITH LIFE'S STRESSES

Stress is a process, not a diagnosis. The level of stress you feel depends a great deal on your attitude towards a particular situation. An event that may be very stressful for you may be a mere hiccup for me. Some people seem to thrive on stress and even need it in order to get things done. As a clinical problem, however, stress occurs when the demands made on you exceed (or you feel they exceed) your ability to cope and you feel distress.

A variety of factors can make you feel stressed, including:

O Environment (work, home, school, and so on).

O Lifestyle.

O Emotional issues.

During recent years, new insights about the causes of human stress have focused on the difference between *obvious* and *non-obvious* causes. Obvious causes of stress include the things that happen to us and around us – the things that we see easily. Non-obvious causes include conversations and behaviour patterns that become triggered within our bodies. These include judgements, expectations, the need for control and the need for approval.

Your attitude, personality and approach to life will influence how you respond to stress and the following factors all play a part:

O How you think about a problem.

O The different ways you cope with difficult situations.

O Your life experiences and life history.

○ Your self-esteem.

○ Whether you have people around you who can give you support.

Patsy was fairly typical of many of those who join my healing circles. About two years earlier, at the age of thirty, she had met her father for the first time since she was a toddler. It was the start of a period of great trauma and she had been seeing a counsellor for the previous six months, after which she had begun to regularly attend yoga classes. She had found this extremely helpful as it released all kinds of emotional problems and freed a stiffness in her lower back and hips. Then, as so often happens with a stress-related problem, her neck completely seized up so that she was unable to turn her head. Since her yoga teacher could not immediately find a cause or a solution, Patsy lost confidence and gave up the yoga. For the next nine months she suffered from chronic headaches, dropped shoulders and 'lots of little illnesses and problems, compounded by four weeks of illness on holiday, followed by another month when I returned'.

'As you came around the circle, my breathing changed and I started shaking,' she told me. 'I could feel tears falling down. When you reached me, you began with your hands on my shoulders and moved almost instantly to the base of my neck. I felt the tension unlock and my shoulders move back, which meant that I could use all of the space in my lungs. When you moved away, I know I was shaking, and probably sobbing, and I spent a few minutes enjoying the release. I walked away feeling taller, happier and healthier. I didn't think I had a major problem but since the stress was released, I realise that I had been in constant low-level pain for months.'

Patsy, like so many people, had been paying the price of long-term stress. Although it had begun with an emotional issue, it had quickly affected her body, leading to restricted joint movements and pain.

Stress is in the Eye of the Beholder

As Dr Brian Roet, a former anaesthetist and now Britain's leading hypnotherapist, once said, 'The only person without stress is a dead person!' Unfortunately there are many stresses common to most of us: we see violence on television, often live in overcrowded circumstances and argue with a boss or our family. But it is important to realise that stress, like beauty, is in the eye of the beholder.

Sometimes stress creeps up on us and we become so used to it that we are unaware of the damage it may be doing to us. How can we tell that we are stressed?

The Four Signs of Stress

○ Being anxious and finding it difficult to relax. Anxiety can actually be divided into two groups. There is *free-floating anxiety*, which has been learned in the past from others, often parents, and incorporated into the system. *Specific anxiety* relates to present-day situations such as coping with mortgages and traffic jams.

○ Becoming angry or irritable when things don't go as you want them to.

○ Worrying about things that worry won't help.

○ Experiencing difficulty in concentrating.

Are You on the Down Slope?

When you are stressed, initially you may find yourself suffering from headaches, sleeping problems or stomach upsets. These signals of vague discomfort and minor ailments are rather like an early warning system. If our present way of thought, emotions and living are reflected in our body, then these signals can make us aware of the possible need for change at a physical, psychological or spiritual level.

We all need an appropriate degree of arousal or wakefulness to achieve anything of course. If we get too relaxed all we can do is sleep! However, the pressures of outer life or inner conflict can force us to become so aroused that we develop a 'hair trigger' and become emotionally fragile, tired but sleepless, more aroused but accomplishing less. At such a point in life, having gone beyond healthy fatigue and ignoring feelings and needs, each extra demand becomes a burden inexorably decreasing over-drawn energy reserves. With no clear way of earning more, we slide into exhaustion and illness.

Dr Peter Nixon works with cardiac patients at London's Charing Cross Hospital and has developed what he calls the Human Function Curve Check List to guide us when we find ourselves, to quote Dr Nixon, 'in the nether land between being well and not having brewed up specific illness'.

Am I on the down slope:

○ Because too much is demanded of me?

○ Because I cannot say 'no' when I should?

○ Because I am not sufficiently in control and I can't cope?

○ Because I am too angry, too tense, too upset, too irritable or too indignant?

○ Because of too much 'people-poisoning'?

○ Because I'm too impatient and have too many time pressures?

○ Because I'm not sleeping *well* enough to keep well?

○ Because I'm not staying fit enough to stay well?

○ Because I'm not balancing the periods of hard effort with adequate sleep and relaxation?

○ Because I'm out of real energy and using sheer willpower to keep going?

○ Because I'm infallible, indispensable, indestructible, immortal?

If you feel you are on the down slope towards stress, it may be because there has been some recent disruption in your life. Change is the situation most likely to cause us stress. Even minor change can cause considerable feelings of helplessness or hopelessness.

It is your ability to *adapt* to change that is important. The Canadian doctor and pioneer stress researcher Hans Selye once said that we are all born with a certain finite amount of what he called 'adaption energy'. Once it has been spent, it cannot be replenished. Lord Moran, the personal physician of Sir Winston Churchill, studied shell-shocked soldiers and referred to this energy as 'courage'. We all have varying levels of courage, or adaption energy, but once it has been used up, burnout occurs. In this sense shell shock in young soldiers and senility in the elderly are very similar because they are both the result of having spent all the adaption energy.

In the 1920s, Dr Walter Cannon, a noted Harvard University physiologist who had first identified and named the 'fight or flight response', began recording connections between stressful periods in a person's life and the appearance of physical ailments. A decade later, Dr Adolf Meyer, a leading American psychiatrist, compiled a 'life chart' that specifically linked health problems with a person's particular life circumstances at the time. This was refined during the 1950s and 1960s.

In 1969 two American medical researchers, Thomas Holmes and Richard Rahe, studied the effects that changes in life brought about in an international sample of 5,000 people from Europe, the United States, Oceania and Japan. They looked for specific events that seemed to precipitate illness and discovered very significant patterns. When a number of changes occurred in life during a relatively short time, the patient was more likely to become ill.

Holmes and Rahe were able to list the life events that seemed to cause the greatest stresses for most people in their everyday lives and give them a quantitive value. These life events included 'positive events' such as marriage, holidays and outstanding personal achievements, 'negative events' such as marital separation or the death of a spouse or family member, and 'neutral events' like changes in working hours or the number of family get-togethers. Some cultural differences surfaced, as in the case of the Japanese, who ranked minor law violations near the middle of the list and jail terms second from the top, but on the whole there was a remarkable uniformity of results cutting across all national and socio-economic levels.

Because Holmes and Rahe were unsure just how stressful certain events were, they asked a group of people how much adjustment different events would need. Setting marriage at an arbitrary value of 50 'life change units' (LCUs) the other relative ranks appeared as shown in the table below. These scores are independent of education, intelligence, sex, race and class. Variations occur between individuals, depending on their personal strengths and weaknesses, but not between social groups.

RATINGS OF STRESSFUL LIFE EVENTS

Life Event	Score
Death of spouse	100
Divorce	73
Marital separation	65
Prison term	63
Death of a close family member	53
Personal injury or illness	53
Marriage	50
Being made redundant from work	47
Marital reconciliation	45
Retirement	45
Change in health of family member	44
Pregnancy	40
Sex difficulties	39
Gain of new family member	39
Business adjustment	39
Change in financial state	38
Death of a close friend	37
Change to a different line of work	36
Change in number of arguments with spouse	35
Mortgage over one year's net salary	31
Foreclosure of mortgage or loan	30
Change in responsibilities at work	29
Son or daughter leaving home	29
Trouble with in-laws	29
Outstanding personal achievement	28
Spouse begins or stops work	26
Begin or end school	26
Change in living conditions	25
Revision of personal habits	24
Trouble with boss	23
Change in work hours or conditions	20
Change in residence	20
Change in schools	20
Change in recreation	19
Change in church activities	19

Change in social activities	18
Mortgage or loan less than one year's net salary	17
Change in sleeping habits	16
Change in number of family get-togethers	15
Change in eating habits	15
Holidays	13
Christmas	12
Minor violations of the law	11

The amount of stress that you experience within a year is considered to be low if your LCU score is 150–199, moderate if it is 200–299 and high if it is over 300 LCU.

When medical researchers began to investigate what happened to people whose stress levels were high, they were astonished by their findings. Those with the highest levels of stress, as measured by LCUs, had more traffic accidents than those who scored lower. Children whose parents moved, divorced or received a large pay increase had all sorts of complications, including higher suicide rates. Those people who had gone through numerous major life events were more likely to suffer from a huge variety of medical conditions such as heart disease, diabetes, leukaemia, rheumatoid arthritis, schizophrenia, depression and difficulties in pregnancy.

According to the Holmes–Rahe Scale of Stress Ratings, if your total score of stress during the previous 12 months is less than 150 LCUs, you have a 30 per cent chance of a serious change in your health in the next 12 months. Up to 300 LCUs gives you a 50 per cent chance and over 300 LCUs gives you an 80 per cent chance.

Taking Responsibility for Your Stress

We will all undoubtedly experience stressful events at some time in our lives, so it is important to know how best to deal with stress. Ultimately, we have to do this for ourselves. As a healer, many people come to me so that I can 'fix' them. I prefer to be thought of as a guide or teacher rather than a 'fixer'. As an analogy, it is as if I am sitting by the side of a seemingly endless road that passes through territory that I know extremely well. I also sell maps and guides to the area to those who stop and ask for directions. People using their own means of transport hear of me in many different ways and come to sit at the side of the road with me, talking about their situations, difficulties and the problems of travel in their own area. Many have become lost and are looking for help to find their way home again; some are searching for a quicker, easier, less painful route; others need maintenance on the vehicle that is transporting them around.

My job is to try to understand each traveller's specific needs and abilities and to offer appropriate help in the form of improved maps of their area or technical advice about the vehicle repairs that are needed. It is most important that I recognise the uniqueness of their situation and the limitations of any drastic change. It would be useless if I offered advice about a Bentley to someone who arrived on a motorbike. It would not be helpful to sell someone a map of a town if they lived on a mountainside. I have to consider carefully my ability to offer help and my client's ability to receive and make use of it. Usually all the client knows is that they need some form of advice to improve their situation.

After their initial visit, my clients need to put some of my advice into practice. I am always surprised at the number of people who won't have a try at something new. They continue to store unused theory without gaining the confidence and optimism that comes from practising it. It is as if there are two sides: one that wants to change and the other that is frightened and cries out, 'Better the devil you know than the one you don't!' Simply take it slowly and move forward at a suitable pace. Here are a few tips.

GUIDELINES FOR MAKING CHANGES

○ Acknowledge and accept that you have a problem and changes need to be made.

○ Take responsibility for the problem and any proposed change.

○ Be flexible and open-minded about the steps necessary to make the required change.

○ Commit yourself to putting in the required time and effort.

O Learn *what* to do and *how* to do it.

O Understand the role *you* are playing in the creation or maintenance of the problem.

O Adopt an attitude of *learning* from experiences rather than one of 'success and failure'.

O Become aware of your own feelings, attitudes, internal 'self-talk' and restrictions.

O Don't expect to notice benefits immediately.

O Realise that 'unless you change the direction you are going you will end up where you are heading'.

You can choose to take potentially harmful stress and turn it into a powerful energy. There are many ways of doing this and we will look at them over the next couple of chapters. Start by realising that you can be the person you want to be and live the life you *want* to live instead of allowing stress to control you. Let me show you how!

Relationships and Stress

Most of the stresses listed by Holmes and Rahe involve either relationships or finances, which are without doubt the greatest stresses of modern life.

There is no doubt that relating to our fellow human beings seems to give us most problems. For some, especially the elderly or the bereaved, the difficulty is not having any relationships at all. Most people need to have intimate contact with other people, so even being involved in a bad relationship may appear to be better than no relationship at all.

We know that cigarette smoking has such an effect on death rates that every packet carries a Government Health Warning telling us of the possible consequences. However, Harold Morowitz, a professor of biophysics, reviewed all the data compiled by the Hammond Report in America which led to the Surgeon General's warnings about smoking and found that the effect of divorce, in terms of mortality risk, was almost the same as smoking over twenty cigarettes a day.[1] This makes one wonder whether divorce should also carry a Government Health Warning!

How to Improve Your Communication Skills

The quality of any relationship always comes down to the quality of communication, so positive communication skills are going to help reduce stress and conflicts of interpersonal relationships. The following guidelines may therefore help you to reduce relationship-based stress.

Be aware of *what* you want to communicate If you are not sure yourself about what you feel, think or sense, your statements can be easily misunderstood. Often a 'thinking' statement is actually covering up a 'feeling' statement. For example, 'I think you are making the wrong choice' can mean 'I feel very upset that you decided to do that.' Likewise an 'intention' statement such as 'I am going to put the garden chairs away' may mask a thinking statement: 'It was stupid of you to leave them out.' How clear and honest we are in our own internal communication will affect how someone else responds to that communication. If you want to be clear in your communication you must be aware of your own 'inner personality' because honesty and directness are part of the extent to which we are willing or able to reveal this 'inner personality'.

Learn to be a good listener It is important that you let the person you are communicating with really share their thoughts and feelings without being interrupted. If you first try to understand, you will find yourself being better understood in turn. Allow the other person to have their say, making sure you have understood them by perhaps saying, 'I think I understand, what you are saying is . . .', and showing that you have recognised what the other person may actually be feeling but not wanting to reveal, by saying something like 'It sounds to me as if you were pretty upset when . . .' This very simple technique shows the other person that you are both listening and understanding. Although restating what you think is being said may cause some short-term conflict in certain situations, it is almost always worth the risk. These are ways of *actively listening* and not just sitting there with unhearing ears. Questions can also be used to get more information or clarification. Remember that good questions open up lines of communication: 'Who said that to you?' 'When did you realise?' 'Where did that happen?' 'How did that feel?' Avoid a simple: 'Why?' It can sound challenging and put the other person on the defensive.

Help other people to become good listeners Ask the other person if they have understood what you have been communicating to them. Ask them to tell you what they have heard. If they don't seem to understand what you are saying, keep going until they do.

Don't try to talk over somebody So many arguments get out of hand because neither side will listen. If you find yourself being interrupted, just relax and don't try to out-talk the other person. If you are polite and let other people have their say, all but the rudest ones will eventually respond in the same way. If they don't, point out to them that they are interrupting the communication process. You can only do this if you have been a good listener, of course. Double standards in relationships seldom work!

Read the other person's words and body language We communicate not only with our words but also with the gestures, facial expressions, postures and vocal tones we use. Improving your communication skills involves becoming more aware of non-verbal cues not only from others but also from yourself. Couples who have lived together for a very long time have usually learned how to 'read' their partner extremely accurately and will often sit together in silence still 'communicating'. Don't just get the other person's story verbally. Get it non-verbally too.

Silence is OK! Unfortunately, many people feel uncomfortable in silence. Remember that some people need quietness to gather together their thoughts and feel safe in communicating. The important thing to remember during silences is to remain an active listener.

Look after a relationship We all like to be liked and noticed, so let your husband, wife or partner know that you appreciate them. Give positive feedback to someone who has helped you or given you pleasure. Let people know if you have been really upset by something and give yourself enough time if you want to discuss something important. Separate quality time from quantity time.

Conflict Resolution

Since we are all unique individuals and we all see things differently, it is inevitable that there will be occasions when we encounter tensions or misunderstandings in our lives. People grow and change, times change, and the faster these changes occur, the more potential there is for conflict.

Conflict itself is not the problem – it is how we *act* or *react* when it happens. Relationships rarely grow without some level of conflict, but that can also be the cause of their break-up if the conflicts continue unresolved. To be able to cope with stress it is essential to develop an awareness of the factors contributing to conflict and also an understanding of the specific skills that can be used to change a situation. Even the medical profession is now beginning to acknowledge what many people like myself have been saying for so long: negative emotions and stresses like anger, blame and regret can smoulder inside and manifest as disease (dis-ease) in our bodies.

We first need to clear the major blocks that exist because of our prior imprinting. From the time we were small children we learned about winning and losing. We learned to blame and that our enemy was the cause of our problems. We perhaps encoded a few winning strategies of our own. We might have learned to play the victim so that someone else, such as a parent, teacher or friend, will come to our aid and rescue us from the enemy or persecutor and perhaps even punish them on our behalf.

It is fascinating to contemplate that the concepts of 'enemy' and 'win/lose' have fuelled most of the major conflicts throughout history. Soldiers and politicians, monarchs and multi-nationals – the 'toys' change, but the games are still the same.

Crisis and Opportunity

By shifting our focus and seeing the *problem* as the enemy and not the person, we can gain a whole new perspective on a situation. In Chinese script the characters for 'crisis' and 'opportunity' are the same; conflict really can become an opportunity for communication for both parties to learn, so communication becomes creative instead of destructive.

(Remember that the people who seem to be most stress-resistant are usually those who see a problem as a chance to learn.) Both parties can use their intelligence to work together as *partners* instead of *opponents* and accept responsibility for the outcome resulting in a win/win solution, which may be compromise.

It is not always easy to break old patterns around conflict, to release the prejudice, judgement and subconscious beliefs, which, although they may not always serve us, have become a part of who we are. But as we dissolve the barriers between 'us' and 'them', we can learn an enormous amount about ourselves. Conflict itself can teach us a lot. In his book *Illusions*, Richard Bach writes: 'There is no such thing as a problem without a gift for you in its hands. You seek problems because you need their gifts.' The same applies to conflict.

We often refer to a conflict situation as being 'highly charged'. This charge can be used constructively as a force to enhance and validate or destructively to violate and diminish the energy of the other, whether they be individual, group, nation or even nature. Without conflict we would not know the meaning of harmony.

Both these states depend very much on how you experience change and whether you resist it or flow with it. 'Finding inner peace' has become rather a cliché and is often prescribed as a solution to those experiencing chronic tension and stress in their lives. Attaining peace within and without is a dynamic process, just as conflict is. Learning the skills of conflict resolution is just a first step – you need to *practise* them at every opportunity. But sometimes just using one or two of the skills on the following checklist can make a real difference to a difficult situation.

CONFLICT CHECKLIST

You can use this checklist by yourself or with someone else. Writing down your answers can be particularly effective.

Do I want to resolve the conflict?

Be willing to fix the problem. Is resentment caused by:

○ Something in my past that still hurts?

○ Something I haven't admitted to needing?

○ Something I dislike in another person because I won't accept it in myself?

Can I see the whole picture and not just my own point of view?

○ Do I need to broaden my outlook?

What are the needs and anxieties of everyone involved?

○ What areas do we have in common?

○ What do we need to work on?

How can we make this fair?

○ Negotiate; consider compromises and toleration of other sides/wishes.

○ Make a clear agreement or contract.

○ Are all parties satisfied?

What are the possibilities?

○ Think up as many solutions as you can.

○ Choose the one that gives everyone more of what they want.

Can we work it out?

○ Treat each other as equals.

What am I feeling?

○ Am I too emotional?

○ Could I get more facts?

○ Could I take time to calm down?

○ Could I tell them how I feel?

What do I want to change?

○ How will I tell them without blaming them?

○ Attack the *problem, not* the person.

What opportunities can this bring?

○ Work on the positive possibilities – 'what is', not the negatives,

○ What cannot be or how it is 'supposed to be'.

What is it like to be in their shoes?

○ Do they know that I really hear and understand them?

Do we need a neutral third person?

○ Could this help to understand each other and create our own solutions?

How can we both win?

○ Work towards solutions where everyone's needs are respected.

○ Always use a strategy that allows the other an escape route.

In order for conflict resolution be work, you must be able to communicate with other people clearly and assertively.

Assertiveness

We have heard a great deal in the last couple of decades about 'personal empowerment' and much of what is offered in the myriad of seminars and courses on the subject is simply assertiveness training. It teaches you how to deal more effectively with demanding people in your job and at home, and it teaches you the communication skills to get their needs met. By learning these techniques many situations that might previously have been stressful to you are now approached from a more relaxed perspective.

If you have ever come away from a confrontation or conversation feeling that something was left unclear or unsaid, or that either person was tricked, used or made to feel guilty, then one of the participants was not being assertive. If you felt that you had expressed what was important to you and allowed the other person to respond in their own way, then regardless of the final outcome, you behaved assertively.

It is important to remember that being assertive refers to a way of coping with confrontations. It does not mean getting your own way every time or winning some battle of wits against someone else. Assertive behaviour is usually most likely to produce a result that is generally acceptable to all concerned, without any feeling that they have been unfairly treated.

Assertiveness is frequently confused with aggression. An aggressive confrontation is when one or both parties try to put forward their desires, feelings and beliefs at the expense of someone else. There may be raised voices, angry personal attacks, emotional blackmail and a total failure of each person to understand the other's viewpoint. In an assertive confrontation, each person stands up for their personal rights, but each shows respect and understanding for the other's point of view. An assertive confrontation is likely to result in fair play on both sides, with each maintaining respect for the other.

GUIDELINES FOR COMMUNICATING WITH ASSERTIVENESS

O State your problem with facts. Do not use interpretation or criticism.

O Express your feelings with care, but without suppression. As the other person acknowledges them, a basis is created for understanding wants and requests.

O As you describe your feelings, show that you understand what the other side feels.

O Describe your problem or difficulty from a detached point of view.

O State your requests reasonably. This step can only be expressed after your wants have been clearly stated.

We are often taught early in life to believe that there are times and places where our own need to express ourselves must take second place. For example, in dealing with a doctor or hospital consultant, you might feel that by speaking honestly and assertively you are, in some way, 'breaking the rules'. However, we all have certain basic human rights and should not have to feel guilty about exercising them.

Your Basic Human Rights

○ The right to change your mind and break commitments that have been made.

○ The right to make mistakes and the need to allow other people to make mistakes.

○ The right to make decisions or statements without having justifications, or even logical bases.

○ The right to feel and express emotions, both positive and negative, without feeling that it is weak or undesirable to do so.

○ The right not to know about something or not to understand.

○ The right not to get involved with someone else's problems, or even to care about them.

○ The right to refuse demands made of you.

○ The right to be the judge of yourself and your own actions and to cope with their consequences.

○ The right to do all or any of these things without giving any reason at all for your actions.

All these are basic human rights that you should be able to follow whenever you wish. If you want to assert these rights effectively, you must be able to also listen to other other people and allow them to express themselves too. At the same time, clearly present your own feelings and opinions. It is important that you avoid excuses or justifications and stay close to a point of confrontation. This is not being difficult; it is being assertive.

The Basic Rules of Assertiveness

Don't:

○ Put forward excuses.

○ Apologise profusely for refusing.

○ Get sidetracked.

○ Be manipulated by emotional blackmail.

○ Be tentative with your refusal.

○ Be rushed into a decision.

Do:

○ Accept your right to say 'no'.

○ Clarify the issues before deciding.

○ Say 'no' firmly and clearly.

○ Give *reasons* (and not excuses).

○ Stand your ground if you believe you are right.

○ Look for *alternative* solutions.

Like with anything else, you need to keep practising your assertiveness skills in different situations until they become second nature. Quite apart from the fact that assertiveness will produce more fruitful solutions, it may also have an effect on your physical and emotional health.

In 1965, George Solomon published a report of his study of women with rheumatoid arthritis and their sisters who did not have the disease. Both sisters had the same genetic inheritance, which is known to play an important role in rheumatoid arthritis, yet while one became ill with the disease the other remained healthy. Solomon wondered if there were psychological differences between the sisters that might explain why one became ill while the other did not. After psychological testing he said, 'In every single case the healthy sibling was more assertive than the sister with arthritis.'[2]

In later research Solomon was able to establish that HIV patients who are more assertive may live longer.[3] Assertiveness skills have also been shown to help people with eating disorders by helping them to change or resolve unhappy relationships.

At the age of thirty-five, Martine, who had her own very successful consultancy company, was diagnosed with breast cancer. After treating her with surgery and then chemotherapy, in what later sounded like a rather odd statement her oncologist told her that it was 'the best type to get if you have to have it'! For almost four years regular checks showed that she was clear and that there were no signs of recurrence, but when I first began treating her she had been suffering from a lot of back pain and it had been found, after an MRI scan, that the cancer had indeed returned and had now metastasised in her spine. In the next few months it spread rapidly to her liver, her brain and her lungs.

Although by nature Martine was usually vivacious, intelligent and determined, now she was depressed, frightened and angry, but committed to fight for her life. She had also endured the painful break-up of her marriage just a few months previously.

As well as going through chemotherapy and radiotherapy, Martine was actively pursuing any other complementary treatments that she felt might help her through this very difficult and painful time. She would spend hours researching new drugs that were becoming available from America and other countries and volunteered for trials that she thought might be beneficial. After a while scans would reveal that she was clear again, but sadly the remissions sadly never lasted very long and a few months later she would be back in treatment again.

I felt strongly that although Martine was highly motivated she was really looking for people to 'fix' her and to do all the real work for her. It was fairly clear that simmering inside her was a cauldron of unresolved issues with her parents and her ex-husband, and anger and frustration at the people who couldn't keep her healthy. Then for eighteen months we lost touch. Cancelling all her appointments with me, she disappeared and I assumed the worst.

One day, out of the blue, Martine called asking for another appointment with me. She looked better than I had ever seen her and something had obviously changed. She had picked up, she explained, on something that I had implied shortly before we last met. She said she had thought long and hard about why her remissions never lasted more than a couple of months and had reached a point where she felt that her body simply couldn't take any further chemotherapy. She therefore decided to take a break from the medical treatments that were providing little more than stopgap remissions and she stopped visiting all the other therapists who had been trying to help and support her. 'I knew that the key to recovery had to be within me, and not outside,' she told me.

Since then Martine had been working on her own, with occasional help from a psychotherapist, on a programme of conflict resolution and assertiveness exercises. She had recovered from the break-up of her marriage and had realised that while she had grown and moved on, her ex-husband had not. Now they were good friends without any rancour.

'When people used to see me they always thought that I was this happy, outgoing and successful woman who could handle anything,' she said. 'But underneath I was aware of my negative patterns. To my friends and colleagues I probably still seem the same, but I've changed so much inside and all the anger and negativity that I had has either gone or no longer bothers me.'

Martine has now been off chemotherapy for two years and is still in remission.

Finance and Stress

Apart from relationship stress, one of the greatest stressors for some of my patients is financial stress, usually caused by loss of income due to illness. Financial concerns can really add to existing stress levels. A financial crisis is not likely to push a financially stable family over the brink, but it may be the last straw for one that is already experiencing difficulties. If you are in such a situation, your first priority should be to survive this difficult period both financially and emotionally. Sit down with other family members to analyse your financial goals, priorities and basic needs.

Sue came to me for treatment having been diagnosed with myeloma, a cancer of the plasma cells in the bone marrow, and was determined to do all she could to help herself in her fight against it. She held a full-time teaching job and Ron, her husband, had his own engineering business that in recent years had been on the verge of collapse on several occasions. Their children had now left home and Sue and Ron lived in a large, rambling house with an unmanageable garden of several acres.

From the start Sue identified their property as the single greatest cause of stress in her life because she felt unable to maintain the garden or keep the house clean and tidy while working full time. When she and Ron discussed the problem, the solution suddenly became clear. They sold the house and bought one that was smaller and much more manageable, and the money that was left over from the sale was helpful in saving Ron's business from collapse. It was the most effective way of dealing with stresses that were affecting Sue's health, Ron's business and their relationship.

Finance-related stress can often affect people who are earning a good salary but who do not have the discipline and organisation to look after their money. It has been said that the difference between spending 5 per cent *more* than you earn and spending 5 per cent *less* than you earn separates financial distress from comfort.

Financial security doesn't have to mean having millions of pounds in your bank account. It is about having sufficient assets, insurance policies, skills and positive cash flow that if you lost your job because of ill health or a downturn in the economy, you would not end up on the street. It gives you a very valuable control button to fight stress.

If all your loans or borrowings can be consolidated into a manageable programme of repayment and if your current spending patterns are within your *net* means, you should be in a very good position to avoid or withstand many of the finance-related stresses. However, remember that temporary decreases in income provide the temptation to use credit as the means to maintain current levels of living. You can rationalise this by saying that when your income is restored, your debts will be repaid. But it is a strain on any budget to repay loans or credit card debts because you are repaying not only the original money that you borrowed, but also the interest and finance charges. Unwise use of credit now can extend a temporary financial situation into years of indebtedness and stress. You may find the following tips helpful in avoiding such stress.

GUIDELINES FOR AVOIDING FINANCIAL STRESS

O Set realistic financial goals.

O Do not panic. You can almost certainly still control your financial situation if you plan carefully.

O Communicate. Analyse your financial priorities and talk with your family or anyone else who is affected by what you will do.

O Do not default on payments. Explain your situation to your creditors and work out adjustments.

O Make sure you are living on your net income, not your gross.

O Avoid impulsive spending and competitive response to peer pressure – 'Keeping up with the Joneses'.

O If you are experiencing difficulties, be prepared to change your standard of living at least temporarily, so that you don't end up sacrificing essentials.

Time Management and Stress

As I know only too well from my experiences with patients and my personal experience when Gig was ill, illness in itself can be an extremely stressful time both for the patient and their family. Not only is there often a fear of the unknown, but there are also numerous hospital visits, whether for check-ups, surgery or extended treatment such as chemotherapy or radiotherapy. On top of all that you may be making changes in your lifestyle, and relaxation exercises, meditation, writing a journal and making dietary changes all take time in themselves. The prospect can be so daunting that often a patient will tell me that they simply don't have the time to do all the things they would like to do. Although that may appear so, it is very rarely the case if you learn to plan efficiently by introducing time management to your days, weeks and months. Time need not be yet another stress!

To become efficient in managing your time you need to have a good grasp of the short, medium and long term, which will provide you with a feeling of being in control. In practice this is achieved by planning at three levels.

1 Plan the day. Do this the night before so that you can go to bed in the knowledge that tomorrow is already arranged. You don't want to find that issues overtake you before you have even started the day.

2 Plan the week. Do this on Fridays so that you have a scheme already set out for the coming week.

3 Plan the month and even the year. Get a bigger picture and update it continuously as entries occur.

Managing Your Time Effectively

Imagine for a moment that you are the leader of an expedition of explorers making your way through dense jungle. You are surrounded on all sides by dark green foliage and the whistling and chattering of thousands of birds and monkeys. You are thinking about how lucky you are to be leading this expedition when suddenly you hear 'Stop! Stop advancing!' It is the expedition navigator and he is approaching you from the back of the line. 'It has become obvious over the last few days that we have veered right off course!' He points to the southwest, saying, 'We must continue that way.'

Hearing this, the bushwhacking guide turns and approaches the two of you from the front. He gazes to the southwest for a few moments and says, 'That's the thickest jungle I've ever seen. Why don't we just keep going this way? We're making great time!'

When you have finished your expedition, what do you tell the rest of the world? Did you follow the advice of the navigator or the bush-whacker?

Hopefully the choice is fairly clear. If you follow the navigator's advice you will certainly have your work cut out for you, but you will eventually reach your destination. If, however, you follow the bush-whacker's path of least resistance travelling should be easy, but you will have no way of knowing what problems lie ahead or where you will end up.

The purpose of imagining yourself as the expedition leader is to clarify the concepts of efficiency and effectiveness. Doing things effectively and efficiently means finding out what is *important* to you. As expedition leader it is unlikely that you would get very far without a map telling you where to go and when. Displaying effectiveness means that you know what you need to study and understand to help your healing processes. Displaying efficiency means that you are familiar enough with it not to be fumbling with concepts, drawing blanks and running out of time.

Recognising that Time is Precious

People who have goals and are serious about their futures always take great care to use their time well; they seem to consider time a precious resource to be allocated to appropriate ends and only after careful consideration. This is in contrast to the wandering masses of people who are confused, lost and unfocused. These people don't consider time as a valuable resource, but simply as a measure of how old something is or when something is going to happen. These differing view-points are both generated by the goals, or lack of them, of the people in question.

If you had only one more day to live, every minute would become cherished and unwasted. Since none of us really knows how much time we have it makes sense to consider our time to be of limited supply and great value. So we should concentrate on some things while ignoring others.

EXERCISE: MAKING TIME

In my seminars I have often discussed how our lives would change for the better if we lived each day as if it was our last. Many participants have had their thoughts focused by a simple exercise that I have shared with them. Taking paper and pen, you may begin to realise that your only time limits are those you create for yourself:

1 List seven things that you love to do and that you haven't done for several months – maybe reading a book, exercising, accomplishing a goal or taking a trip somewhere.

2 Beside each of these seven things, list what stops you from doing it – something either inside (such as your feelings) or outside (someone or something, such as lack of money, that keeps you from it).

3 Take the two or three things that give you the greatest pleasure or enjoyment, and think of one step you can take to bring each one into your life.

4 Mark your calendar with a date and a time by which you will bring each of these pleasurable activities into your life.

Importance and Urgency

A helpful strategy in clarifying your present time perspective is to think of your activities in terms of importance and urgency.

Not important and not urgent You might wonder why anybody would want to spend their time doing things that are neither important nor urgent, but a huge amount of your time is probably spent in engaging in such throwaway tasks as sleeping in, chatting for hours on the phone or watching television for hour after hour. Be careful, because you might be engaging in activities that will not achieve your goals and doing things that are neither important nor urgent is senseless.

Not important but urgent Engaging in tasks that are urgent but not really important is a potentially dangerous way to spend your time because it may keep you from achieving your goals. Imagine feeling rushed and pressured to get something done while you think about how useless the task really is in terms of what you want to accomplish. Unfortunately, too many people misinterpret urgency for importance and consequently spend a great deal of their time rushing around doing things that, in the end, probably don't yield any real accomplishment.

There is a simple solution to this problem. If you are feeling rushed, stop for a moment and ask yourself: 'What would be the consequences to me if I didn't do this?' The answer to this question will put the activity's importance and urgency into perspective. Urgency has a personal dimension and it is crucial that you understand to whom the urgency really applies. Often the consequences to you are so small that it seems ridiculous to continue with the activity.

Important but not urgent The activities in this category can be tricky. Quite often we put off until tomorrow a very important activity only to engage in something else that is not as important and more urgent. A self-help programme is best started as a preventive measure but so many people find a comedy on television more compelling than writing a journal or spending thirty minutes relaxing with yoga exercises. Be sure of your reasons for doing what you do.

Important and urgent Activities that are both urgent and important are the most likely to be acted on. For many of my patients it is the urgency of their situation that prompts them to spend time working on it. Sadly, some of them leave it until the last moment before they start doing anything for themselves.

According to Stephen Covey, author of *First Things First*, most people spend their time in the *important and urgent* and in the *urgent, not important* categories. 'Doing things faster is no substitute for doing the right things,' he says. He believes that the third category, *important but not urgent*, is where quality time happens and you 'learn to live, to love, to learn, to leave a legacy'.

GUIDELINES FOR FINDING TIME

○ Plan your timetable well ahead.

○ Set priorities of what you have to achieve.

○ Put off non-urgent matters.

○ Learn to say 'no'. Often in saying 'yes' to someone else, you are saying 'no' to yourself.

○ Reduce the amount of time you watch television or spend playing games on the computer.

○ Get up half an hour earlier. One of my patients once calculated that by doing this he was gaining an extra *five working weeks* a year!

○ Try to handle paperwork only once.

○ Take the telephone off the hook if you don't want to be disturbed.

Finally, remember what is known as the Pareto Principle. This states that typically 80 per cent of unfocused effort generates only 20 per cent of results and that the remaining 80 per cent of results are achieved with only 20 per cent of focused effort!

Chapter 8

YOUR PHYSICAL WELL-BEING

Exercise, diet and relaxation all have a role to play in both decreasing stress levels and boosting the immune system. The way that we move and rest and the foods that we eat have a huge impact on how we cope, feel, react and think.

While you might think that watching television or staring out of the window are good ways of relaxing after a stressful day, one of the best ways to unwind is actually to do something else that is also stressful! It should, however, be something that needs all your concentration but involves *different* circuits of your brain. That is why some people find skydiving, white-water rafting or playing sport to be relaxing. A professional sportsman may find that something more peaceful such as fishing or playing chess is relaxing, because it is the opposite of what he does professionally.

Why Exercise is Good for You

There are times when we are in a *low-energy* state and times when we are in a *high-energy state*. Exercise can be used to increase low-energy states and decrease high-energy states. It can be used as 'first aid' to bring about a more balanced mood, and regular exercise is now known to improve long-term depression as well as long-standing chronic anxiety states.

Some of the benefits of exercise occur because it reduces the level of lactic acid, a measure of how tense we are, and increases the level of endorphins, which give us a feeling of well-being and happiness. Dennis Lobstein, a professor of exercise psychobiology at the University of New Mexico, compared the endorphin levels and depression profiles of ten joggers to those of ten sedentary men of the same age. The sedentary men were found to be more depressed, perceived greater stress in their lives and had more stress-circulating hormones and lower levels of endorphins.[1]

The Mental Benefits

Quite apart from the physical benefits of exercise, there are numerous mental benefits too. Exercise can:

○ Provide a natural release of pent-up feelings.

○ Help to reduce tension and anxiety.

○ Improve mental outlook and self-esteem.

○ Help to relieve moderate depression.

○ Improve your ability to handle stress.

○ Stimulate improved mental functions.

○ Induce relaxation and improve sleep.

Psychologist Diane Tice, of Case Western Reserve University in America, has found that aerobic exercise is one of the most effective tools for combating mild depression as well as other bad moods. She also noted that the mood-changing benefits of exercise were most effective with people who were physically lazy and rarely exercised. Ironically, those who exercised regularly found that they felt worse if there was a day when they couldn't exercise.

In a study of 135 college students, those who exercised on a regular basis were more likely to take life's daily stresses in their stride compared with their less physically active counterparts, claimed a report in the *Annals of Behavioural Medicine* in 1999. Study participants filled out questionnaires assessing the daily hassles they encountered during the previous week, such as car trouble, running late for appointments or arguments with colleagues, as well as questionnaires on major life events, mood, physical activity and overall health. During periods of high stress, those who reported exercising frequently had 37 per cent fewer physical symptoms than their counterparts who exercised less often. In addition, highly stressed students who engaged in less exercise reported 21 per cent more anxiety than students who exercised more frequently. Exercise helps people to take their mind off stressors, allowing for a temporary escape from the pressure and so acting as a kind of 'rejuvenation' process, the researchers reported.

The Physical Benefits

Regular and moderate exercise, even walking for half an hour each day, has been shown to affect the immune system and to reduce stress. The key is moderate and regular activity. Researchers at the Copenhagen Muscle Research Centre discovered that heavy training, such as that practised by professional athletes, reduces the levels of T cells and natural killer cells for up to twenty-four hours after the session.[2] There is a well-known connection between overtraining in athletes and an increased susceptibility to infections.

Another study that was carried out with elderly women, rather than professional athletes, found that exercise appeared specifically to promote the ability of natural killer cells to destroy tumours if the women maintained a moderate exercise programme.[3]

Exercise increases your metabolism, which is the rate at which your body ticks over, and the resulting metabolic rate is the largest single user of energy. After strenuous exercise it remains raised by about 10 per cent for up to 48 hours. When your metabolism functions faster and more efficiently you feel better and you burn more fat from your body stores because your need for oxygen is increased.

When we exercise, our body produces stress hormones such as cortisol, which affects the metabolism of protein, glucose and fats; adrenaline, which stimulates the sympathetic nervous system and increases cardiac output; and beta-endorphins, which relieve depression and create feelings of well-being and optimism. Exercise also oxygenates the blood.

Extended exercise or training sessions can decrease some of the blood's amino acids such as glutamine. Under normal circumstances our muscles will automatically make large amounts of glutamine, which is also known to be an important energy source for the cells of the immune system. Again, the key is regular and moderate exercise.

Exercise and the Immune System

The number of leukocytes, our immune boosters, all increase during exercise, although the effect seems to diminish after about an hour of exercise. Macrophages also show signs of greater activity after exercise.

It would also seem that you do not have to be a professional athlete in order to benefit by such boosting of the immune system. A study published in 1994 showed that exercise reduced the risk of breast cancer in women 40 years old or younger, particularly those who had children, by as much as 60 per cent. The researchers, led by Leslie Bernstein and her colleagues at the University of Southern California's North Cancer Center, worked out the average exercise level of the women in the study from the start of menstruation to a year before they were diagnosed with cancer. Those who exercised an average of at least 48 minutes each week were less likely to have developed breast cancer than those who exercised less or not all. The greatest protection from cancer was found in the women who exercised the most, more than 3.8 hours each week. The report concluded that the decrease in ovarian hormones associated with exercise was a protective factor.[4]

A few years earlier, Dr Rose Frisch had analysed 5,398 women who had graduated from university between 1925 and 1981 and found that those who exercised consistently were two and a half times less likely to develop cancer of the reproductive organs than their more sedentary counterparts and nearly two times less likely to develop breast cancer. This proved to be true regardless of whether the women used birth control pills, hormone replacement therapy, smoked or had family histories of cancer.[5] More than a hundred other recent studies have also shown that exercise can increase bone density before and after the menopause, reducing the risk of osteoporosis or bone fractures.

Alan became a patient of mine in the mid-1980s, a few years after discovering that he was HIV positive. With a vindictive controversy being encouraged by a fearful media, it was probably about the worst time to receive such a diagnosis. Being infected was terrible enough, but the stress that went with the diagnosis and the reactions of others was enormous. I can think of no more demoralising stress than being made into a pariah. As Alan said at the time, 'People stand up in the pulpit and denounce you, shun you. They do not want to know. They do not want to help. There are very few willing hands to hold yours.'

With the support of his wife, Alan did not act on his initial impulse to hang himself, but, as he said, 'Everything we had ever dreamed of suddenly went down the chute. No children. No nothing.'

Alan was convinced that self-esteem, a positive frame of mind and a low-stress lifestyle would be crucial if he were not to develop AIDS. 'I have every chance of surviving,' he said, 'and I cannot see any reason for not surviving . . . am not under stress. I am perfectly calm and nothing is going to worry me.'

Alan took up swimming, which he had always enjoyed, and it became his life. Since then he has won countless swimming competitions at a county level and is now an exercise instructor. He is convinced that this is what has kept him so healthy and he is now one of the longest surviving people infected with HIV in Britain.

Becky is another patient whom I have treated for several years. At the age of seventeen she was diagnosed with Hodgkin's lymphoma, a cancer of the lymphatic system. Five years later she had received so much medical treatment that her doctors told her there was no further chemotherapy or other treatment they could offer. But Becky wasn't about to give up. As she said at the time, 'Although the doctors can't give me any hope, as far as I'm concerned there is always hope.'

While Becky was still ill she saw an advertisement for a training course for fitness instructors and, although she had never really been involved with exercise before, she decided to enrol on the course. She now runs aerobic and fitness classes five days a week. It was, she believes, the turning point in her recovery because not long afterwards her cancer went into remission and several years later she is still clear. 'I'm convinced,' she told me, 'that exercise and diet have played a major role in my recovery.'

With such evidence for the health benefits of exercise it is probably not surprising that Dr Robert Butler of New York's Mount Sinai Medical School once said, 'If exercise could be packaged into a pill, it would be the single most prescribed and beneficial medicine in the nation.'

Why not try it? All the medical research points to the fact that you don't have to run marathons or do heavy weight-training to get the physical and psychological benefits of exercise. Moderate exercise a few times a day will give you the same benefits. If, for example, you walk up and down your stairs for ten minutes three times a day, it has the same effect on your body as an intensive half-hour workout in a gym. One study even found that washing and waxing the car and other household activities, when undertaken regularly, could extend your life.[6] All it takes is thirty minutes of moderate exercise a day.

Aerobic and Anaeobic Exercise

There are two forms of exercise: aerobic and anaerobic. Anaerobic exercise is high-intensity activity of a short duration and does not need oxygen, but if you sustain the activity at higher levels of intensity, it becomes aerobic (does need oxygen). Anaerobic exercise burns stored glucose in the body and helps to build muscle, while aerobic exercise is beneficial to the heart and helps to burn fat.

EXAMPLES OF AEROBIC AND ANAEROBIC EXERCISE

Aerobic	Anaerobic
Walking	Weightlifting
Jogging	Short-distance sprinting
Rowing	or swimming
Swimming	Callisthenics
Cycling	Push-ups
Aerobics	Sit-ups
Cross-country skiing	Pull-ups
	Yoga
	Tai chi

Fitness instructors advise you to get 70 to 80 per cent of your exercise from aerobic exercise and the remaining 20 to 30 per cent from anaerobics. But is there one definitive type of exercise that is of universal benefit? Probably, like everything else, what is good for one person may not be good for another. For somebody with cardiovascular problems, twenty minutes of aerobic exercise three times a week may act as a preventative. For the woman suffering from osteoporosis, weight-bearing anaerobic exercise which does not put excessive strain on the joints is a better choice.

When researchers looked at brisk walking compared with aerobic exercise, they found that walking was just as good for heart health. Walking three or more hours per week was associated with a 30 to 40 per cent reduction in the risk of a heart attack.[7]

You can use the following quick test to determine your own level of fitness.

HOW FIT ARE YOU?

How active are you? How often do you take physical exercise (including keep fit classes and sport) that makes you out of breath?

a. Four times or more a week.
b. Two to three times a week.
c. Once a week.
d. Less than once a week.

How far do you walk each week?

a. More than 5 km (3 miles).
b. Up to 5 km (3 miles).
c. Less than 1 ½ km (1 mile).
d. Less than 1 km (½ mile).

How do you travel to work or to the shops?

a. All the way on foot/cycle.
b. Part of the way on foot/cycle.
c. Occasionally on foot/cycle.
d. All the way by car or public transport.

When you have a choice do you:

a. Take the stairs, up and down, always?
b. Take the stairs unless you have something to carry?
c. Occasionally take the stairs?
d. Take the lift/escalator unless it's broken?

At weekends do you:

a. Spend several hours gardening, decorating, doing DIY, or some sport?
b. Usually sit down for meals and sit still in the evening?
c. Take a few short walks?
d. Spend most of the time sitting reading or watching television?

Do you think nothing of:

a. Doing the household chores after a day's work?
b. Rushing out to the shops again if you've forgotten something?
c. Getting other people to run errands for you even if you have time?
d. Paying for a telephone call when you could make a personal visit?

Add up your score:

4 points for every *a* answer
3 points for every *b* answer
2 points for every *c* answer
1 point for every *d* answer

20+	You are naturally very active and probably quite fit.
15–20	You are active and have a healthy attitude towards fitness.
10–15	You are only mildly active and would benefit from some more exercise.
Under 10	You are rather lazy and need to think again about your attitude towards activity. Try to reorganise your day to allow time for some exercise.

Yoga

Many of my patients, especially those who are elderly, have gained great benefit from yoga, which is an ancient art practised in Tibet, India and China. The word 'yoga' means 'union' or 'joining' and in its more literal sense refers to man's union with God or the universe, but in the context of helping your body it means the joining of two breaths. Correct breathing is the basis of yoga and most of the movements and correct bodily positions (or 'asanas', as they are called) are associated with deep breathing. Yoga tones up the body, delays ageing and develops your mind and spirit. Some of the techniques are physical, others mental.

I had been treating Kathleen for about fifteen years and had never really given a thought as to how old she might be. To my amazement, she told me that her family were planning a big party for her *ninetieth* birthday! Had I not known, I would have thought she was in her mid-sixties. Her agility and looks were, she explained to me, the resulting benefit of sixty years of practising yoga.

It reminded me of an old legend of a romantic wise man at the court of a Chinese king who was so moved by the beauty of his beloved succumbing to the ravages of old age that he withdrew from the world. After sitting cross-legged, deep in trance for three days, he emerged having developed yoga, a system designed to preserve her youth and loveliness.

Yoga recognises the intimate link between physical and mental health, and seeks to improve both through many different exercises, meditation, correct breathing and complete relaxation by focusing your mind on each part of your body in turn until the whole of you is completely relaxed. Your concentration is then brought to bear on a particular body movement. Yoga encourages a feeling of inner peace and calmness. However, it should always be learnt from a competent yoga teacher; don't try to learn it from a book because some of the positions and exercises can be potentially damaging without supervision.

Combating Stress through Diet

Diet has a strong impact on how well our body functions, yet for many people diet and weight are stressors that can affect us just as much as marital problems, physical illness, job pressures or family conflicts. This needn't be so – eating is good for us and it should be fun, not stressful!

Also, a stressed person is likely to be more interested in meals that can be prepared and eaten quickly than in foods that constitute a more correctly balanced diet. Eating too quickly and mindlessly can be a symptom of using food as a stress-reducer, an attempt to suppress anxiety or fill an emotional void. When you eat, chew slowly, tasting the food. Don't take more until you have swallowed the last mouthful and give yourself time to breathe properly as you eat. Plan your meals ahead so you can avoid eating under stress or 'snatching' something to eat in between tasks or while working.

Poor nutrition may well be one of the most neglected causes of disabling stress. While you may know that good nutrition contributes to good health, you may not realise that your eating habits have a profound influence on your daily stress level. Low levels of nutrients have been linked to stress-related symptoms such as insomnia, irritability, depression and fatigue.

Many doctors and complementary therapists have created a very profitable market in the field of nutrition, often telling us how highly complicated the subject is. This is not true. Briefly, like people, all living cells need food to survive and for cells this means oxygen, without which they die very rapidly. Oxygen is continually involved in chemical reactions within the cells and these reactions in turn produce waste products known as 'free radicals'. These are highly unstable molecules and you can imagine them as wandering, aimless people who have nothing better to do than to get into trouble. Free radicals form scar tissue in the collagen of your skin so you get wrinkles. They find their way into your bloodstream, forming cholesterol plaque in your arteries, which can lead to heart attacks and strokes. They can get into your joints, causing inflammation and arthritis. They can break down your cells' DNA and cause cancer. Dr Bruce Ames of the University of California, Berkeley, reckons that the DNA in your cells gets hit about 10,000 times a day by free radicals which can cause a great deal of damage.

Research has shown that free radicals can be 'disarmed' by antioxidants, which you can think of as social workers. Antioxidants attack the very causes of illness, depression of the immune system and indeed the ageing process. The crucial antioxidants – vitamins A, C, and E, and the minerals selenium and zinc – can be found in tomatoes, dark green vegetables, seafood, grains, seeds and nuts, root vegetables and almost all colourful fruits, such as apples, pears, strawberries, and cherries.

Unfortunately, because of the intense cultivation and numerous chemicals, herbicides, insecticides and growth restrictors and promoters used today, many nutrients that should be taken up by crops and vegetables have been leached from the soil so there is enough to support only the growth of the plant. The 'goodness' from the plant also starts to deteriorate as soon as it is harvested, so by the time it reaches our plate all that may be left is cellulose, or roughage. Freshly harvested organic fruits and vegetables are able to offer much higher levels of essential nutrients.

Balancing DHEA and Cortisol

There are two hormones that take on a dramatic role in the immune system if you are under a great deal of stress. They are dehydroepiandosterone (DHEA) and the main stress hormone, cortisol. DHEA is produced in the adrenal glands but, under stress, they start to produce cortisol instead. It is now known that cortisol does the most to damage immune system functioning, as it affects lymphocytes, macrophages and leukocytes, and depresses certain cytokines. Many people with chronic conditions have decreased levels of DHEA and raised levels of cortisol. However, the correct balance of DHEA and cortisol can be restored both by relaxation techniques and by certain foods that will help to support the adrenal glands.

To support the adrenal glands the body needs vitamin B5, vitamin C and magnesium.

Vitamin B5, also known as pantothenic acid, is found in broccoli, sweet potatoes, whole grains, cauliflower, salmon, liver, peas and beans. Nutritionists recommend that if you are suffering from chronic stress, you should supplement your diet with 100 to 500 mg of vitamin B5 daily.

Vitamin C is the only vitamin that we cannot store in our bodies, so you should ensure that your diet is high in it. It is well known that under extreme stress, whether it is chemical (for example smoking and pollutants), emotional, psychological or physical, you need far more of this vitamin because the urinary excretion of vitamin C is increased. Foods rich in vitamin C include broccoli, cabbage, chilli peppers, and green peppers, as well as all black or red berries, kiwi fruit and citrus fruits. Extra vitamin C, either through an increased dietary consumption or through supplements, is recommended during periods of great stress.

Magnesium is the primary mineral needed by the adrenal glands. It is found in mackerel, cod, whole grains, leafy green vegetables, beans, nuts and fruits. Because magnesium is so widely abundant in most foods, many dieticians believe that we receive a sufficient supply through our diet. However, many people are not eating a natural and balanced diet, but rather large quantities of refined foods. Since the process of food processing removes a high proportion of magnesium it is again a good idea to take it in supplement form during times of stress.

The best time of day to take vitamins is at breakfast, as certain nutrients are better absorbed when the digestive system is working at its peak. Taken before bedtime, vitamins are less easily absorbed and can cause mild indigestion and disrupt sleep.

Caffeine

Many people who are under stress will reach for stimulant drinks such as tea, coffee and alcohol (see below). These actually deplete nutrients from the body, however, and lead to an increased production of adrenaline, which can increase anxiety.

The stimulating effects of caffeine can last for as long as seven hours after drinking a cup of coffee. I will only drink one cup of coffee a day, in the morning, because I know that if I drink it in the afternoon or evening I will not sleep properly that night.

People who are prone to stress or anxiety are known to be much more sensitive to caffeine[8] and we all become more sensitive to caffeine as we get older. Also, a high intake of caffeine can adversely affect bone quality, so menopausal women worried about osteoporosis should be particularly careful with their intake.

Alcohol

Although many people think that alcohol has a calming influence and will therefore help to combat stress, a study in which ninety healthy men were given either a placebo or alcohol showed significant *increases* in anxiety scores after drinking the alcohol.[9] If you are anxious or stressed it is probably best not to drink alcohol at all.

Quite apart from this, excessive alcohol can damage almost every one of our biological systems, causing gastrointestinal problems, liver disease, and brain and heart disorders. It also increases the adrenal hormone output. A high consumption of alcohol increases the risk of high blood pressure, and research suggests that women who drink more than two glasses of wine a day may be at greater risk of breast cancer than women who do not.

Refined Carbohydrates

Eating 'comfort foods' is not the way to combat stress. Such foods, with their high levels of sugar and refined carbohydrates, not only deplete many stored nutrients, especially magnesium, but are known to also contribute to problems with blood sugar control, especially hypogly-caemia. This is because they put excessive demands on the pancreas to produce more insulin so that eventually it gets tired and works less effi-ciently. The link between hypoglycaemia and mental impairment is well established and studies have also linked it to depression.[10] Depression itself often causes feelings of stress and anxiety, forming a vicious circle. Reducing or better still eliminating sugary foods will take a lot of pres-sure off the liver, which is the primary cleansing organ of the body.

Herbs to Help You Relax

There are several botanical medicines (herbs) that clinical studies have found to significantly reduce feelings of stress and anxiety by supporting adrenal function and preventing the negative effects of stress.

It is suggested that herbs for stress are taken in a 'stressless' manner, the daily dose being divided in three and taken after meals. Those to promote sleep should be taken as a hot drink, or with a hot drink, half an hour before going to bed.

Make a note on your calendar or in your diary when you start taking your 'tonic' so that you not only remember when to take a recommended break from it, but also so that you can note any improvements.

If you are taking prescribed medication, herbal preparations may interfere with or alter the effect of these drugs. Therefore tell your herbalist or nutritional therapist what drugs you are taking, or consult them before self-administration.

Valerian

Valerian is a plant found both in Europe and North America and its root has been used in folk medicine as a sedative and in lowering blood pres-sure. It also helps to increase the flow of bile and relax intestinal muscles. Valeric acid and valepotriates, two of the active compounds in the plant, have been found to bind to the same brain receptors as Valium.

Valerian is used most frequently in the treatment of insomnia and as a mild sedative can be taken half an hour before going to bed. You should never use valerian with barbiturates, as it may cause excessive sedation.

Chinese/Korean Ginseng (*Panax ginseng*)

This is used as a revitalising tonic after a long illness and to improve the ability to cope with stress, which it does primarily by working on the adrenal glands. One study showed that its stress-relieving effects were comparable to those of Valium. However, while Valium can affect motor movement, cause behaviour changes and have sedative effects, Chinese ginseng, in the correct dosage, normally causes none of these negative side-effects.[11]

Chinese ginseng is also a potent immune booster. Another study showed that after eight weeks of taking one capsule every twelve hours, volunteers were found to have an improved neutrophil function, increased numbers of lymphocytes, increased helper T cells and increased natural killer cell activity.[12]

It is best to start with the lowest recommended dose and gradually increase it, dividing the amount into three daily doses after meals. There may possibly be side-effects, such as euphoria, diarrhoea and skin eruptions, if it is taken over an extended period. It may therefore be best to use it for a period of say, two to three weeks, then forgo it for another two weeks.

Ginseng may cause headaches, tremulousness and manic episodes in people treated with phenelizine sulphate. It should not be used with oestrogens and corticosteroids because it may increase their effect, nor should it be used with warfarin. It may also affect blood glucose levels and should be completely avoided, or used with great caution, if you are diabetic.

Siberian Ginseng (*Eleutherococcus senticosis*)

Known to Chinese herbalists 4,000 years ago, some consider Chinese ginseng to be stronger than Siberian ginseng, so if you have been under mild to moderate stress with no really obvious impaired adrenal function, Siberian ginseng may be considered. It has been used to treat chronic fatigue syndrome and has also been shown to lower elevated serum cholesterol and reduce blood pressure, which also improves kidney function.

Curiously, Siberian ginseng can lower blood pressure in individuals with high blood pressure but can raise blood pressure in those with low blood pressure; this is known as an adaptogen. In one clinical trial it was found to cause a significant increase in helper T cells and an increase in natural killer cell activity.[13] Siberian ginseng does not contain ginsenoides, which therefore makes it less toxic than Chinese ginseng.

The Relaxation Response

Learning to calm the mind is an extremely important part of relieving stress. The easiest way of stilling the mind and body is through the use of relaxation exercises. These produce a real physiological response now known as 'the relaxation response', which is exactly the opposite of a stressed response.

Transcendental meditation, or TM as it is more commonly known, allows the mind to settle into a quiet, relaxed state. Gradually, quieter and deeper levels of mental stillness are reached until there is a point of complete mental stillness, during which the mind is said to have transcended the everyday level of thought while still experiencing full inner wakefulness. Introduced into Britain in the 1960s by Maharishi Mahesh Yogi and popularised by the Beatles, the transcendental meditation movement now has over 130,000 followers in Britain, of whom about 1,000 are doctors who are using it in medical application.

Also in the 1960s, a group of practising transcendental meditators approached a respected Harvard cardiologist, Dr Herbert Benson. They believed that they could lower their blood pressure simply by meditating. When Benson tested their claims he was surprised to find that when the meditators were sitting quietly and focusing their minds on a single image, their metabolism decreased, their heart and respiratory rates slowed down and their brainwaves took on a distinctive pattern. He termed this 'the relaxation response'. In this quietened state the parasympathetic nervous system controls bodily functions such as breathing, heart rate and digestion. While the sympathetic nervous system protects us from immediate danger with the fight or flight reaction, the parasympathetic nervous system is designed for repair, maintenance and restoration of the body.

Even though the results spoke for themselves during Benson's early research, it made no sense to him that meditation was the only way to invoke this response. He soon discovered what he believes is at the heart of the changes. Repetition of any activity, whether it is speaking the same word over and over again, praying or exercising, can cause the body to relax and promote healing.

EXERCISE: THE RELAXATION RESPONSE

You can try for yourself the following simple relaxation exercise that I have used in hundreds of seminars. As with Herbert Benson's technique, it is simple, quick and very effective:

1 Sit quietly in a comfortable position.

2 Close your eyes.

3 Deeply relax all your muscles, beginning at your feet and progressing up to your face. Keep them relaxed.

4 Breathe through your nose. Become aware of your breathing. As you breathe out, say the word 'one' silently to yourself. For example, breathe in . . . out, 'one', in . . . out 'one'. Breathe easily and naturally.

5 Continue for ten to twenty minutes. You can open your eyes to check the time, but don't use an alarm. When you finish, sit quietly for several minutes, at first with your eyes closed and later with your eyes open. Do not stand up for a few moments.

Do not worry about whether you are successful in achieving a deep level of relaxation. Maintain a passive attitude and let relaxation happen at its own pace. When distracting thoughts occur, try to ignore them by not dwelling on them and return to repeating 'one'. With practice, you will be able to relax with little effort. Practise the technique once or twice a day, but not for two hours after any meal, since the digestive processes seem to interfere with it.

You may want to try this next exercise as well. It is one that I have frequently used in my workshops as a prelude for helping participants to relax before a longer meditational journey.

EXERCISE: COMPLETE PHYSICAL RELAXATION

Find a comfortable position in a chair, or lying on the floor. Let your hands rest gently in your lap and your feet lie heavily on the floor or a cushion. Close your eyes and look down. Accept that there will be some level of noise around you, even if it's just the ticking of the clock. Let life go on around you as you start to relax. Turn **within** to that quiet centre within yourself and sigh deeply. . . . And again. Let the breath settle and come and go of its own accord.

Bring your attention to your feet. Screw up your toes tightly and then let them soften and relax. Lift your feet off the floor and let them drop. They will remain heavy and still.

Tighten up your calves and then let them soften and relax.

Pull your knees together tightly, then release them and let them stay parted a little.

Tense up the big muscles of your thighs. Feel them pushing against the chair or the floor and then let them go.

Pull your buttocks together. Now release them and let your bottom sink into the seat of the chair or onto the floor below you.

Tighten everything between the legs, pulling up your under-carriage. Tight . . . tighter . . . . Now slowly let it go.

Pull your tummy in towards your spine and then . . . slowly release.

Now all the lower part of your body feels heavy and relaxed. Let it rest in this way while you take your attention to:

Your hands. Clench them into fists, then stretch out your fingers and let them relax and curl the way they want to. Lift your hands and drop them into your lap, letting them rest where they fall.

Keeping your hands relaxed, tense your arms. Then let them go.

Lift your shoulders a little and then let them drop.

Your chest feels open and free, moving gently as your breath comes and goes.

Your neck feels comfortable, straight and in line with your spine.

Be aware of your jaw. Clench your teeth together. Feel the tension. Then release and feel the teeth part.

Screw up the whole of your face. Then let it out slowly. . . . Cheeks soft, eyelids heavy.

Raise your eyebrows as if very surprised. Let them go and feel that there is lots of space between the brows.

Let go of any tension around your ears.

Even your scalp feels a little looser now.

At this stage it's nice to imagine relaxation climbing your spine. Take your attention to its base and imagine relaxation slowly rising. As it climbs you can feel that part of your back relaxing and letting go. Pay particular attention to the area between your shoulder blades, where tension so often starts.

Your whole body is now pleasantly relaxed.

Your breath comes and goes, flowing the way it wants, like waves breaking on a shore, dissolving away any tension, bringing relaxation.

As your body has relaxed so too your thoughts have slowed down. Don't try to make your mind a blank. Just be aware of your thoughts. Don't concentrate on any one in particular. Just watch them come and go.

After a few minutes, move on to the next stage. If you are fidgeting, you've had long enough.

Bring your thoughts back to the here and now.

Without opening your eyes, be aware of your body again and its position, its place in the room.

Tune in again to the sounds around you.

Allow the breath to flow more deeply, bringing in energy ready to move again.

Move your head slightly from side to side and wriggle your fingers and toes.

Straighten up if you've slumped a little.

Have a really good stretch and yawn, sigh, whatever your body tells you.

Open your eyes if you haven't already done so and SMILE.

Don't rush away as soon as the relaxation has ended. You may well feel rather dreamy and slow to begin with, but that's good. You will probably find that a little later you get an energy surge that the relaxation releases.

The Benefits of Meditation

For thousands of years, religions all over the world have extolled the benefits of meditation and quiet contemplation. In Islam and Catholicism,

Judaism and Buddhism, Hinduism and Taoism, and in religious practice from the West to Africa and Asia, the value of sitting quietly cultivating stillness or focusing the mind has been well recognised.

There is now an impressive array of scientific documentation so substantial that it can be said without fear of contradiction that meditation and relaxation techniques have been scientifically shown to be highly beneficial to our health. Over 1,000 research studies, most of them published in well-respected scientific journals, attest to a wide range of measurable improvements in human function as a result of meditative practices. For example:

○ People suffering from insomnia were found to fall asleep four times more quickly after learning the relaxation response. Many of them then returned to what are considered normal patterns of sleep.

○ Chronic pain patients who practised relaxation techniques were able to reduce visits to their doctors by an average of 36 per cent.

○ The relaxation response resulted in a 58 per cent reduction of symptoms among women with severe pre-menstrual tension. (Another report, praising Prozac, showed a 52 per cent reduction of symptoms among women taking this anti-depressant drug.)

Numerous methods have been found to be effective at relaxing people, including self-hypnosis, progressive relaxation, prayer, meditation and biofeedback. The important thing is to select one that appeals to you and then spend fifteen to twenty minutes once or twice a day to perform it.

The most successful recording that I ever made, which was also used in many health centres and hospitals, only ran for fifteen minutes each side but many people told me that it was so effective that they never heard the end of it. Although I have reproduced it here, you might find it easier to either make your own recording of it or have someone read it to you.

EXERCISE: JUST RELAX

I'd like you to find a quiet, comfortable place to sit or lie down with your eyes closed and your hands resting gently in your lap or by your sides. I want you to breathe easily and naturally, breathing in through your nose and exhaling through your mouth. As you breathe in, slowly count to four and imagine the warm air flowing in. Imagine this warmed air flowing to every part of your body. Pause for a second and then slowly breathe out to a count of four. As you breathe in, imagine that you are breathing in a sense of peace and serenity. As you exhale, you are releasing any stress or worry.

As you inhale, you are breathing in peace and tranquillity. As you exhale, imagine all your tension and stress leaving your body.

Your entire body begins to ease as you start to drift, deeper and deeper, into relaxation with each breath.

Your breathing becomes deeper and easier . . . deeper and easier.

Every breath is slow and easy, slow and relaxed.

You are becoming completely at ease.

A pleasant feeling of lightness begins to flow through every part of your body as you continue drifting, deeper and deeper . . . deeper and deeper.

A soothing picture now comes to your mind.

You are slowly walking on a clear spring morning down a country lane. The air is crisp and fresh, the scent of flowers hangs in the air and the plants are a gentle green and covered in early morning dew. The soft sunlight catches the dewdrops and they sparkle like crystals.

You are perfectly at ease.

Tall trees reach up to the soft blue sky and sway in a gentle breeze.

The hedgerows are alive with birds that greet with joy a new day. In the distance is the sound of sheep calling out to their lambs.

The scene fills you with happiness and the joy of a new day.

You have now reached a green grassy meadow. As you walk slowly across it, a cuckoo calls out from a nearby hedgerow.

Not too far away is the sound of water, trickling, bubbling water. You find yourself beside a stream of clear water and, as it dances and splashes over seemingly polished stones, the movement of the water creates cascading silvery lights.

A dragonfly darts across the water's surface, the early morning light catching its lace-like wings.

A little further upstream you suddenly catch a rainbow glimpse of a fleeting kingfisher.

All around you, pushing through the soft grass, are buttercups, deep yellow in the early morning light.

You are now resting on a beautiful green mossy bank . . . soft, gentle and restful.

You are completely at ease . . . perfectly at ease . . . a part of this magical creation.

Soft, fluffy clouds are lazily drifting by. The golden sunlight is soothing and relaxing. During your rest, all the healing energies of nature are flowing through your body.

Feel yourself being renewed.

Your mind is filled with a feeling of deep peace and contentment. It is so peaceful in this quiet place. You are having a wonderful rest.

Rest and relaxation are good.

You feel good. You feel healthy. You feel happy.

Relax and enter an even deeper, healthier level of mind.

I'd like you to repeat silently to yourself these thoughts for your day:

'My inner conscious mind will relax any tension from my body whenever I repeat to myself three times the word "relax". Upon hearing the word "relax", a flow of energy will revitalise my body. Relax . . . relax . . . relax.

'Today, I will confront any situation that presents itself to me in a positive and constructive way.

'Today, my confidence in my ability to deal with any difficulties that may arise will continue to grow.

'Today, I will find a way to do my job more effectively and the better I become at it, the more interesting it will become.

'Today, I can and will succeed, and whatever the problem, I will find a way around it.

'Today will be a good day and it will be great just to be alive, whatever happens.

'Today creative ideas and inspiration will come easily to me.

'Today my inner wisdom is guiding me towards my goals and I feel good.

'I am now ready to accept all the joy and prosperity that life has to offer me.'

The Beneficial Effects of Music

Naturally, different things will relax different people. Throughout most of *my* life it has been music, which is also a very important component of my healing work. Music makes a world of difference to the healing experience, softening the atmosphere and enhancing people's receptivity to energies. It can dissipate the hard, cold edge of silence and help people to relax. I deliberately choose descriptive music that I hope will conjure up visual images and transport my patients to the furthest reaches of their imagination.

I also use music in my work to fix an association with the healing experience and so enable people to revisit that experience whenever they choose. Many of my patients will ask me for the details of the music I've been playing and will then buy a copy of it to play at home. They find that they are able to prolong the benefits of the healing by linking the music they hear during the healing session with the act itself. In some cases this connection is very intense and people experience vivid imagery. They can sense changes occurring and also say that they can feel the heat of my hands again.

I am always careful to use music that people are very unlikely to have heard in another connection, because a piece of music, like a perfume, can have very powerful emotions attached to it. Although there are many well-known compositions that I find positive and uplifting, I prefer not to use them because they may arouse some painful memory or association in someone else.

Years ago I was treating a lady who had cancer. She had her own cassette tape of relaxation music, which included many well-known pieces of classical music played on the harp and flute. She carried this tape everywhere with her and even when she was going through chemotherapy treatment in hospital she would be listening to it.

Almost a year later she was watching television one night when an advertisement for a particular brand of paint was shown. She immediately felt really nauseous and ran to the bathroom because she thought she was going to be sick. This feeling passed very quickly and she felt fine again. She could not understand what had happened. Later the same week the same advertisement came on while she was watching television, and again she felt really sick. Then she remembered: the background music used in the commercial was one of the pieces on the cassette tape she had used during her illness. She also realised that she will never be able to listen to that piece of music again without her mind associating it with her experience of illness and the side-effects of chemotherapy.

I should have remembered this lesson when I treated orchestral conductor Arthur Davison, although his aversion turned out to be for quite a different reason. Charming and courteous though he was, I was a little intimidated by having to select music for someone with his professional background. Somehow it didn't seem appropriate to select one of my favourites from Vangelis, Kitaro or Tony O'Connor. I chose a classical recording in my collection and began the healing session. After about a minute he turned to me and said: 'I don't know whether you put this music on for your benefit or mine, but if you've put it on for my benefit I don't find it relaxing at all. I'm sitting here counting in all the instruments! Have you got any good modern jazz?'

Bernie Siegel is another advocate of music for relaxation and healing and he too has had the experience of choosing inappropriate music. He was playing harp music to a patient that he was about to operate on when the patient turned to him and said, 'It's a good thing I heard that while I'm awake. If I woke up and heard it, I wouldn't know where I was!'

Of course the use of music in healing is not new. The ancient Egyptians called music the 'physic of the soul' and the Persians were said to have cured various illnesses with the sound of the lute. Confucius believed that music was an aid to harmonious living while Plato believed that health in mind and body could be obtained through music. George II, who was subject to great bouts of depression, found solace in music.

Interestingly, the word 'health' comes from the old English word *heol*, a root word signifying whole, healing, hale and inhaling. *Heal* in northern Middle English means 'to make sound', 'to become healthy again'. We use the word 'sound' as a synonym for health and whole-ness and to signify the unshakeable foundation for whatever we do – we speak of a sound judgement, sound advice, sound investments and sound business procedures. When things are going smoothly we are in tune and in harmony with others and the world around us. In romantic relationships we hope to set the right tone, strike a sympathetic chord or communicate on the same wavelength. If something unexpected happens, we decide to play it by ear. Musical metaphors and sonic imagery permeate our lives.

When I am healing I tend to play music that other healers might not immediately think of using. I have never subscribed to the idea that music for healing has to be pretty and emotionally bland. Music that lifts us and makes us want to fly, in our hearts and minds, does far more by way of engendering a positive outlook. I feel that many of my patients need to find a winning strength, and music can represent energy and grit as well as inspire hope.

Depending on their waveform and other characteristics, sounds can have a charging and releasing effect. In some cases they can positively charge the brain and the body. At times loud, pulsating music can energise us and mask or release pain or tension. Some of the most positively charged sounds are made by our own voices. But sound can also bring about negative changes. Loud sounds, such as those from a factory or a jet engine, can deplete the body. A piercing, high saw-tooth frequency close to an ear can bring about immediate headaches. Low-frequency sounds can create stress, muscle contractions and pain.

Through the brain stem the auditory nerves connect with all the muscles of the body, hence muscle tone, flexibility and equilibrium are directly influenced by sound. Through the vagus nerve the inner ear connects with the larynx, heart, lungs, stomach, liver, bladder, kidneys and the small and large intestines. This suggests that auditory vibrations from the eardrum interact with the parasympathetic nerves to regulate control and actually influence all the major organs of the body.

As anybody who has ever been into a fast-food restaurant will know, the piped music tends to be bright and briskly paced to encourage the customers to eat their food as fast as possible. Classical music, especially slow string music, makes you eat more slowly and consume less.

Music can also affect your breathing. Both are rhythmic. A deeper, slower rate of breathing is optimal in contributing to calmness and control of the emotions, deeper thinking and better metabolism. Shallow, fast breathing can lead to scattered and superficial thinking, impulsive behaviour and a tendency to make mistakes. By listening to music with longer, slower sounds you can usually deepen and slow the breath and relax the mind, especially if abdominal breathing is used.

Music Therapy

Music reduces muscle tension and improves body movement and co-ordination. In the 1980s, a Norwegian teacher called Olaf Schiller began using music therapy for children with severe physical and mental disabilities. He devised what he called a 'musical bath', a special environment in which youngsters could be immersed in sound, and discovered that a range of New Age, ambient and popular music could reduce muscle tension and relax the children. Now known as 'vibral acoustic therapy', Schiller's methods have spread to other parts of Europe. Music is also widely used in rehabilitation centres to restructure and repattern repetitive movements following accidents or illness.

Scientists at the University of Buffalo, led by Dr Karen Allen, a pioneer researcher on the effect of music on cardiovascular response to stress, and Dr Lawrence Golden, a clinical professor of medicine, found that older people who listened to their choice of music during out-patient eye surgery for cataracts or glaucoma had significantly lower heart rate, blood pressure and cardiac workload than patients who did not listen to music. In addition, when asked to rate how the surgery affected them, the music listeners rated themselves significantly less anxious and significantly better at coping with the experience than their non-music-listening colleagues. Music was responsible for two effects, both important to successful surgery: it decreased stress on the cardiovascular system and helped patients to relax.

Patients in the experimental group listened to music through headphones before, during and after surgery, while those in the control group did not listen to music at all. The researchers found that the heart rate and blood pressure of all of the patients in the control group increased on the morning of surgery, but then dropped significantly in the music group within ten minutes of tuning in and remained low. Only in the music group did cardiovascular measures reach a near normal baseline.

As Dr Allen noted, patients like music because it is 'cheap and effective, and has no negative side-effects'.[14]

The Mozart Effect

Don Campbell, an American who is an internationally acclaimed expert on the transformative power of sound, tone and music, first coined the now well-known phrase 'the Mozart effect'. He had discovered that in many different parts of the world, Mozart's music had quite extraordinary benefits for its listeners. In France, monks found that if their cows listened to Mozart they produced more milk; in Washington State immigration department officials found that if they played Mozart to Asian immigrants their learning process was accelerated; in Edmonton in Canada it was found that when Mozart was played in string quartets in city squares, the pedestrian traffic was calmed and drug dealing was reduced. In northern Japan it was claimed that one particular brewery discovered that Mozart made the best saké. The density of the yeast used for brewing the traditional Japanese rice wine, a measure of its quality, increased by a factor of 10. In the 1990s, researchers at the University of California found that graduate psychology students scored 8 to 9 points higher on a special IQ test after listening for 10 minutes to Mozart's double piano sonata, although the effect only lasted for about 15 minutes. At St Agnes Hospital in Baltimore, half an hour of Mozart's music played to patients in the intensive care unit produced the same effect as 10 milligrams of Valium, according to Dr Raymond Barr, director of the coronary care unit.

Scientific research does seem to show that compositions by Mozart reliably produce good moods in those who listen to them. This happens even if the listener is not particularly keen on classical music, which suggests that good composers tap into universal musical preferences. Recent neuroscientific research would seem to bear this out, because when someone listens to a classical melody, the neurons in different brain regions fire more synchronously than when they listen to a random sequence of notes. The reason for this sense of melody is still a mystery.

Of course, what is beneficial to one person does not always work for another. I used to treat an elderly gentleman who really did not enjoy music at all, unless it was by the 1930s Latin bandleader Edmundo Ross. If I played music that I considered to be relaxing, he would say that it sounded like bathwater! He is not alone in his opinion, because many people find strength and comfort in silence.

The Power of Silence

Ian, one of my silence-loving patients, told me, 'I find solitude with silence helpful, but usually it is only available between the hours of

11 p.m. and 2 a.m. before bed. Sometimes concentration helps, or some-times a passive enjoyment of this rare commodity of silence.'

I believe that one way to access your healing power is to practise silence. Practising silence means making a commitment to simply *be*. Turn off the television or the radio, put away your books and simply hear the silence. If this is something that you are unaccustomed to, your internal dialogue may distract you for a while. You may feel an intense need to speak and you may find that your thoughts flow in rivers of turbulence. You may find that you feel a sense of urgency and anxiety. However, as you stay with your experience your mind will eventually give up and begin to quiet itself. As your internal dialogue begins to quieten, you will begin to experience the field of all possibilities.

This is a method of experiencing pure awareness. Imagine throwing a small stone into a still pond and watching the ripples softly spreading outward, expanding into the stillness of the pond. Once the ripples settle down, throw in another small stone. Now imagine that the stone is an intention. In this silence even your faintest intention will ripple across.

Chapter 9

THE HEALTHY DIET

So far on our healing journey we have discovered the extent to which our body is so extraordinarily influenced by our thoughts and our emotions, but what really keeps our body working most efficiently is the food that we eat. Food is the fuel that makes us function, gives us energy, and builds the body and repairs it. Food for health does the job properly.

While in many parts of the world people eat to survive, in affluent countries our eating habits have become divorced from our real nutritional needs. Here, the food we eat, far from enhancing our health, is a major contributing factor in serious, widespread health problems, notably heart disease, obesity, cancer and digestive disorders – the so-called 'diseases of civilisation'. The situation is cruelly ironic since, unlike many millions in the Third World, the West has an abundance of good food. Diet, of all factors involved in health, should be one of the easiest to control.

A Balanced Diet

Eating is a pleasure and so is good health. Yet when we eat, we do not usually think about how the food will affect our health. High-fat meals, high-sodium meals and high-cholesterol meals have become part of our lives. More and more people are suffering from diet-induced illnesses such as heart disease, high blood pressure and certain types of cancer and diabetes.

For good health, we need good nutrition. Eating enough, but not in excess, of each type of nutrient is essential to keep our bodies in proper condition. Any food, even if it is healthy, can be harmful if we take too much of it.

Changing to a good diet should not be a matter of making stressful adjustments, such as avoiding all sweet or fatty foods, or living on a monotonous fare of brown rice and vegetables. Fad diets are not the

answer to ill health either. They can deprive the body of essential nutrients and lower the body's metabolic rate. What counts most is estab-
lishing a good ratio of nutrients, choosing good-quality foods and being
aware of special individual requirements. Within a sensible framework,
there is scope for infinite variation, and occasional treats can be enjoyed
without harm. The simplest rule is to choose foods that are as close to
their natural state as possible because they are likely to yield the fullest
range of nutrients that your body requires.

Traditionally, a balanced diet was defined as one that included foods
from each of the four major food groups – carbohydrates, proteins, fruits
and vegetables, and fats – but current nutritional wisdom is suggesting
that a low-fat, high-fibre diet is better at disease prevention. It is now
recommended that we eat more grains, vegetables and fruits and less
meat, dairy products, fats, oils and sweets.

The evidence from published scientific studies linking disease to diet
is now so overwhelming that advice to people to consume more fruits
and vegetables and reduce fat intake has already been integrated into the
UN, US, European and UK government dietary guideline policies.

There is such a myriad of dietary information, however, sometimes
seemingly conflicting, that occasionally my patients have told me that
they no longer know what a 'balanced diet' consists of, and how much
of any particular food they need to consume in order to gain the optimal
nutritional intake.

Accordingly, next to each of the food groups listed below is a range
of recommended daily servings. The highest numbers are for tall, active
men; the lowest are for short, inactive women.

Bread, cereal, rice and pasta: six to eleven servings A serving
equals: 1 slice of bread; 25 g (1 oz) of ready-to-eat cereal; ½ cup
cooked cereal, rice or pasta.

Vegetables: three to five servings A serving equals: 1 cup of raw,
leafy vegetables; ½ cup of other vegetables, cooked or chopped raw;
3/4 cup of vegetable juice.

Milk, yoghurt and cheese: two to three servings A serving
equals: 1 cup of milk or yoghurt; 40 g (½ oz) of natural cheese; 55 g
(2 oz) of processed cheese.

Meat, poultry, fish, dry beans, eggs and nuts: two to three servings A serving equals: 55–85 g (2–3 oz) of cooked lean meat, poultry or fish; ½ cup of cooked dry beans, 1 egg, or 2 tablespoons of peanut butter (the latter count as 25 g/1 oz of lean meat).

Fats, oils and sweets Limit calories from these, especially if you need to lose weight. Limit fat to 30 per cent of your diet. Remember that 1 gram of saturated fat has 9 calories. Having said that, there are some oils that are essential to your diet and ideally should make up part of your limited intake of fat. The two families of oils are known as the Omega 3 and Omega 6. The best sources of Omega 3 are fish and flax seed, while Omega 6 can be found in sunflower and sesame seeds.

Eating a healthy diet is possible with a little planning. While no diet is perfect for everyone, there are several steps you can take to determine what works for you:

GUIDELINES FOR A HEALTHY DIET

○ Write down a list of your favourite foods. If you like to eat junk food, include it!

○ Plan each meal. Try to include a high-fibre source, at least one fruit or vegetable, and at least one lean protein source for breakfast, lunch and dinner.

○ Include one serving from your favourite food list each day. Limit the amount of servings from the less-healthy choices, but don't deprive yourself of the foods that you enjoy.

○ Try to incorporate seafood or other sources of Omega 3 fatty acids, such as flax seed oil, at least every third day.

○ Include plenty of legumes. Beans are rich in fibre, high in protein and low in dietary fat.

○ Make sure you eat additional fruits, vegetables and side salads to ensure you have three to five vegetables and two to four fruit servings every day.

○ If you do not eat dairy produce, make sure you incorporate plenty of kale, broccoli and/or soy into your diet. If you do eat dairy produce, still make sure that you include two to three servings a day.

○ Limit sugar and alcohol intake. If you enjoy sugary foods, only eat them when they are included in your plan.

○ Drink water. Include plenty of fluids in every meal.

○ Stick to your plan. If you get off it, get back on track the next day.

Supplements

Some people mistakenly believe that taking a supplement in the morning will erase or counteract a poor diet. The fact is that it won't. A supplement does not provide all the nutrients and other substances, such as fibre, that your body needs. It only provides the ones listed on the label. Besides that, vitamin pills do not satisfy your appetite. Eating an apple (full of potassium and fibre) or a ripe slice of cantaloupe melon (filled with vitamins A and C) is far more fulfilling, and filling.

On the other hand, supplementing a good all-round multivitamin and mineral does help to ensure you are getting an optimal intake. There are some people who may benefit from additional supplements. Elderly people who may not get enough sunlight to make up a steady supply of vitamin D, or who are not consuming adequate calcium and foods fortified with vitamin B12, may be supplement candidates. Some pregnant women may find it a challenge of Olympic proportions to meet their iron needs without a supplement.

Strict vegetarians who do not eat any animal foods should ensure that their diets are adequate in vitamins B12 and D, iron, calcium and zinc. If you are unable to eat a healthy diet because of a medical condition, or because your lifestyle prevents it, you may also benefit from a supplement. But beware: when it comes to vitamins and nutrients, more may not be better. Certain nutrients, such as vitamin A, can be toxic when taken in large doses.

Your body needs vitamins and minerals to form blood cells, build strong bones and regulate the nervous system, but it can't generate them on its own, so it needs to take them in through food or in the form of supplements.

While taking therapeutic doses of nutrients for better health, one thing that you should bear in mind is that vitamin and mineral supplements should be treated with the same care and concern for safety that you reserve for prescription and over-the-counter medications. As you will see, large doses of certain nutrients can be toxic, they can cause side-effects and they can sometimes interact with medications that you might be taking.

RDAs

Recommended dietary allowances (RDAs) for vitamins and minerals were originally prepared by the US Food and Nutrition Board of the National Research Council in 1941 and were developed to reduce the rates of severe nutritional deficiencies such as scurvy (lack of vitamin C), pellagra (lack of niacin) and beriberi (lack of vitamin B1). Another important consideration is that RDAs were designed to serve as the basis for evaluating the adequacy of diets of groups of people, not individuals. However, individuals vary too widely in their nutritional needs and, as the US Food and Nutrition Board has stated, 'Individuals with special nutritional needs are not covered by the RDAs.' These focus only on the prevention of nutritional deficiencies in population groups and do not define optimal intake for an individual. The RDAs do not take into account environmental and lifestyle factors that can destroy vitamins and bind minerals. While the US Food and Nutrition Board acknowledges that smokers, for example, need twice as much vitamin C as non-smokers, they do not take into account alcohol consumption, food additives and other chemicals that are known to affect our nutrient function.

Although RDAs have done a good job of defining nutritional deficiencies, fewer than three in a hundred people manage to meet the recommended daily amounts (RDAs) set down by the EU and there is still a great deal to be learned about the *optimum* intake of nutrients. Patrick

Holford, founder of the Institute for Optimum Nutrition and author of the bestselling *The Optimum Nutrition Bible*, explains that to achieve maximum health, you need optimum nutrition. If you eat the average 'well-balanced diet', you will have average health. This is why nutritional consultants have devised the suggested optimal nutrient allowances (SONAs) index, with levels two to ten times higher than the RDAs. Over thirty different studies have shown that a daily intake of 1,000 mg or more of vitamin C reduces the incidence, severity and length of colds, for example, yet the RDA is just 60 mg.

The following guide will show you how to get the most vitamins and minerals from your diet. The amounts given are the basic maintenance intake, based on research carried out by the Institute for Optimum Nutrition to establish optimal nutrient allowances, not RDAs. In italics is a suggested therapeutic level that can be used to correct a deficiency, which you can then reduce once your symptoms improve.

Vitamins

Vitamin A

Daily value: 5,000–7,500 iu (*15,000–20,000 iu*)

What it does Vitamin A is a fat-soluble vitamin which comes in two forms. The first is retinol, which is found in meats. The other is provitamin A, which is found in plant foods in the form of compounds called carotenoids. The best-known and most prominent carotenoid is beta-carotene, which provides about two-thirds of vitamin A in our diets. Beta-carotene is not as well absorbed as retinol, and it is only about half as active in vitamin activity. It helps to maintain good vision, build and maintain skin, teeth, bones and mucous membranes and is necessary for the production of bacteria-fighting chemicals in the ears, saliva and sweat. It also aids the efficient production of T cells, helps the kidneys in filtering and removing debris from the blood, and stimulates fighting T and B cells against infection. A deficiency of vitamin A can lead to an increased susceptibility to infections.

What it may do Current clinical trials on prevention of cancer of the cervix and of the lung and breast are using beta-carotene. It may also be helpful in the prevention of colon cancer and melanoma. It may increase resistance to infection in children.

Food sources Milk, eggs, liver, cheese, fish oil, also fruits and vegetables that contain beta-carotene.

Supplementation Vitamin A is stored in the liver and additional supplementation is not normally recommended as it can be toxic in high doses. Pregnant women need to be particularly careful, as large doses of vitamin A have been linked to birth defects and sponta-neous abortions. Beta-carotene is non-toxic and should be taken with vitamin E.

Vitamin B1 (Thiamine)

Daily value: 25 mg (*50 mg*)

What it does It helps to convert carbohydrates into energy and is necessary for healthy brain, nerve cells and heart function.

Food sources Whole grains, enriched grain products, beans, meats, liver, wheat germ, nuts, fish, brewer's yeast.

Supplementation Supplementation in addition to a good multivit-amin is not usually necessary.

Vitamin B2 (Riboflavin)

Daily value: 25 mg (*50 mg*)

What it does It helps to convert carbohydrates into energy. It is also essential for growth, the production of red blood cells and healthy skin and eyes.

Food sources Dairy products, liver, meat, chicken, fish, enriched grain products, leafy greens, beans, nuts, eggs and almonds.

Supplementation Supplementation in addition to a good multivit-amin is not usually needed, although both oral contraceptives and alcohol seem to reduce the body's ability to absorb riboflavin. You may want to take a B-complex vitamin to cover all the bases.

Vitamin B3 (Niacin)

Daily value: 50 mg (*100 mg*)

What it does It is useful in protecting the cardiovascular system – dilating the blood vessels helps keep blood pressure down. Vitamin B3 is also effective in the treatment of diabetes, a condition that carries with it a high risk of cardiovascular disease. It has been shown to be effective in helping to manage depression, along with B6 and zinc. Dopamine, a neurotransmitter, requires vitamin B3 and iron for its formation. Dopamine is involved in the laying down and maintenance of memory. B3 also helps in the release of energy from foods and in maintaining healthy skin, nerves and digestive system.

What it may do Megadoses may lower high blood cholesterol.

Food sources Nuts, meat, fish, chicken, liver, enriched grain products, dairy products, peanut butter and brewer's yeast.

Supplementation Supplementation in addition to a multivitamin is not normally needed. Large doses may be prescribed by your doctor to lower blood cholesterol. In some forms, for example niacin, it may cause flushing, and in extreme cases liver damage and an irregular heartbeat.

Vitamin B5 (Pantothenic Acid)

Daily value: 50 mg (*100 mg*)

What it does It is vital for the metabolism and the production of essential body chemicals. It can improve the ratio between good and bad cholesterols and is also involved in reducing stress.

Food sources Unprocessed whole grains, beans, milk, eggs and liver. Up to 50 per cent of pantothenic acid is destroyed by processing, canning or cooking.

Supplementation Supplementation in addition to a multivitamin is not normally needed. It may cause diarrhoea in large doses.

Vitamin B6 (Pyroxidine)

Daily value: 35 mg (75 mg)

What it does It enhances the ability of the white blood cells to destroy offending pathogens. The thymus gland also needs good levels of B6. It is vital in chemical reactions of proteins and amino acids. It helps to maintain brain function and form red blood cells. Together with vitamin B12, it is essential for preventing the build-up of homocysteine, which can be partly responsible for the 'furring up' of the arteries.

What it may do It may help to boost immunity in the elderly.

Food sources Whole grains, bananas, meat, beans, nuts, wheat germ, brewer's yeast, chicken, fish and liver.

Supplementation Supplementation in addition to a multivitamin is not normally needed. Large doses can cause numbness and neurological disorders which are reversable once the dose is stopped.

Vitamin B12

Daily value: 5 mcg (10 mcg)

What it does It is necessary for the development of red blood cells and helps to maintain normal functioning of the nervous system.

Food sources Liver, beef, pork, poultry, eggs, milk, cheese, yoghurt, shellfish, fortified cereals and fortified soy products.

Supplementation Strict vegetarians and vegans may need additional supplementation. Vitamin B12 should not be supplemented on its own but taken with the other B vitamins as it can mask deficiencies in folic acid. If you have any of the following conditions, check with your doctor before using B12: folate deficiency, iron deficiency, any kind of infection, Leber's disease, polycythemia vera or uraemia.

Vitamin B complex

This affects all aspects of the immune system, increases antibody response, keeps the thymus active, maintains the body's bacterial destruction abilities and keeps cellular immune responses efficient.

The B vitamins are water soluble and are not stored in the body. They should be taken with food in the stomach.

Vitamin C (Ascorbic Acid)

Daily value: 400–1,000 mg (*4,000–5,000 mg*)

What it does Vitamin C is probably the most important vitamin for the health of the immune system. It has potent antiviral properties, which is important because viruses, even when dormant, have been shown to undermine immunity. It is also antibacterial, detoxifying bacteria and preventing them from spreading. It is essential for the process of disarming and destroying invading pathogens. This process is enhanced by the presence of zinc. Vitamin C also helps to promote healthy gums and teeth; it aids in iron absorption; maintains normal connective tissue and helps in the healing of wounds. As an antioxidant, it combats the adverse effects of free radicals. It helps the thymus make T cells. It is also important for the production of interferon, a substance that battles viruses. A deficiency can show up in decreased activity of bacterial-eating cells and slow wound healing. Vitamin C is probably one of the most powerful nutrients for fighting cardiovascular disease. It has been shown to lower cholesterol levels and helps regulate blood pressure by thinning the blood.

What it may do Canadian studies have shown a decreased number of colon polyps in patients taking high doses of vitamin C. Such polyps are precursors for colon cancer. Although vitamin C has been claimed to decrease cancer growth and cause remissions in cancer patients, major trials using high-dose intravenous vitamin C fail to confirm any anti-cancer effect of this vitamin in patients with *established* cancer. It may reduce the *risk* of lung, oesophagus, stomach and bladder cancer, as well as coronary artery disease. It may also prevent or delay cataracts and slow the ageing process. Smoking and alcohol consumption both increase the excretion of vitamin C.

Food sources Citrus fruits and juices, strawberries, tomatoes, peppers, broccoli, potatoes, cauliflower and Brussels sprouts.

Supplementation 250–500 mg daily with an additional 250–500 mg a day for smokers and anyone not consuming fruits or vegetables rich in vitamin C daily. Vitamin C usually works better in the presence of bioflavonoids which are often included in some vitamin C supplements. Larger doses may cause diarrhoea. Chewable vitamin C tablets can cause enamel loss from the surface of the teeth and other dental problems. If you are taking vitamin C in the form of powdered ascorbic acid, make sure that you drink the mixture through a straw to prevent enamel erosion.

Vitamin D

Daily value: 10 mcg (*20 mcg*)

What it does It strengthens bones and teeth by aiding the absorption of calcium. It also helps to maintain phosphorus in the blood.

What it may do It may reduce the risk of osteoporosis and forestall breast and colon cancer.

Food sources Milk, fish oil and fortified margarine. It is also produced by the body in response to sunlight.

Supplementation Supplementation in addition to a multivitamin is not normally needed. Vegetarians, the elderly, and those who don't drink milk or get exposure to the sun should make sure they get at least 400 iu in their supplementation. It is toxic in high doses.

Vitamin E

Daily value: 100–300 iu (*1,000 iu*)

What it does It helps to form red blood cells and combats the adverse effects of free radicals. It also stimulates antibody production and accelerates T cell reactions.

What it may do It may reduce the risk of oesophageal or stomach cancers and coronary artery disease. It may also prevent or delay cataracts and boost immunity in the elderly.

Food sources Vegetable oil, nuts, margarine, wheat germ, leafy greens, seeds, almonds, olives and asparagus.

Supplementation 200–800 iu for everybody. You can't get that much from food, especially if you are on a low-fat diet. You should not take vitamin E supplements if you are on anticoagulants like Warfarin, however. Large doses of vitamin E are associated with hair loss. Vitamin E is stored in the liver.

Biotin (*Vitamin B*)

Daily value: 50 mcg (*100 mcg*)

What it does It is important in the metabolism of protein, carbohydrates and fats.

Food sources Eggs, milk, liver, mushrooms, bananas, tomatoes and whole grains. Biotin is destroyed by certain food-processing techniques such as canning and heat curing, so it is always better to choose fresh fruits, vegetables and meats rather than canned or cured foods.

Supplementation Supplementation in addition to a multivitamin is not normally needed.

Folic acid (*Vitamin B*)

Daily value: 200 mcg (*400 mcg*)

What it does It is important in the synthesis of DNA, in normal growth and in protein metabolism. It reduces the risk of certain birth defects, notably spina bifida and encephaly.

What it may do It may reduce the risk of cervical cancer and heart disease.

Food sources Leafy greens, wheat germ, liver, beans, whole grains, broccoli, asparagus, citrus fruit and juices.

Supplementation Supplementation should include at least 400 mcg, for all women who may become pregnant, to help prevent birth defects. It should be noted that folic acid supplementation alone can mask B12 deficiency anaemia so it is best taken in the form of a B vitamin or multivitamin supplement which contains both in it.

Vitamin K

Daily value: 100 mcg

What it does It protects us from bleeding excessively due to cuts and wounds or internal bleeding. It is also used in the formation of prothrombin and other blood-clotting proteins.

Food sources Leafy green vegetables such as broccoli and spinach, olive oil and soybean oil, beef liver and green tea.

Supplementation Not usually included in multivitamin supplements as it is normally made in sufficient amounts in the bacteria in the digestive tract.

Co-enzyme Q10

Daily value: 30 mg (*90 mg*)

What it does Naturally produced by the body, this remarkable nutrient is found in every human cell and in all living organisms. It has been dubbed 'vitamin Q' because of its essential role in keeping all systems running smoothly. It works together with other enzymes to break down and convert food into energy and is particularly abundant in high-energy-demanding cells, such as those found in the heart. Q10 can be made in the body from other enzymes, although our ability to do this declines as we age.

What it may do It may help congestive heart failure, angina and high blood pressure. It may benefit breast or prostate cancer and counter Alzheimer's disease and memory loss.

Food sources Sardines, mackerel, green beans and spinach.

Supplementation For supplementing conventional cancer therapy, 200 mg each day. It is best absorbed in an oil-soluble form.

Minerals

Calcium

Daily value: 150 mg (*600 mg*)

What it does Calcium plays many roles in the immune system. It is involved in the synthesis of the enzymes that T cells use to defeat pathogenic invaders and, like vitamin C, is essential for enabling the white blood cells to digest and destroy certain viruses. Together with vitamin D, it helps to build and maintain healthy bones and teeth. It also helps lower blood pressure and control the heartbeat; helps regulate muscle contractions; plays a role in blood-clotting and prevents fatal bleeding from breaks in the walls of blood vessels; aids in the absorption of vitamin B12; and activates enzymes such as lipase, the fat-splitting enzyme.

What it may do It may offer protection against osteoporosis.

Food sources Dairy products, sardines with bones, shrimps, broccoli, spinach, almonds and tofu.

Supplementation Supplement 200–600 mg per day. The most absorbable forms include calcium citrate, amino acid chelate or gluconate. It should be taken alongside magnesium which helps its utilisation in the body. Most people do not get enough calcium in their diets. Very high doses can cause nausea, constipation, lethargy, abdominal pains and possible urinary stones.

Iron

Daily value: 10 mg (*20 mg*)

What it does It plays an essential role in the production of all white blood cells and is involved in the synthesis of antibodies. However, if iron levels are too high, bacteria thrive. This does not mean that if you have an infection you should exclude iron-rich foods from your diet, but you should not take supplements containing iron at this time. Iron also prevents anaemia.

Food sources Meat, eggs, fortified cereals, breads, rice and pasta.

Supplementation Supplementation in addition to a multivitamin is not normally needed. Dosages exceeding 100 mg can interfere with calcium and zinc absorption.

Magnesium

Daily value: 75 mg (*300 mg*)

What it does It is essential in ensuring proper thymus function and is also needed for the formation of prostaglandins (hormone-like compounds found in all tissues) and for controlling histamine levels. It also plays a part in the transmission of nerve impulses to muscles, the transporting of calcium and potassium, the production of body proteins and DNA, and the regulating of blood pressure, in conjunction with calcium and potassium.

What it may do Magnesium in the form of magnesium oxide in combination with vitamin B6 has been shown to dissolve certain types of kidney stone (calcium oxalate stones).

Food sources Nuts, legumes, whole grains and green vegetables. Milk of magnesia, which provides 1,000 mg of magnesium in just two tablespoons, is a commonly used toxic source. Elderly people who take it frequently as a laxative can be at risk of magnesia intoxication because their ageing kidneys may not function well enough to clear it as well as a younger person's kidneys.

Supplementation Supplement 75–300 mg per day. The most absorbable forms include magnesium citrate, amino acid chelate or gluconate. The often-typical fast-food and refined diet of many people does not generally provide enough of this mineral.

Potassium

Daily value: 100 mg *(2,000–5,000 mg)*

What it does It helps the body to transmit nerve impulses, maintain normal blood pressure, keep a normal water balance between the cells and body fluids, and ensure proper functioning of cellular enzymes.

What it may do Potassium in amounts of around 2,300 mg a day, whether from foods or supplements, has been shown to lower blood pressure by relaxing the arteries and reducing blood volumes, especially for people who use a lot of salt. In fact, this amount of potassium lowers blood pressure about half as much as drugs, without the side-effects.

Food sources Bananas, potatoes, oranges, dates, tomatoes, spinach and broccoli.

Selenium

Daily value: 100 mcg *(200 mcg)*

What it does It boosts the antioxidant effect of vitamin E. Also, immune cells are inefficient at reproducing themselves when faced with repeated infection and selenium is involved with antibody synthesis.

What it may do It may reduce the incidence of some cancers, help in the prevention of cataracts and improve mental alertness in older age.

Food sources An average brazil nut provides 70 mcg of selenium. It is also found in garlic, onions, wheat products, grains, fish, lobster, clams, crab, liver, asparagus, brown rice and sesame seeds.

Supplementation Supplementation in addition to a multivitamin is not normally needed. Works in harmony with vitamin E. Caution should be taken in doses that exceed 500 mcg as selenium can be toxic at relatively low levels.

Zinc

Daily value 10 mg (*25 mg*)

What it does The thymus gland needs zinc to manufacture the T cells that fight pathogens entering the body. It is also needed to encourage the T cells towards active maturity. In addition, zinc enables the activity of more than 200 biological enzymes, helps to achieve normal growth, assists in hormonal activity, reproduction and lactation, and carries out immune functions such as protecting against infection and cancer.

What it may do It can be helpful in the treatment of acne and can hasten the healing of peptic ulcer disease and burns.

Food sources Meat, liver, eggs and seafood (especially oysters).

Supplementation Supplementation in addition to a multivitamin is not normally needed. Ironically, too much zinc, like too little zinc, can depress the immune system. Excessive zinc can cause anaemia, copper deficiencies and lowered levels of good cholesterol (HDL) in the blood. It is important that zinc is taken one to two hours after iron because it interferes with the absorption of iron. Chelated zinc will not affect the gastrointestinal tract as zinc sulphate does.

Omega 3 fatty acids

Daily value: 360 mg (*1,200–3,000 mg*)

What they do These are essential fatty acids that our bodies cannot create without first obtaining them from food. Linolenic acid, the primary Omega 3 fatty acid, can be obtained through some fats, oils, nuts and soybeans. However, while eicosapentaenoic acid (EPA) and docosahexaenoic acid (DHA), also from the Omega 3 family, *can* both be created by the body in the presence of linolenic acid, they are best available through breast milk for infants and seafood for adults. EPA and DHA are very important for normal brain development, communication and vision. They also play a protective role in arthritis, lupus, high blood pressure, cancer and heart disease.

What they may do They may be helpful in treating multiple sclerosis, and some cases of diabetes and skin cancer, and appear to help arthritic joint pain.

Food sources Shellfish, sardines, tuna, salmon, herring, trout, mackerel and anchovies. Non-meat sources include canola oil, soybeans, flaxseed, walnuts and wheat germ.

Supplementation Cold pressed flaxseed oil (also known as linseed oil), which is a good source of the Omega 3 oils, would be a good addition to the diet, especially for vegetarians and non-fish eaters. This can be added to salad dressings but should not be used to cook with as high temperatures destroy its beneficial properties.

Bear in mind that vitamins and minerals work over a long period of time, so patience is needed.

Do You Need Supplements?

Do you need to take a vitamin and mineral supplement? This is a difficult question to answer as it depends on many factors including your age, sex and possible familial risk for a certain illness. Scientists know that certain vitamins and minerals can help prevent a number of different illnesses. However, what is not known is whether the benefits of these vitamins and minerals are the result of a single nutrient or combinations of nutrients or other factors. Before you consider taking supplements, first examine your lifestyle habits such as diet, drinking habits and whether or not you smoke.

If you have a particular health problem or are undergoing certain medical treatments, your body may be under strain or depleted of some vitamins or minerals, in which case supplementation is going to help you. Your best bet may well be a multivitamin supplement. This should contain at least 7,500 iu of vitamin A, 400 iu of D, 100 iu of E, 250 mg of C, 25 mg of B1 and B2, 50 mg of B3, B5 and B6, 10 mcg of B12 and 400 mcg of folic acid and 50 mcg of biotin. Often the supplement will also include calcium, magnesium, iron, zinc and manganese – all nutrients in which people are often deficient. However, additional calcium, magnesium and vitamin C may also need to be taken as these nutrients are required in larger doses than can fit into a single multivitamin or mineral supplement.

Strengthening the Immune System

Since our immune system is so crucial in defending us from illness and disease, it is obviously best to support it by eating foods that are going to strengthen it. The quantity you eat does not matter so much as the quality of the food. Saturated fats, sugar and salt all contribute to a weaker immune system. For example, when you digest sugar, there is a measurable slowdown in activity by certain classes of white blood cells involved in the immune system. Although the effect only lasts for a few hours, if you continually graze on sugary foods you may be experiencing constant suppression.

This does not mean that you should focus on certain foods and fill yourself with them. The consensus of experts in the field is that any one nutrient, or any one food, may help to a degree, but the best thing you can do is to develop an all-round healthy diet. Indeed, it is even possible to have too much of a good thing. For example, garlic, which in low doses has demonstrated immune-building properties, has the opposite effect in large doses. Speaking of a research project that had to be abandoned, Johanna Dwyer of Tufts Medical School is quoted as saying, 'Patients developed 'flu-like symptoms. Researchers realised it was some kind of immune response to the very large doses being administered to the volunteers.' This does not mean giving up using garlic for colds, but it does mean not taking it in massive quantities.

The ability of your immune system to fight disease depends on cellular communication and anything that can improve normal communication will almost certainly be beneficial, especially if it is safe and natural. Mainstream medical journals are now publishing reports of compelling and consistent data associating diets rich in fruits and vegetables with significant health benefits and reduced risk of many different diseases.

GUIDELINES FOR OPTIMUM IMMUNE SYSTEM SUPPORT

❍ Eat a variety of foods and not just 'immune system foods'. The immune system is varied and so needs many different nutrients. If you stick with only a few foods, you may deprive or hurt your body's other nutritional needs.

❍ Eat generous amounts of fruits and vegetables. They contain important vitamins as well as phytochemicals that can help your body to fight disease.

❍ Eat foods that contain minerals, especially zinc, iron and copper. Nuts, seeds and whole grains are good sources but don't overdo it with a lot of additional supplementation above a multi-mineral because too much of any of these is as bad as not enough.

❍ Eat complex carbohydrates such as grains and legumes. This results in longer-lasting energy. If you do not get enough carbohydrates, your body will draw on protein, robbing immunological cells of important foods.

❍ Eat foods that are high in fibre. Try to consume 30–40 g (1–1 ½ oz) of fibre a day.

❍ Eat before or during times of stress. This way the body does not have to find energy from the immune system.

❍ If you have a baby, try to breastfeed. This ensures that important antibodies and hormones are passed to the child.

❍ Try not to make fats any more than 20 per cent of your daily caloric intake.

❍ Don't eat sweets, as they suppress the immune system.

Chapter 10

FOODS FOR SPECIFIC AILMENTS

Good nutrition can help keep us in good health and also help combat a variety of ailments. If an animal is sick or injured it seems to instinctively know what to eat in order to try to heal itself. I believe that we are all much more like wild animals than we might care to admit. If we really listen to our bodies, I think that they too will tell us what they need. If you have ever had too much to drink, you will wake up feeling hung over and in need of orange juice. It's the body's way of telling you that it needs vitamin C that has been depleted and excreted by excessive alcohol. Unfortunately, we now don't listen as intuitively to our bodies as perhaps we did in the past

In the 1920s, a long time before scientists had discovered what we now know about vitamins and minerals, a young British nutritional expert, Dr Robert McCarrison, undertook a fascinating experiment. He had been posted out to India and while there had noticed the great variations in the health of the Indians in different areas of that huge country. The Madrassi people of the south lived on a diet that consisted mostly of boiled white rice, with few raw vegetables, and they rarely ate meat or dairy products. Physically they seemed undernourished and in a poor state of health. However, the Sikhs who lived in the north invariably looked wonderfully fit and in good physical condition. They lived mostly on wholewheat chapattis, a little butter, lots of unpasteurised milk, sprouted peas and plenty of vegetables, which they nearly always ate raw.

McCarrison wondered whether the different diets of the Madrassi people and the Sikhs could be the explanation as to why they looked physically so different. To test his idea, he took large numbers of healthy baby rats, all bred from the same stock, and reared them on different diets. All the rats lived in clean, airy surroundings but it soon became clear that those fed on the Madrassi diet grew up to be sickly, weak and quarrelsome, while those on the Sikh diet were much healthier – big, sleek, glossy, furry and good-natured animals.

From that point on, all McCarrison's rats were fed the Sikh diet and he himself said for the rest of his life that the best foods of all were 'the unsophisticated foodstuffs of nature' grown on healthy soil, eaten as fresh as possible and, as far as possible, eaten whole. Many decades later we are learning that numerous diseases, such as multiple sclerosis, depression, some cancers, migraine and headaches, may result from poor diet.

Heart Disease and Diet

You might think that anybody, given the opportunity, would rather look like the sleek Sikh than the sickly Madrassi – especially if they are healthcare professionals who deal with ailing patients on a daily basis. In 1980, Dr Frank Hu of the Harvard School of Public Health began monitoring the heart disease rates of over 84,000 nurses. They were questioned every two years from 1980 to 1994 about their lifestyle habits, whether they were exercising regularly and eating healthy foods. When the study began, the women were between the ages of 34 and 59, and over the years the researchers documented 1,129 cases of coronary heart disease, 296 of which were fatal.

Hu and his colleagues classified a subject as 'low risk' for heart disease or stroke if she did not smoke, exercised each day for half an hour or more, had an occasional alcoholic drink but not more, on average, than half a drink a day, had a body mass index (a measure of obesity) of 25 or lower, and ate a healthy diet.

A healthy diet was classified as one low in saturated fat and partially hydrogenated oils, and high in fibre, folate, Omega 3 fatty acids from fish, whole grains and vegetable oils. Hu discovered that only 1 to 2 per cent of the research subjects followed all of the guidelines, despite the fact that they were all healthcare professionals.[1]

Cardiovascular disease is still the main killer of both men and women in Britain and few people follow the recommended guidelines, even though they offer an 80 per cent reduction in risk. Heart disease is a lifestyle disease. It was rare at the turn of the twentieth century, and it is still relatively rare in places with different lifestyle and eating habits, like rural China.

In the early 1960s, researchers discovered that Eskimos eating their traditional marine diet were virtually free of heart disease compared to other nationalities, and that they had lower levels of rheumatoid arthritis. It was also interesting to note that they ate a predominantly high-fat diet, consisting of blubber and seal meat. Researchers eventually came to realise that the high level of polyunsaturated fats in the Eskimo diet, particularly Omega 3 fatty acids, were responsible for this cardio-protective effect.

The protective effect of a high fish diet against the incidence of heart disease was demonstrated in Japan. Japanese farmers consume around 90 g (3 oz) of fish per day, compared to Japanese fishermen, who consume around 250 g (8 oz) per day. The fishermen have lower blood pressures and lower incidences of heart disease than do the farmers, and the Japanese population as a whole has a *sixfold* lower incidence of heart disease compared to Americans, who consume an average of less than 20 g (³/₄ oz) of fish per day.

Garlic also has a documented ability to help prevent heart disease by lowering cholesterol, reducing overall blood lipids and decreasing blood pressure. In high doses of about eight cloves a day, garlic can lower blood cholesterol levels by as much as 20 per cent. Excessive stickiness of blood platelets, called 'increased platelet aggregation', is known to be a high risk factor for heart disease and strokes. Once platelets stick to one another, they can form a clot that can get stuck in small arteries and produce a heart attack or stroke. In one study conducted over a period of 4 weeks, 120 patients with increased platelet aggregation were given either 900 mg per day of a dried garlic preparation, or a placebo. Among several benefits experienced by those in the garlic group was that the platelet aggregation disappeared altogether and diastolic blood pressure dropped from an average of 74 to 67 mmHg.[2]

The Reversal Diet and Prevention Diet

Dr Dean Ornish has developed what he calls a Reversal Diet for people with heart disease who want to reverse its effects and lower their risk of heart attack, and a Prevention Diet for people without heart disease whose cholesterol levels are above 150 without cholesterol-lowering medication. He highlights epidemiological research studies supporting his claims regarding a very low-fat diet and improved cardiovascular health. (Epidemiological studies are based on analyses of the incidence of disease in the population.) For most people, the more cholesterol and saturated fat consumed, the higher the cholesterol and blood pressure levels, which are both risk factors for heart disease. Lowering these levels can reduce the risk of developing or advancing heart disease.

Dr Ornish's beliefs about diet and heart disease rest on several principles. Each gram of fat contains nine calories, while protein and carbohydrates contain four calories per gram. You can eat more food on a very low-fat diet since fewer calories are consumed in each meal. Eating fat makes you fat and causes heart disease. Dietary fat is easily converted into body fat whereas complex carbohydrates, such as grains, beans, fruits and vegetables are the staple of low-fat diets and are less easily converted to body fat. Saturated fat is converted to cholesterol by the liver and raises blood cholesterol levels. It is found primarily in animal products. Monounsaturated fat and polyunsaturated fat of which large amounts are found in avocados, nuts and seeds, do not raise cholesterol levels.

The Reversal Diet is primarily a vegetarian diet since vegetarian foods do not contain cholesterol and are low in saturated fat.

The Reversal Diet has the following restrictions:

O Less than 10 per cent of calories are from fat, little of it saturated.

O Foods high in saturated fat are excluded.

O The diet is high in fibre.

O Moderate alcohol consumption is allowed, but not encouraged.

O All oils and animal products except non-fat milk, non-fat dairy products and non-fat yoghurt are excluded. All meats, poultry and seafood are excluded.

O Egg whites are included.

O Caffeine, monosodium glutamate and other stimulants are excluded.

O Moderate use of sugar and salt is allowed.

O The diet does not restrict calories.

Interestingly, in spite of the fact that tens of thousands of people have benefited from Dr Ornish's Reversal Diet, he has critics who claim that his diet is too difficult for most people to follow. I think that if you are seriously worried that you are at a high risk from a heart attack and you want to prevent it, you will overcome any perceived difficulty in following a restricted diet, especially as it will not only reduce the risk of heart disease, but also help you lose unwanted weight, maintain a healthy weight and boost your energy.

Eyesight and Diet

Vitamin A is the nutrient most clearly associated with healthy vision. A diet deficient in vitamin A quickly leads to an impairment of night vision commonly known as 'night blindness'. This connection was discovered in the 1930s, although the condition had already been recognised in ancient Egypt and treated with cooked liver, an organ rich in vitamin A. In spite of the common saying, eating carrots won't make you see in the dark, but the vitamin A they supply can help the eyes well beyond its capacity to prevent night blindness.

Vision, particularly colour vision, is most acute in the macula, the central region of the retina. The entire retina of the eye has a high metabolic demand for oxygen, which means that the retina, especially the macula, produces an exceptionally high level of free radicals. In many otherwise healthy people the macula deteriorates over time, leading to progressive visual impairment and blindness.

In one study, vision loss in 39 patients suffering from advanced age-related macular degeneration was stopped during the 18 months that they took antioxidant tablets.[3] Researchers have also found that patients with the lowest levels of serum beta-carotene had double the likelihood of developing age-related macular degeneration.[4]

In a study of more than 3,000 people aged from 45 to 74, researchers claimed that drinking wine reduced the risk of macular degeneration by 50 per cent.[5] Since other alcoholic drinks were not found to have any effect, the probable mechanism is the flavonoid content of the wine. During the 1990s alone, over 50 reports were published in medical journals about the benefits of diet and nutritional supplements in preventing macular degeneration.

Lung Function and Diet

If you don't want to drink wine, you might well find that fruit juice also has healing qualities – at least on your lung function. A study was carried out on over 2,500 Welshmen aged between 45 and 59 to investigate associations between diet and lung function[6] and it was discovered that there was indeed an improvement among those men who had high intakes of vitamin C, vitamin E, beta-carotene, citrus fruits, apples and the frequent consumption of fruit juices or squashes. Allowing adjustment for confounding factors such as body weight, smoking history, social class, exercise and total energy intake, only the associations with vitamin E and apples persisted, with lung function estimated to be 39 ml higher for vitamin E intakes and 138 ml higher for those eating 5 or more apples per week compared with non-consumers.[6]

The very positive association between lung function and high vitamin E intake, and the number of apples eaten each week, substantiates the known protective effect of hard fruits rather than soft or citrus fruits.

In the United States there is growing evidence to suggest that eating apples may help prevent lung cancer. The National Cancer Institute has reported that foods containing flavonoids (the naturally occurring plant compounds that also have potent antioxidant properties), like those found in apples, may reduce the risk of lung cancer by as much as 50 per cent, although the exact mechanisms for this have yet to be identified. Still, it seems that new research is finally giving the old adage 'An apple a day keeps the doctor away' the scientific support it has long needed.

Parkinson's Disease and Diet

There is some evidence that vitamins E and C can slow the gradual progression of Parkinson's disease. Diet was first identified as a potentially important variable in the management of Parkinson's disease in the late 1960s, when a new drug, 1-3,4-dihydroxy-phenylalanine, or L-dopa, was introduced to treat the disease. It was first noticed that high levels of both dietary protein and vitamin B6 interfered with the action of L-dopa by somehow blocking the use by the brain of the drug. It was therefore suggested that Parkinson's disease sufferers should modify their diets so as to decrease their B6 intake.

In 1979, Dr Stanley Fahn began a pilot study in which patients with early Parkinson's disease were asked to take 3,200 iu a day of vitamin E and 3,000 mg a day of vitamin C prior to starting any other anti-Parkinsonian therapy. Patients in the early stages of the disease were able to delay the standard treatment with L-dopa for two and a half to three years. The gradual progression of the disease was slowed down, allowing afflicted patients to live a longer and fuller life.

Researchers at the Leonard Davis School of Gerontology, University of Southern California, have been continuing Fahn's earlier work and have found that multiple vitamins and minerals also affect the treatment of Parkinson's disease, although their mechanisms are not clearly understood.

Multiple Sclerosis and Diet

Possibly some of the most persuasive evidence of dietary influence upon health can be found in links between multiple sclerosis (MS) and diet. MS is an inflammation of the protective fatty layer surrounding the nerve cells, known as the myelin sheath. As inflammation progresses, the myelin sheath breaks down and is replaced with scar tissue, making the enclosed nerve ineffective.

Worldwide, the incidence of MS crosses all racial barriers. It is common in northern Europe, Canada and the United States, but rare in Japan, elsewhere in Asia and in Africa. However, when people migrate from a country of low incidence of MS to a country of high incidence, their chance of developing this disease increases. The culprit appears to be the food we eat each day.

One general observation that can be made is that countries with lots of cases of MS are also wealthy countries, but an exception is the wealthy country of Japan. There is an explanation for this: even though the Japanese have money, stress, pollution and the smoking habits characteristic of people in other industrialised countries, their traditional rice-based diet is more characteristic of the foods consumed in poorer countries.

A diet filled with rich foods assails us with many different substances that may be related to diseases that trouble us, but animal fats, especially those from dairy products, have been most closely linked to the development of MS. One important theory suggests that cow's milk consumed in infancy lays the foundation for injuries to the nervous system that appear in later life. Cow's milk contains one-fifth as much of an essential fat, called linoleic acid, as human mother's milk. This essential dietary-derived substance helps to make up some of the chemical components in nervous tissues.

Children raised on a linoleic-acid deficient, high-animal-fat diet, as most children are in our modern affluent society, quite possibly start life with a damaged nervous system, which is susceptible to insults and injuries in later life. Analysis of brain tissues has shown that MS sufferers have a higher content of saturated fats than do people who do not have the disease.

During the Second World War, civilians across Western Europe were under enormous stress as one enemy or another occupied their countries, but doctors observed that patients with MS needed two to two-and-a-half times fewer hospitalisations during this period. At that time all kinds of food were scarce and the civil populations could no longer afford to eat their meat-producing animals. Instead, they ate grains and vegetables that had earlier nourished their cows, chickens and pigs. The overall result was a significant reduction in the amounts of animal products they ate and therefore the amount of animal fat they consumed.

Following the publication of these observations, Dr Roy Swank, former head of the University of Oregon's Department of Neurology, began treating his MS patients with a low-fat diet. His landmark research, based on more than 20 years of experience while studying over 3,000 MS sufferers, shows that if the disease is detected early, and if attacks have been few and the patient adopts a low-fat diet, they have a 95 per cent chance of remaining stable, or even improving, over the next 20 years.[7] Even people who have had MS for a long time and have already suffered severe neural damage will slow the progress of the disease with a change to a low-fat diet.

More recently, Dr Swank has published further research results from patients he has studied for more than 35 years. He and his colleagues found first of all that every incremental increase in intake of saturated fats (animal fat) is associated with a corresponding increase in frequency of MS attacks. To arrest the disease, the diet must contain as little fat as possible. Those patients on a low-fat diet (17 g/½ oz per day) lived almost three times as long and generally improved their level of function. On a high-fat diet (42 g/1½ oz per day) the average patient went from active to wheelchair and bedridden (or dead) over the 35 years of the study.[8]

A number of those people I treat for MS have experienced enormous benefit from following a fat-free or low-fat diet.

Within a year of diagnosis with MS, Simon was being affected by bouts of weakness in his legs, pins and needles, and visual disturbances that seemed to come in waves every two or three weeks. Once he had eliminated, as far as he could, all fats from his diet his symptoms improved markedly and the attacks occurred with much less severity only every two or three months.

Rosemary has managed to keep to a low-fat diet for over twenty years and is convinced that, for her, it is the key to preventing her MS from worsening.

Even before I first knew of the link between MS and a high intake of animal fat, I had noticed that a high proportion of my MS patients were members of butchers' families, although no research has yet been undertaken to determine any association between the two. From observation, I would certainly recommend trying to follow Swank's guidelines if you suffer from MS.

Rheumatoid Arthritis and Diet

Rheumatoid arthritis sufferers may experience some improvement by adopting a vegetarian diet, according to a study in the *British Journal of Nutrition*. In a thirteen-month study of forty-four patients with active rheumatoid arthritis, those who stopped eating meat experienced fewer arthritis symptoms than the volunteers whose diets contained meat and other animal products. One explanation is that vegetarian diets contain different types of fat from those found in diets that include meat products. While saturated fat is used as a source of energy or to store energy, certain classes of polyunsaturated fat form powerful, hormone-like compounds called prostaglandins, or PGs.

There are several different families of PGs, each causing the body to behave in a different way. Where arthritis is concerned, some PGs can encourage inflammation while others will not. The type of fat we eat is one of the factors that determine how much of each type of PG the body makes. Research has shown that Omega 3 fatty acids, which are found

in fish oil as well as flaxseed oil, are able to decrease the painful symptoms of arthritis. It seems that the body turns them into PGs that do not
encourage inflammation. The Omega 6 fatty acids found in evening primrose oil and borage oil are also able to be converted into anti-inflammatory PGs. However, under unfavourable conditions, this may lead to the
potential formation of pro-inflammatory PGs. This is promoted by a diet
high in saturated fat, alcohol and sugar. An inadequate supply of the
nutrients vitamin B6, biotin, zinc, vitamin B3 and vitamin C means that
the enzymes that help to make the anti-inflammatory PGs may not function as effectively.

A study published in 1996 in the journal *Epidemiology* found that
regular intake of high Omega 3 fish, such as salmon, mackerel, herring,
trout and tuna, reduces the risk of rheumatoid arthritis. This probably
explains why so many of my arthritic patients swear by fish-oil capsules,
which they find extremely helpful in alleviating pain and swollen joints.
Fried food was associated with a higher risk.

Another possible explanation for the effect of the vegetarian diet is
again connected with the greater intake of antioxidants (contained in
fruits and vegetables), which have the ability to prevent fats from reacting
with oxygen in inappropriate ways that can lay the groundwork for
major health problems such as heart disease and cancer. This errant
'oxidation' is also believed to kick into high gear during the inflamma-
tory process associated with arthritis.

A study in the *Annals of the Rheumatic Diseases* reported that vitamin
E might be of help in alleviating some of the stiffness experienced by
arthritis sufferers. Those taking 600 mg of vitamin E twice daily for
twelve weeks reported a significant decrease in pain.

Numerous small studies have concluded that fish-oil supplementation leads to a marked improvement of rheumatoid arthritis symptoms.
However, precisely because these studies had been small, their publication did not have much impact on the medical treatment of arthritis.
In the 1990s a team of researchers from the Harvard Medical School
combined and analysed the results of all the small studies, which
involved 368 participants who had taken fish-oil supplements for at
least 3 months. Their meta-analysis revealed a highly significant
decrease in the number of tender joints and a significant shortening in
the duration of morning stiffness among patients taking fish-oil supplements.[9]

Stroke and Diet

Dr Hiroyasu Iso and his colleagues at the Channing Laboratory and at Harvard Medical School followed almost 80,000 women over 14 years, from 1980 to 1994. At the start of the study, which collected information on lifestyles and medical history from female nurses in 11 states, the women were aged from 34 to 59. Over that time 574 strokes were recorded, but the researchers found that the more fish a woman consumed, the lower the risk of a stroke. In particular, eating fish reduced the risk of the type of stroke caused by a clot blocking the supply of blood to the brain, which accounts for around half of all brain attacks. Women who ate fish once a week had a 22 per cent risk reduction, while those who ate fish 2 to 4 times a week had a 27 per cent lower risk. The biggest fish-eaters, who consumed fish 5 or more times a week, had the greatest risk reduction of around 52 per cent.

The researchers took account of factors such as age and smoking, and examined the effect of fish and Omega 3 fatty acid consumption on the risk of different types of stroke, and on women who regularly took aspirin. Aspirin can potentially lower stroke risk by reducing the stickiness of blood and its tendency to clot. It was found that eating fish gave the greatest amount of stroke protection to women who did not usually use aspirin.[10]

Crohn's Disease and Diet

Research has shown that Omega 3 fatty acids help not only heart disease and rheumatoid arthritis but also Crohn's disease, as well as kidney disorders, preeclampsia risk, depression and menstrual problems.

In Italy, researchers observed the effect of Omega 3 fatty acids on Crohn's disease. This is a condition in which parts of the intestines become inflamed, thickened and ulcerated. The study followed a group of patients who at the start of the project were all in a period of remission. Half of the patients were treated with a placebo and the other half with capsules of Omega 3 fatty acids. After a year 59 per cent of those taking the fish-oil capsules were still in remission, while only 26 per cent of the placebo group were.[11]

Prostate Problems and Saw Palmetto

For over a year, Alan had brought his wife to me for healing but had never thought of asking for help for his own problem. Like many men of his age he was suffering from an enlarged prostate gland and, to use his words, he 'didn't want to go under the knife', which is what his doctor was proposing if his problem did not improve fairly quickly.

Up to 60 per cent of men will find themselves in Alan's predicament with what is known medically as benign prostatic hyperplasia (BPH). It is one of the most frequent problems for which men seek my help. The prostate gland surrounds the urethra and if you imagine a rubber washer (prostate) with a straw (uretha) passing through it, you can get a fairly good picture of what happens. As the prostate gland swells and pinches closed the urethra, problems start. It becomes painful to urinate, there is a decreased flow, difficulty in stopping or starting the flow and worst of all, as Alan had discovered, nocturnal urination. Like many men with an enlarged prostate, Alan was having to get up seven or eight times a night.

Alan started taking saw palmetto and within a very short time he was sleeping through the night without the need to endlessly get up to go to the bathroom. It also meant that he did not need my help.

As early as 1892, an article by A. L. Marcy appeared in the *American Journal of Urology* noting that nine out of ten men will eventually suffer an enlarged prostate. In those days drugs were not available for treating it, so doctors had to fall back on the knowledge of the Native Americans. They used saw palmetto berries in the treatment of genitourinary tract disturbances and as a nutritional tonic to support the body. They gave it to men to increase the function of the testicles and relieve irritation in mucous membranes, particularly those of the genitourinary tract and prostate.

Saw palmetto is a dwarf palm that grows in the sandy, windswept coastal areas of the southeastern United States. It shrinks the prostate with at least ten different mechanisms and has a track record in reducing the severity of BPH in mild to moderate cases that is better than that of the most commonly prescribed medication for BPH. The berries are a rich source of oils, powerful fatty acids that have shown a remarkable affinity for the male genitourinary tract and for inhibiting excesses of a testosterone by-product, dihydrotestosterone (DHT), thus enabling the prostate to shrink back to a more youthful state, reducing the blockage of the urethra and eliminating symptoms of an enlarged prostate without surgery or drugs.

One final word about saw palmetto: it contains tannic acids that may inhibit your absorption of iron, and as in the case of all other supplements, if you are taking any medication consult your doctor or nutritional therapist first before self administration.

Chapter 11

NUTRITION AND CANCER

It is very clear that diet has a role to play in preventing cancer. An American study published in 1994 reported a sharp fall in the incidence of colon cancer between 1985 and 1988. The authors found that dietary fat, particularly animal fat, was associated with high risk but dietary fibre was associated with a low risk. Fruits, vegetables and vitamin D were seen to have a protective effect, whilst a sedentary lifestyle and obesity were linked with a higher incidence of colorectal cancer. This was a highly significant finding because it implicated diet and seemed to reduce the risk of genetic factors. It is now well known that immigrant families, after as little as a generation or two, develop the cancer profiles of their host countries.

In 1997, the British government published a report entitled *Nutritional Aspects of the Development of Cancer*, which found that as many as two-thirds of cancer cases are linked to the types of food that we eat. This was the first officially sanctioned report to make a connection between diet and cancer. It recommended that Britons adopt 'Mediterranean' eating habits, replacing traditional meat dishes with a southern European menu, which places much greater emphasis on vegetables, fibre and fresh fruits.

Almost simultaneously with publication of the British report came the first global report on diet and cancer, published by the World Cancer Research Fund in association with the American Institute for Cancer Research: 'Food, nutrition and the prevention of cancer: a global perspective'. The report was prepared by a panel of 15 scientists from 9 countries, supported by over 100 reviewers, who assessed more than 4,000 studies and studied the links between a wide range of foods and drinks, nutrients, methods of food processing and storage, body size and level of physical activity, and each of 18 common cancers. It claimed that a diet high in fruits and vegetables may reduce the incidence of cervical cancer by 10 to 20 per cent; breast cancer by 10 to 20 per cent;

pancreatic cancer by 33 to 50 per cent (if alcohol is also eliminated); laryngeal cancer by 33 to 50 per cent; and cancer of the oesophagus by 50 to 75 per cent (also if alcohol is eliminated).

Scientists are always cautious as it is hard to single out one lifestyle factor as the one that prevents cancer. However, it would seem that diet is a definite factor in cancer prevention.

The World Cancer Research Fund and American Institute for Cancer Research made fourteen dietary recommendations aimed both at policy makers and individuals which include:

○ Eat a plant-based diet with a variety of 400–800 g (15–30 oz) of fruits and vegetables a day, 600–800 g (20–30 oz) of legumes, roots, tubers and plantains a day and minimally processed starchy staple foods. Limit unrefined sugars.

○ If you feel you need red meat, have no more than 80 g (3 oz) a day. Preferably eat fish, poultry or non-domesticated animal meat; this will also reduce the consumption of animal fat. Avoid charred meat and fish and only occasionally have cured or smoked meat and fish, and then preferably dry cured and traditionally smoked.

○ Use olive oil to cook with as it tends to be more stable in high temperatures. Add herbs and spices to flavour food and dressings, rather than salt.

○ Use refrigeration to preserve perishable food. Food stored at ambient temperature may become contaminated with mycotoxins (fungal toxins).

○ Unregulated or improper use of additives, contaminants and other residues can be a health hazard, particularly in economically developing countries.

○ Limit alcoholic drinks, if consumed at all, to fewer than two drinks a day for men and one for women.

○ Maintain a reasonable body weight.

○ Take a brisk walk daily and have at least an hour's aerobic exercise per week, especially if your occupational activity is low or moderate.

It was also suggested that you should eat vegetables as fresh as possible, as the nutritional value deteriorates with age, and they should prefer- ably be organic. Though 'scientific tests' show that the nutritional value may be the same in both organic and non-organic fruits and vegetables, there may be residues of herbicides or pesticides in fruits, vegetables and meat, due to today's intensive agricultural practices.

Treating Cancer Through Diet

Although there is now a wealth of material from scientific studies showing that diet and nutrition can indeed prevent many forms of cancer, there is little published evidence that diet supplements, vitamins, minerals or special diets actually *change* the course of cancer once it has developed.

Misleading Claims

After Gig had been diagnosed with cancer we were inundated with advice on nutrition and diet and, like anybody else in the same situation, discov- ered just how easy it is to clutch at straws. Somebody told us about a form of colonic cleansing that involved taking capsules containing 500 mg of magnesium peroxide. The claim was that 'a clean colon can lead to more effective absorption of vital minerals and nutrients, allowing for more vibrant health'. This seemed sensible, though at £40 for 180 capsules, the magnesium peroxide was not cheap, and the suggested use was *up to 15* capsules a day. However, the capsules were added to Gig's arsenal of 'natural cancer cures'.

One morning, having popped her capsules, Gig suddenly had thick white smoke pouring out of her nose and mouth, and an acrid taste in her mouth. Although it gave us a good laugh, which we needed at that time, it was also rather frightening. Gig decided not to risk taking them again because I had never heard of smoking out cancer.

Intrigued by what magnesium peroxide was used for under normal circumstances, I discovered that it is used in the oil and petrol industry and as an active ingredient in washing powders and dry-cleaning fluids, and as a bleach for dyes and silks. According to Hummel Croton Inc., one of the large American pharmaceutical companies which manufac- ture it for industrial use, 'Acute ingestion' – which presumably includes swallowing it in capsule form – 'may cause gastroenteritis with abdominal pain, nausea, vomiting and diarrhoea. Systemic effects may follow and may include ringing in the ears, dizziness, elevated blood pressure, blurred vision and tremors. If swallowed, call a physician immediately.' This was the same chemical that was being sold as a *natural health aid*!

Appalled, I called the supplier and asked if there was any scientific or medical evidence which could justify their claims. With a rather cavalier laugh, I was told, 'We don't get into scientific proof but we sell thousands of them.' This was a useful reminder of just how easy it is when you are in a vulnerable situation to blindly accept whatever sales pitch you are offered. My advice is to do good research before parting with large sums of money for products that may at best be harmless and at worst downright dangerous.

Like most people who look into natural or 'alternative' treatment for cancer, we were recommended to use Essiac by many people who swore by it. Essiac is a herbal remedy that was perscribed and promoted for about 50 years by Rene M. Caisse, a Canadian nurse who died in 1978. She claimed that the formula originally came from an Ojibwa medicine man and she named it after the backward spelling of her own name, Caisse. She claimed that many of the people she had treated for cancer reported that they were miraculously cured by taking it, while others claimed that it relieved their pain and made their lives with cancer more bearable. Shortly before her death, she passed the formula and manufacturing rights to the Resperin Corporation, a Canadian company that has provided it to patients under a special agreement with Canadian health officials. She hoped that it would be clinically validated, which at the time of writing Resperin has not done. Resperin now licenses Essiac to companies around the world, who offer it as a food supplement, not a medical product.

Although it will not do you any harm, tests conducted in the United States and Canada using samples of Essiac have failed to show any anti-tumour activity. The Resperin website states that the formula contains burdock, Indian rhubarb root, sheep sorrel, and slippery elm, all known individually to remove toxins from the body. However, I am unaware of any evidence, other than anecdotal, that it has any benefit, and personally I remain sceptical, but its popularity with cancer patients remains undiminished.

In recent times, some of the most hyped claims have been made for shark cartilage. My patients frequently ask me about it, but most of them are dissuaded from using it by its high cost rather than by the fact that it does not work. From the observation that sharks rarely get cancer, a huge multimillion-dollar industry of books and shark-based medicines has developed – despite the absence of any reliable, scientifically proven benefit to cancer patients. It is claimed that shark cartilage contains a protein that inhibits the growth of new blood vessels needed for the spread of cancer. Although a very small anti-angiogenic effect was observed in laboratory experiments, it has not been found that feeding shark cartilage to humans significantly inhibits angiogenesis in patients with cancer. (In medical terminology *angiogenesis* derives from the Greek *angio*, meaning blood vessel, and *genesis*, meaning to form.) Anti-angiogenesis is an active area of mainstream cancer research. Even if direct applications were effective, oral administration would not work because the protein would be digested rather than absorbed intact into the body. If the proteins could enter the body, they would cause an immune response that would make the individual allergic to them which could trigger disastrous allergic responses with further exposure to the protein.

In November 1998, the *Journal of Clinical Oncology* published a report of sixty patients with a variety of previously treated, advanced cancers who were given shark cartilage as their only treatment.[1] After three months, none of them achieved a complete or even partial remission. Ten patients showed no progression of their disease during that time which, to mainstream medical researchers is not significant, as many cancers do not progress rapidly or consistently. However, to those who were predisposed to shark cartilage, this was highly significant.

In the US the authorities have been quick to take action against at least three companies marketing shark cartilage. In September 1997, the Federal Drugs Agency warned Lane-Labs-USA to stop claiming that its shark cartilage product BeneFin can help fight cancer, arthritis and psoriasis. In December 1999, the US Department of Justice filed a lawsuit intended to stop the company from continuing its illegal marketing. In 1998, the Federal Trade Commission obtained two consent agreements, barring unsubstantiated claims for shark cartilage products, against two companies who had claimed their product was effective against cancer, rheumatism, arthritis, diabetes, fibroids, bursitis, circulatory problems and cysts! In June 2000, the FTC announced that Lane-Labs USA and Dr I. William Lane, a biochemist/entrepreneur and author of the book *Sharks Don't Get Cancer*, had signed consent agreements to stop illegal claims for BeneFin and to pay $550,000 in penalties and $450,000 towards the cost of an approved clinical trial involving shark cartilage.

I am often asked about a variety of 'miraculous cancer cures', but while I am sure it could be argued that there is a strong placebo effect in some cases, sadly there is little or no good evidence from suitable studies to suggest that any of these has a demonstrable benefit against cancer. As Gig and I discovered, you can spend a great deal of money on dubious products and a great deal of time consuming them several times a day to no good effect.

Despite anecdotal accounts of the benefits of intensive nutritional programmes, including high-dose intravenous vitamin regimens, cleansing diets and macrobiotics, none of these approaches has been scientifically proven to be beneficial in treating cancer *once it has begun*. Sometimes they can pose real risks and potentially harmful effects. Nevertheless, they remain attractive to many of my patients.

Cancer and Vitamin C

For a long time it was believed that very high doses of vitamin C were useful in the treatment of cancer. This was largely attributable to Linus Pauling who, in 1976 and 1978, reported that he and a Scottish surgeon, Ewan Cameron, had treated patients with high doses of vitamin C and that they had survived three to four times longer than similar patients who did not receive vitamin C.[2] In 1979, two Japanese researchers affiliated with the Linus Pauling Institute, Drs Murata and Morishige, of Saga University in Japan, published a report claiming that cancer patients on 5–30 g of vitamin C lived six times longer than those on 4 g or less, whilst those suffering from cancer of the uterus lived 15 times as long on vitamin C.[3]

However, Pauling and Cameron's findings were discredited after three apparent replications of their study by the Mayo Clinic in the United States could find no correlation between taking high doses of vitamin C and extended life expectancy.[4,5,6] It was later argued that the 'terminal' patients in the original trial kept taking vitamin C every day, while those in the Mayo Clinic trial stopped after an average of seventy-five days. The book was closed and mega-dose vitamin C was considered quackery.

It is interesting to note that in the 1970s the average Scottish diet had little variety of vegetables, mainly turnips, potatoes, carrots and kale, well cooked, as well as a high consumption of meat, fried foods and sugar, mainly in the form of confectionery, so the large doses of vitamin C given may have influenced Linus Pauling and Ewan Cameron's study.

Cancer-preventive Foods

In the 1950s, scientists had begun to identify enzymes that allow the detoxification and excretion of toxic and carcinogenic compounds from the body. By the 1970s, laboratory studies were showing that there is a variety of components within fruits and vegetables that 'switch on' these enzymes. Thus a diet high in fruits and vegetables makes it easier for the body to defend itself by detoxifying carcinogens before the cancer process starts.

Over the years, many naturally occurring plant components have been shown to play a key role in protection. Some, like the antioxidant vitamins C and E, prevent the kind of genetic damage that is important both early and late in the cancer process. Others, like folate, may be important in ensuring that damage to DNA is less likely and even repaired. Still others, like retinoids and fatty acids, seem to play a defensive role later on in the process by encouraging cancerous cells to stop multiplying or even commit a kind of suicide.

Broccoli, Cauliflower and Cabbage

Among all the cancer-fighting vegetables, broccoli, cauliflower and cabbage stand out, especially in bladder cancer. Broccoli is recognised by nutritionists as one of the most healthy foods available. It is a rich source of sulforaphane, which was first identified in 1992 as a compound that mobilises the body's natural cancer-fighting resources. Some 5 years later, scientists at the prestigious Johns Hopkins University found a new and highly concentrated source of sulforaphane: 3-day-old broccoli sprouts. These were found to 'consistently contain 20 to 50 times the amount of chemoprotective compounds found in mature broccoli heads', according to Professor of Pharmacology Dr Paul Talalay. His work, published in the *Proceedings of the National Academy of Sciences* in 1997, is now the subject of issued and pending patents.

One study has shown that regardless of how many different types of fruit and vegetable a group of 48,000 men ate, only those consuming broccoli and related cruciferous vegetables reduced their risk of bladder cancer. It is believed that broccoli may fight cancer by detoxifying organisms in the gut that would otherwise trigger malignancies in bladder tissue.

Tomatoes

Researchers have known for some time that men who eat cooked tomato products, such as pasta sauces, tend to have lower rates of prostate cancer than those who do not. A study reported at the 1999 annual conference of the American Association for Cancer Research showed that daily doses of lycopene, an antioxidant that ripens tomatoes and gives them their red colour, may not only prevent prostate cancer but also shrink existing tumours. Men who took 20 mg of the supplement (the quantity found in 1–1½/kg 2–3 lb of tomatoes) had lower levels of prostate-specific antigen (PSA), an indicator of cell growth, and smaller tumours.

Selenium and Vitamin E

Another researcher from the Johns Hopkins University, Dr Kathy Helzlsouer, reported at the end of 2000 that a form of vitamin E not usually found in vitamin supplements might help guard against prostate cancer.[7] This form of vitamin E, known as gamma-tocopherol, is found naturally in vegetable and seed oils, nuts, whole grains and leafy greens. Earlier studies have shown that the form of vitamin E found in supplements, alpha-tocopherol, and selenium may reduce prostate cancer risk. However, in this new study, this was only beneficial when gamma-tocopherol was also high. So taking vitamin E supplements alone may not reduce the risk of prostate cancer, but if they are taken with selenium and a dietary intake of vitamin E, the prospects look encouraging.

It has also been suggested that vitamin E and selenium supplements, taken in combination, resulted in a 13 per cent reduction in cancer mortality in a population with high rates of oesophageal and stomach cancer.[8]

The findings of Finnish scientists investigating the selenium and vitamin E link were even more pronounced. Dr Paul Knekt and his colleagues in Helsinki found that people with high levels of selenium and vitamin E had a much lower risk of developing lung cancer.[9]

A very striking result involving the use of supplementary selenium was reported by researchers from the Arizona Cancer Centre at the University of Arizona, who found that 200 mcg of selenium per day taken over a period of 4^1/$_2$ years, affected a variety of cancers. The volunteers taking selenium had 63 per cent fewer prostate cancers, 58 per cent fewer colorectal cancers and 46 per cent fewer lung cancers than the group taking a placebo.[10]

British researcher Dr Margaret Rayman, of the Centre for Nutrition and Food Safety at the University of Guildford, published a comprehensive review article about the importance of selenium in the *Lancet* in 2000. She noted that since selenium enters the food chain through plants, which take it up from the soil, selenium deficiency is likely to occur in areas with soil low in selenium. These include many parts of Europe and the United Kingdom.

Cancer and Folic Acid

Folic acid, a B vitamin which, like vitamin E, is found in green, leafy vegetables, is the latest of a growing list of micronutrients thought to protect against cancer. The theory rests on its relationship to DNA defects that are widely believed to lead to cancer.

In 1998, a report was published which confirmed that an increased intake of folic acid might protect against colon cancer. Higher intake of all forms of folate, including supplementation, was clearly related to a lower risk of colon cancer.[11]

Breast Cancer and Diet

Breast cancer is a terrible disease which kills thousands of women each year. I treat dozens of women who are battling it each week. The causes are many and research into the genetic basis of the disease as well as new therapies continues at a frenetic pace. It is promising that simple dietary changes may help to reduce cancer risk or even improve the prognosis of people who currently suffer from this devastating disease.

According to a report published in 2001 in the *British Medical Journal*, eating less and taking more exercise could help to reduce a woman's risk of developing breast cancer.[12] This may explain why women from less affluent countries, who tend to eat less food and lead lifestyles that involve more daily movement, have less breast cancer than women in the West. Breast cancer rates in the US are 87 cases per 100,000 women, while those in the Congo are as low as 10. In Britain the rate is 124 per 100,000.

The incidence of breast cancer differs widely across industrialised nations and all the known risk factors cannot explain this. Therefore diet, which varies greatly between different countries, has been given a lot of attention, particularly different patterns of dietary fat intake. Breast cancer incidence in Europe and the United States, where women eat a diet containing high levels of polyunsaturated fats, is five times greater than in Japan, where women tend to eat a low-fat diet with a high fish consumption.[13] There is experimental evidence that Omega 6 fatty acid metabolites promote breast cancer tumour growth and invasion, whereas Omega 3 fatty acids inhibit it.[14] It has also been suggested that a high-fat diet may adversely affect the recurrence rate after surgical removal of a primary breast cancer.[15]

Changing Your Diet

While scientists continue the years of investigation, patents and medical trials, we needn't wait to benefit from their research. A diet full of fresh fruits and vegetables clearly has a far-reaching impact on our health and various supplements can help too.

Many of my cancer patients make changes to their diets or take supplements not because they believe them to be a cure but for one or more of the following reasons:

The Benefits of Dietary Change for Cancer Patients

O Supplements and dietary change can boost the immune system, benefit wound healing and reduce opportunist infection.

O A healthy diet encourages rapid healing after surgery, chemotherapy or radiotherapy.

O It reduces the side-effects of chemotherapy or radiotherapy.

O It replaces chronic deficiencies brought about by poor or imbalanced diet.

○ It brings about an improvement in coping with the effects of stress (particularly with B complex vitamins).

○ It has a protective effect through the reduction of free radical and carcinogenic factors.

Don't Feel Guilty about Breaking a Diet!

Although eating a healthy diet can be highly beneficial, if you are finding it difficult, I feel strongly that any longer-term gain that may be made is probably negated by the detrimental effect of the stress experienced in achieving it. The experience of living with cancer and undergoing surgery, or chemotherapy, or radiotherapy, is stressful enough and the last thing you need at such a time is more stress. Unfortunately, I have seen this occur so many times as patients of mine try to religiously follow a particular diet or regime.

James had come to me suffering from lung cancer and although he was undergoing chemotherapy, he knew that the odds of his longer-term survival were not in his favour. As soon as he had completed his medical treatment, he flew out to Mexico to a clinic that specialised in diet and had also, unsuccessfully, treated the film actor Steve McQueen. He returned to Britain several weeks later and began the laborious practice of making endless juices, eating virtually only salads and raw vegetables, and drinking teas that he said made him feel quite nauseous.

Over the next few months I watched as James lost frightening amounts of weight that he could ill afford to lose as he stuck unwaveringly to his dietary regime. His wife called me one morning because he had an appointment with me that afternoon that he was not going to be able to keep. 'What can I do?' she asked me. 'He's just withering away in front of me and is now so weak that he can barely move.'

I suggested that she tell him to drop the diet, as it was obviously causing him distress. 'I'm so glad to hear you say that,' she said. 'He so hates it that he has simply stopped eating.'

I never heard from James again and so assumed, in view of how ill he had been, that he had probably died not long afterwards. Over two years later, I gave a lecture in London and at the end was answering questions from a group of people. After a while, the gentleman I was talking to said, 'You don't know who I am, do you?' I was amazed to find that it was a now-recovered James and I asked him what had happened.

'I followed your advice and gave up the diet. I absolutely hated it, so the morning that you spoke to my wife I ate a big fried breakfast washed down with Guinness. It was just what I wanted and I've not looked back since!'

While I am not suggesting that you try fried food and Guinness as an anti-cancer diet, do be aware of the harmful effects of the stress of trying to keep to a rigid diet that you don't enjoy.

Countering the Side-effects of Cancer Treatment

Nausea, vomiting, taste abnormalities, diarrhoea and constipation are all quite common side-effects of cancer therapies, which makes sticking to strict diets even more difficult. Loss of appetite is common and weight loss can therefore be a major problem. Many of the cancer therapies contribute to potential nutritional changes by reducing food intake, decreasing nutrient absorption or altering metabolism. Many of my patients cannot understand why their foods and drinks taste metallic while undergoing chemotherapy or radiotherapy, or why they get cravings, almost as if they were pregnant, for junk food.

Once Gig had embarked on her chemotherapy and radiotherapy, any thought of the well-balanced diet with plenty of fruits and vegetables was quickly jettisoned. Instead she wanted chips with everything, even with pasta. She liked this most of all. It was as if her body were craving carbohydrates as an antidote to the treatment.

Unlike many people in her situation, she never had any problem in keeping food down. She did, however, find that drinks often tasted metallic, which in particular put her off coffee and wine. Had she been able to have a glass or two of wine with her chips and pasta, her recovery may have been even quicker! Researchers have found that an antioxidant called resveratol, which is found in many grapes, helps to fight cancer.[16]

GUIDELINES FOR COUNTERING THE SIDE-EFFECTS OF CANCER TREATMENT

Loss of appetite

○ Eat small, attractive meals.

○ Make sure that your meals are nourishing.

○ Try eating snacks between meals.

○ Try a high-calorie supplement like Complan or Build-Up.

○ Eat slowly and in a relaxed atmosphere.

Inability to prepare meals, fatigue, weakness

○ Take advantage of convenience foods, canned foods, packets and pre-cooked meals.

○ Use high-calorie supplements.

○ Prepare meals in bulk and freeze them.

Quickly feeling full up

○ Eat small but frequent meals.

○ Decrease your fatty food intake.

○ Do not drink with meals.

○ Drink nourishing fortified drinks.

Nausea and/or vomiting

O Stay away from cooking smells.

O For morning nausea try dry toast with Marmite or Bovril, cream crackers or plain biscuits.

O Decrease your intake of sweet or greasy foods.

O Eat cold foods, as they have less smell than hot foods.

O Avoid liquids at mealtimes.

O Avoid fizzy drinks.

O Try not to lie down straight after eating.

Altered taste in mouth

O Avoid offending foods such as coffee, wine, tea and red meat.

O Enhance the flavour of food wherever possible by using flavourings and seasonings.

O Avoid very hot or very cold foods.

Dry mouth

O Drink frequently.

O Suck ice cubes or boiled sweets.

O Wash your mouth regularly.

○ Use artificial saliva if necessary.

○ Avoid dry foods, hot, spicy foods and alcohol.

○ Eat foods with a high moisture content.

Stomatitis/mucositis

○ Eat soft, moist foods.

○ Drink nourishing drinks.

○ Avoid salty or spicy foods.

○ Eat cold or cool foods.

○ Use a straw if needed.

Difficulty in chewing/swallowing

○ Eat a soft diet (*see page 221*).

○ Eat small but frequent meals.

○ Drink nourishing drinks.

○ Drink fizzy drinks to clear your tubes (where applicable) pre- and post- meals.

Cramps

○ Eat a low-fibre diet.

○ Avoid gas-forming foods.

Diarrhoea

○ Eat a low-fibre diet, but include sources of soluble fibre such as oats and oatbran, dried beans, peas, lentils, barley, apples, citrus fruits and peaches.

○ Drink plenty of fluids.

○ Omit dairy products if you are lactose intolerant.

Constipation

○ Eat a high-fibre diet, increasing your fibre intake gradually.

○ Drink plenty of fluids.

○ Exercise as much as you can.

Malabsorption

○ Follow a low-fat diet.

○ Follow a low-fibre diet.

○ Avoid lactose-containing foods.

GUIDELINES FOR A SOFT DIET

If your treatment leaves you with any difficulty chewing or swallowing, you will benefit from a 'soft diet'.

○ Eat *slowly*. Chew your food well. Drink with your meals and again after you have eaten.

○ Eat at least six small meals a day. Small, frequent meals are easier to digest than three large meals.

○ Eat your favourite foods, but use a blender, sieve, fork, knife or spoon to soften them.

○ Make stews and casseroles, adding more liquids to make them softer.

○ Choose soft foods such as:

- mashed potatoes with added milk
- pumpkin, eggs or softly cooked vegetables
- soft fruits
- yoghurt, cottage cheese, ricotta cheese and custard
- macaroni, spaghetti, noodles and rice
- minced meat, fish or chicken
- home-made soups

○ Avoid rough or coarse foods such as:

- raw vegetables like broccoli, peas or sweetcorn
- cereals such as bran
- toast and wholegrain breads
- nuts

○ Acidic fruits such as oranges, grapefruit and tomatoes can sting your mouth. Try bananas, canned pears and peaches instead, as they should be easier to swallow. Also, do not eat the skin, pith or pips of any fruit.

○ Avoid salty or highly seasoned foods. Do not use spices such as chilli powder, pepper, nutmeg and cloves, as these may further irritate the lining of your mouth.

○ Eat cold or lukewarm foods rather than hot foods.

○ Cold foods can be soothing. Try yoghurt, cold drinks, milk, or Build-Up.

○ Drink lukewarm drinks rather than hot ones.

○ Avoid drinking alcohol, as it can be irritating.

○ Rinse your mouth often, especially after sweet foods or drinks, as your resistance to bacterial invasion of tissue and teeth will be reduced due to lack of saliva.

○ Chew sugar-free gum to stimulate saliva production.

Other Remedies to Counter the Side-effects of Treatment

There are numerous remedies, many of which are of botanical origin, for minimising the worst side-effects of cancer treatment. They can all be quite easily obtained and they have all been tried, tested and reported in scientific journals. However, it is important to check with your doctor or a healthcare professional that they are safe for you to take with your particular condition and that they will not clash or cause an adverse reaction with any medical treatment you may be receiving.

Astragalus A non-toxic botanical medicine that boosts the ability of the spleen to prevent cancer cells from spreading and helps to prevent degeneration of the liver, which is a side-effect of chemotherapy. Astragalus root is a superior immune tonic which nourishes and balances the white blood cells.[17]

Co-enzyme Q10 This has been shown to counteract the toxic effects of the chemotherapy drug doxorubicin.[18] The anti-cancer activity of the chemotherapy drugs mitomycin and fluorouracil is not affected when CQ10 is taken to prevent malfunction of the kidneys and liver.

Dialy sulphide Also known as aged garlic, this has been demonstrated to protect against radiation damage. It can reduce the leakage of intracellular enzymes into the bloodstream, and lower the loss of white blood cells and platelets.[19]

Krestin (PSK) This is a polysaccharide extract from the fungus *Coriolus versicolor*, known more commonly in the West by its nickname 'Turkey Tail'; it is a non-toxic immune-stimulating anti-cancer drug. PSK has been available in Japan for almost twenty years, where it has government approval to be used for a number of cancers. There have been nearly 400 scientific studies carried out on the safety and effectiveness of PSK, some of which show increased survival rates and improved quality of life without toxic side-effects.[20] It has also been shown to counter the side-effects of the chemotherapy drug cyclophasphmide.[21]

Siberian ginseng (*Eleutherococcus senticosis*) This has been found to boost the immune system during chemotherapy or radiotherapy, and is non-toxic.[22] (*See page 158.*)

Superoxide dismutase (SOD) This is a non-toxic enzyme that converts free radicals to hydrogen peroxide, which in turn breaks down into water and oxygen. Breast cells are less likely to become cancerous the more superoxide dismutase they contain.[23] It can also help prevent the fibrous tissue formed after radiotherapy. In addition, there is a long-lasting formulation of superoxide dismutase called Orgotein which as been used, via injection, to effectively prevent the side-effects of high-energy radiotherapy in bladder tumours.[24]

Supplements during Cancer Treatment

I am often asked for advice on vitamins and minerals when people are undergoing cancer treatment, if for no other reason than to replace nutrients that may have been depleted by chemotherapy or radiotherapy. When Gig was ill, she would have rattled if shaken due to the number of vitamin and mineral pills that she was taking both before and during her treatment. She used the guidelines recommended by the Bristol Cancer Help Centre, as do most of my patients who are using supplements.

During Active Phases of Cancer and Its Treatment

Beta-carotene 15 mg or 3 x 6 mg tablets once daily. 6 mg equals 10,000 iu, although equivalence may vary from firm to firm. 10,000 iu of beta-carotene is equivalent to half a pint of carrot juice. To get your daily requirement in juice you would therefore need one and a half pints of carrot juice. You may mix juice and tablets to make up the daily dosage as convenient. This is the safe way to take vitamin A. **Beta-carotene is a pigment and may sometimes cause the skin to turn orange. If this happens, there is no need to worry. Simply reduce your dosage until the problem disappears.**

Vitamin C (as calcium or magnesium ascorbate), 2,000 mg (2 g) three times daily. If you get an upset stomach, a gradual increase in dosage or a different form of the vitamin should be tried. The ascorbic acid form is best avoided. In some cancer centres, dosages of vitamin C as high as 25 g per day are taken for brief periods when the cancer is active. This comes close to using vitamin C as a form of chemotherapy. (Intakes over 10 g daily are considered as therapeutic; i.e. are being given to treat cancer.) **You should not take vitamin C with the chemotherapy drug Methotrexate. Avoid using it for twelve hours either side of treatment.**

Selenium 200 mcg daily.

Zinc Orotate 300 mg, Gluconate 100 mg or Citrate 50 mg, one tablet daily.

For non-hormonal cancers

Evening primrose oil 500 mg, one tablet three times daily. There is some controversy about the use of vitamin E and evening primrose oil in hormone-dependent cancers (breast, ovarian, uterine, prostate and testicular) as they may raise hormone levels. However, there are also studies demonstrating the protective effect of vitamin E and essential fatty acids in hormone-dependent cancers. **In view of this concern, it is probably best to omit these items with hormone-dependent cancers.**

Vitamin E 267 mg (400 iu) one tablet daily. **If you have high blood pressure or are taking anti-thrombotic drugs, consult your doctor before taking this vitamin.**

When You Are In Remission

Vitamin C (as calcium or magnesium ascorbate), 1 g. One tablet three times daily.

Beta-carotene 15 mg capsule or 3 x 6 mg tablets once daily.

Vitamin B complex 50 mg. One tablet daily. **This is a high level of B vitamins and you should take care to ensure that these levels are present in the product you buy. Although B vitamins may turn your urine yellow, there is no need to be concerned.**

Selenium 200 mcg. One tablet daily.

Zinc Orotate 40 mg (or Citrate 15 mg). One tablet daily. Zinc supplementation may reduce copper absorption, hence supplemental copper is sometimes taken with zinc, while various foods interfere with zinc absorption. These include soya, cow's milk, iron supplements, whole-wheat bread and bran. **Therefore zinc should be taken separately from other supplements and not with food.**

For non-hormonal cancers

Vitamin E 267 mg (400 iu). One tablet daily.

Additional Factors

○ You might wish to continue taking pantothenic acid (250 mg daily) if there is still considerable cell repair and healing taking place.

○ For abdominal disturbances during chemotherapy take slippery elm powder as 1 teaspoon three times daily, or aloe vera juice as 1 tablespoon three times daily. Comfrey tea three times daily may also help. Arnica Montana and Nux Vomica, both homoeopathic remedies, can help reduce the dull pain or achiness and lessen the nausea associated with chemotherapy.

○ A homoeopathic remedy, Radium Bromide, may help the side-effects of radiotherapy. There are various aromatherapy creams to prevent skin burning. Use of echinacea helps to maintain your white cell count.

○ For problems with swallowing and digesting tablets, many vitamins and minerals can be obtained in liquid or sub-lingual (under the tongue) form. Alternatively you can open or pierce capsules or crush tablets and mix the contents with soup or juice.

Botanical Supplements and Cancer

In an age in which so much of medical science is quite incomprehensible, even to other scientists, it is comforting to remind ourselves occasionally that a lot of what passes for modern medicine is simply the refinement and repackaging of ancient remedies. For example, we get opiates from poppies, aspirin from the bark of willow trees, and Taxol and Taxatere (both chemotherapy drugs) from yew. Almost 60 per cent of the best-selling prescription drugs in our pharmacies are based on compounds taken directly from Nature's well-stocked medicine cabinet. It is as if there is a bright healing thread running from the medicine bags of shamans and witch doctors to today's pharmaceutical drugs. Here are two that may help in the treatment of cancer.

Bromelain

Bromelain is a very useful adjunct in cancer therapy. It is obtained from the pineapple plant and is a group of sulphur-containing enzymes that digest protein. Over 200 scientific papers have now been published in medical journals on its therapeutic uses since it was first introduced into cancer therapy in 1957. It has been reported to work as an anti-inflammatory, to enhance wound healing, prevent swelling (oedema), enhance the absorption of antibiotics and prevent ulcers.

> I was treating Julie for breast cancer that had metastasised into her bones after she had been told that she could not take any further chemotherapy. At my suggestion, she began taking bromelain and within days noticed that many of her bone pains had gone and that she could move much more freely. At her next check-up, her consultant told her that it was the first time in over two years that she had started to produce her own bone marrow again.

I have now heard several anecdotal accounts like Julie's. I have also been struck by the number of my patients who, when told about brome-lain, have said that they have had cravings for pineapples. Again, they are probably listening to their own bodies and giving them something that may help the healing process. Unfortunately, in order to get the correct dosage of bromelain, you would have to eat about sixty pine-apples a day, so it is best taken as a supplement!

Was Julie's experience merely one of coincidence or placebo? From much of the scientific research that has been conducted, it was probably neither. In one German study, bromelain given with chemotherapy drugs such as 5FU and vincristine resulted in significant tumour regression, although doses of less than 100 mg a day had no apparent benefit.[25] Professor Hans Nieper, who carried out this research, believes that bromelain has an ability to somehow 'deshield' the tumour cell's fibrin coat, making it much easier for the immune system to attack it.

A French study had even more persuasive results. Twelve patients with different kinds of tumours were treated with 600 mg of bromelain each day for periods ranging from six months to several years. Ovarian tumours disappeared, and most breast cancers and metastases decreased markedly compared to standard cancer therapy treatments alone.[26]

Mistletoe

Outside my home stands an enormous and magnificent lime tree that is believed to be over 200 years old. From my healing room I can see its lower branches as they almost sweep the driveway. The tree is admired by many of my patients and passers-by, who are often seen pointing to its upper reaches. There, high above the ground, is an extremely large cluster of mistletoe.

A parasitic plant, mistletoe usually lives on fruit trees and poplars by tapping nutrients from its host. According to ancient folklore, the wood of the cross carried by Christ was made from mistletoe and the plant was therefore 'punished' by being banished from the ground and forced to depend on other plants to survive. The custom of kissing under the mistletoe at Christmas is thought to be connected with the plant's legendary (and unproven) power to increase fertility. Considered sacred in ancient times, it has been used for centuries in Europe to treat a variety of acute and chronic health problems. The leaves, twigs and berries are all medicinal.

Mistletoe is used to relieve the symptoms of malignant tumours, though it is not known to produce a cure. Quite a large number of my patients have attended the Royal London Homoeopathic Hospital (a National Health Service hospital), for treatment with a mistletoe extract known as Iscador. It is known to have properties that will stimulate the immune system and has been used in complementary medicine to treat cancers for over sixty years.

Iscador has been studied over the past twenty years by researchers who have reported that it can increase DNA stability and inhibit cell growth. Two reports have shown that it increases macrophage, T cell and natural killer cell activity, all of which are beneficial in fighting cancer.[26,27,28] It seems to be most effective when injected near a tumour.

Dr Immaculada Marti, a Spanish physician working at Davies Hospital in San Francisco, and Dr Robert Gorter, a Dutch physician and Associate Professor at the University of California in San Francisco, have carried out some of the most extensive clinical work with Iscador, especially with people who are infected with HIV, and have found that it appears to enhance five specific immune responses.

In several European countries and in South Africa, Iscador is registered for commercial purposes and can be legally prescribed.

Chapter 12

FAITH AND HEALING

Like so many people before her, in the weeks after Gig's cancer diagnosis she asked, 'Why me?' We also found ourselves experiencing
many of the myriad feelings and emotional reactions that many of my
patients were already familiar with. In the beginning it seemed so unfair
that this had happened to us. I began to appreciate why people quite
often get angry when they have to face up to an illness. Both Gig and
I, at different times, found ourselves irritable, frustrated or just downright mad. You might feel this way too – about your condition or about
what caused your condition, about the care you are receiving or the care
you are not receiving, about family members, friends, doctors, yourself,
even God.

Sometimes that anger is actually a mask for other emotions, such as
fear – fear that we'll not be able to cope or fear that we will fall apart.

There were times of sadness too. I know that some people experience
despair because they doubt that life will ever be the same or as good as
it was before their illness. You may have days that seem grey. Your future
may seem bleak. You might find that you seem to have no energy at all.

There may be feelings of guilt as well. You may blame yourself for
certain things that have happened, or for certain relationships, or certain
attitudes. You may feel guilty about the pain that others are suffering
because of your condition.

Gig and I found that the first step was to release our feelings, and in
doing so we began to discover an inner strength growing inside us, giving
us hope and leading us on.

A Time of Choices

Although you may have no control over what has happened to you, you
do have control over how you *respond* to what has happened. It is a
time of choices. You can hide, from yourself or others, or you can choose

to be as open and honest as possible. You can choose to give up, or you can use all your reserves and resources in a drive to rebuild a future. You may choose to become embittered, or you can learn to become more understanding, more accepting, wiser. You can choose to get locked into unending anger, or you can release yourself to give your love more freely.

As you learn more about this crisis in your life, it is worth remembering what crisis means: it is a turning point that challenges our ability to cope. It is a time when forces collide and we don't know the outcome. Life can go one way or another when it is ripe with possibility.

Although Gig and I wanted to know why this had happened to us, we came to realise that 'Why me?' is not a particularly helpful question. We found that better questions were:

'What can I now do to make the most of this experience?'
View your illness as a means of growth. Physical challenges can offer a great opportunity for psychological and spiritual advancement. Many people have found that once they have dealt with certain emotional issues, they have recovered their physical health. So rise to the challenge and try to see everything that happens to you in relation to your illness as a chance to move in a more positive direction.

'How can I learn and grow from my illness?' Don't view your illness as punishment or judgement. It's more constructive to focus on developing self-love and self-esteem. As we have discovered, your body responds to both positive and negative emotions, so if you concentrate on giving yourself the love and care you deserve, your immune system will fight harder for you.

'How can I use this experience to discover and fulfil the purpose of my life?' Accept your illness. This doesn't mean that you give up but rather that you see your illness as just one thing to deal with and not something that completely rules your life. Placing trust in a higher power as well as your own ability to cope gives you more space to focus on other things. Don't make physical change your only goal, because although physical recovery is important, the lessons you can learn from your experience are equally important. Your healing process should include learning about happiness, forgiveness, hope and peace of mind.

We also found that a particular meditation, 'The Gift', which I have used in my seminars, was now as helpful to us as it had been to thousands of others before us. You might like to try it. Again, you might like to get a friend to read it for you or make a copy for yourself on a tape.

EXERCISE: THE GIFT

Take in a few deep breaths and, as you let them out, let go of any tension in your body. Be aware of any feelings and try to let them go too. Notice if there are any thoughts in your mind. Just watch them like clouds crossing a blue sky on a warm summer's day.

Imagine yourself enjoying a wonderful sunny day . . . in a beautiful place in the countryside . . . or on a beach . . . or in a forest . . . or in a garden . . . whatever is best for you. Feel the warmth of the sun on your skin . . . A cool breeze gently caresses you . . . See the brightness of the colours. Notice any movement around you . . . leaves, blades of grass, flowers, ocean waves, birds or animals. Hear the sounds of your scene . . . wind in the trees . . . birdsong . . . the splash of water. Experience the happy vitality all around you.

Imagine yourself getting up and exploring this wonderful world. Look at it with different eyes and notice what you discover about it. Imagine yourself running through this scene . . . and experience a sense of joy permeating and filling you.

Imagine now that you find a nice quiet place where you sit down and make yourself comfortable. When you look up you notice a friendly and, in a strange way, familiar figure standing by your side . . . You indicate to this person to sit beside you . . . and feel the warmth of affection and love that is there for you.

Your friend takes your hand and you can feel this warmth flow through you as you listen to their words: 'I am always with you. I am here to love and support you now.'

As you hear these words, you experience a deep sense of reassurance. A profound peace fills and surrounds you totally in a way that you have never known before. When you look once again towards your friend, you become aware that both of you are within a radiantly clear white light . . . and you notice that some of the darkness that was previously in your consciousness is now being lifted from you, as though this light were a magical healing agent of great power and gentleness. As this light seems to be growing brighter, you notice that your friend has a gift for you.

You open your hands to receive it and explore the package. How is it wrapped? How large is it? Is it light or heavy? What might be inside?

Life really is a gift that unfolds, wrapper by wrapper. You might sometimes glimpse the most precious essence within the gift-wrapping. Imagine, for a moment, that your life is a gift-wrapped package. How you feel at the moment may influence the quality of the wrapping, so don't be upset if your package looks like a crumpled brown bag. Some of the greatest gifts are hidden and concealed in the most deceptive coverings. The wrapping may not give you any clue as to the true contents of the package. The wrapping is, in itself, a gift of learning. As you receive the learning, symbolically represented by the wrapping, you will begin to discover your greater gifts contained within it.

All the loving you have ever longed for can come to you. You do not have to put up with less than you really want. You are living in a world rich with gifts of love . . . Reach out and you will receive.

What is it that you would most like to receive? Is it appreciation? Tenderness? Affection? Intimacy with someone you really trust? The strength of someone you know is really there for you? Acts of consideration or kindness? Generosity being extended towards you? Perhaps freedom to express yourself to someone who is accepting and not critical of you? An acceptance of who you are? Maybe space to feel your vulnerability . . . to feel emotional . . . safe . . . with a loving, understanding heart . . . What is the most important gift for you to receive?

Experience now a sense of gratitude as you unwrap your gift. With a sense of excitement, you start to remove the wrapping. What do you find inside? See it in as much detail as possible . . . the colour . . . the size . . . the shape . . . the feel . . . the texture. What does this gift mean for you? How can you use it to improve the relationship with yourself?

Your friend is now standing up and helping you to your feet. You thank this special person for the gift and share a warm embrace. With a squeeze of your hand, you are reminded that you are loved. You have a special place in your friend's heart. And now, once again, you are on your own . . . but filled with loving.

Very gently now, slowly return your attention to the world around you. While these good feelings are still present in your consciousness, take a few minutes to think about your experience . . . especially the gift and its meaning for you.

The first time I shared this meditation in my seminar it had a profoundly moving effect on one participant. He told us that the friend who appeared by his side was his wife and her gift to him was a ticket for a round-the-world cruise. She had led him to a large harbour where a huge ocean-going liner was moored. At the bottom of the gangplank she had kissed him goodbye and told him to have a wonderful time. The ship then set sail and as it steamed out of port, he stood on the stern waving goodbye to his wife on the quayside. She became smaller and smaller as the ship went out to sea, until she eventually disappeared altogether.

As he recounted his experience, tears were pouring down his face. His wife had died almost a year before and he had been going through terrible waves of grief over his loss. The image from the exercise was, he explained, as if his wife was telling him that he had to get on with life by himself. In many cultures an image of water symbolises life and he felt strongly that she wanted him now to go out and enjoy himself. It was the healing he had been looking for.

The Search for Meaning

Although neither Gig nor I are particularly religious in so far as we are not churchgoers, we share strong spiritual beliefs. I have always believed that there is a purpose to life and that it is not some bad joke being played on us by an old man with flowing beard and robes, sitting up in the clouds randomly casting the dice by which our lives will be governed. My personal belief is that we are all spiritual beings inhabiting a physical body and experiencing life in the physical world. You may have asked yourself at certain times in your life: 'Who am I?' 'Am I my body?' 'Am I my mind?' 'Am I the feelings in my heart?' 'If I have a body, mind and heart, can I also *be* those things?' 'If I am not those things, then what am I?' If you are confronted with a serious and perhaps life-threatening illness, you find that you have a much more pressing need to look at the question of who you really are and it quickly becomes a far more focused question. Finding the most enlightened answer is the ultimate reward of the healing journey.

I believe that the purpose of life is a spiritual one and that each and every one of us is here to learn. Life is a series of lessons to be learned. We choose our lives and we may choose many different lives in order to learn the lessons we need to learn. It is through this learning process that we grow and evolve on a spiritual level.

Every experience in life is an opportunity to learn. We choose our own experiences by our thoughts, actions or feelings, because those experiences are going to allow us to learn. Sometimes we learn best from difficult or painful experiences. Suffering can unlock the door to many truths; we can learn so much from pain. It is not, as some people may believe, a punishment, but an opportunity to gain what you need to move ahead on your journey.

Every time we go through what may seem to be a negative or threatening experience, we have a chance to challenge the fear that lies behind it and to choose to learn. If we decide that we can learn from the situation, our fears start coming to the surface so that we can release them. We all have a choice to confront our fears or to suppress them. It is fear of growing and evolving that makes us want to escape from the present situation and find another one. But we are all evolving all the time and all experiencing the results of our own actions, both positive and negative, which is known as karma.

The good passes, but so does the bad. To use that oft-repeated phrase, 'Without darkness, we would not appreciate the light when it comes.' An apt analogy is that the wave wants to experience itself as a wave, with all its ups and downs, before falling back into the ocean and remembering its true identity.

At one time I felt that we were all on a ladder of spiritual evolution, with some of us being lower down the rungs than others, but as I contemplated it, I felt that this image was too rigid, because it did not give enough possibility for free will. Whatever befalls us in life, we have a choice as to how we respond to it and deal with it. So I felt that an image of a tree was more appropriate. It seems to me that, symbolically, we are all trying to climb a tree in order to reach the top. We start by climbing up the trunk and, at some point, find our first branch. The choice is ours. We can either continue, climbing higher up the tree, or we can start moving along the branch. If we do so, we find that the branch divides, sub-divides and divides again so that we are constantly offered a choice of direction. However, all the branches of the tree are reaching up towards the light.

I believe that we choose a physical life so that the spirit can take its lessons and evolve further from the experiences of that life. Sometimes the choice is one of service, in helping others further along the path to experience and know forgiveness and love. There is no death but a constant cycle of rebirth, an endless chain as we grow towards spiritual perfection. Soul-wise, I think we are migratory and we tend to move in groupings. We and the other souls making up the group are like a dandelion clock that has been blown on, scattering us so that we replant in a different part of the universe and yet are within reach of one another in our various lives. We may reconnect as lovers, spouses, friends, parents or children.

Some years ago I treated a youngster, Mark, who had been born with Down's syndrome. This had led, as it so often does, to a multitude of other problems and difficulties both physical and mental. However, Mark had an adoring brother and sister and parents whose understanding, patience, tolerance and love were quite exceptional.

After he had passed away, Mark's mother told me how some of their friends implied that it must now be a relief to be able to have a normal life without the worry and burden of a disabled child. Understandably, the parents were most upset by suggestions like this, explaining that both they and their two other children had learned and grown so much from their time with Mark. 'We would never have traded that time for anything in the world,' they told me. 'Mark was full of unconditional love and happiness, and that was our gain as a family.'

Mark had given them all a great gift.

Children do not remain children forever, but move through various stages towards maturity, and so it is with consciousness. We outgrow people, places and things as we unfold. We let go of the old self to make way for the new self. I believe that each life has its own special design and that we only acquire and keep what truly belongs to us. Sometimes we can be violently moved away from someone or something that we have wanted and we may rage against the stroke of fate that breaks up the alliance. But it may have been a disaster if we had stayed. We find our right place, at the right time and with the right person.

Many of the people who come to my seminars are looking to healing to fill a spiritual vacuum. Perhaps my perception is distorted, because the people I see tend not to be respecters of orthodoxy in any of its forms, but I believe that many people nowadays are questioning the establishment, whether in the area of science, religion or politics. Science was once a god for many people. Now it has been found to have feet of clay. Orthodox religion, too, has had its influence eroded. We seem to be reaching a coming of age and people want to 'do it for themselves'.

Wired for Faith

In 1996 *Time* magazine carried a front cover story entitled 'Faith and Healing. Can spirituality promote health? Doctors are finding some surprising evidence'.

Dr Herbert Benson of the prestigious Beth Israel-Deaconess Hospital in Boston, who in the 1970s introduced the phrase 'the relaxation response' (*see page 159*), has since carried his research far further. In his latest book, *Timeless Healing*, he moves beyond the purely pragmatic use of meditation into the realm of spirituality. He suggests that humans are actually 'engineered for religious faith', an idea based on his work with a group of patients who reported that they sensed a closeness to God while meditating. In Benson's view, prayer operates along the same biochemical pathways as the relaxation response – in other words, praying affects the production of adrenaline and other 'stress hormones', leading to lower blood pressure, and a more relaxed heart rate and respiration and other benefits.

It is probably no coincidence that the relaxation response and religious experience share the same headquarters in the brain. Research has shown that the relaxation response is controlled by the amygdala, a small, almond-shaped structure. Together with the hippocampus, gyrus fornicatus and hypothalamus, it makes up the limbic system, which plays a key role in emotions, sexual pleasure, deep-felt memories and, it seems, spirituality. When either the hippocampus or the amygdala is electrically stimulated during surgery, some patients experience visions of angels and devils, while patients whose limbic systems are chronically stimulated by drug abuse or a tumour often become religious fanatics.

This particularly interests me because in 1974 I participated in a series of tests at the New Horizons Research Foundation in Toronto, Canada. Psychiatrist Dr Joel Whitton devised one experiment that was subsequently to attract a great deal of excited interest. He wanted to find out what, if anything, was going on in my brain while I was engaged in what the researchers called 'paranormal activity'.

I was connected to a machine called an electro-encephalograph (EEG) by means of electrodes that were attached to my scalp in order to measure my brainwave patterns. Our brainwave patterns, which are made by the various levels of electrical activity in the brain, alter depending on what we are doing. My brainwaves were measured while I was in various states: resting with eyes closed, making head, neck and eye movements, talking and being involved in a paranormal or psychic task. The experiment was conducted on several separate occasions, each time in the presence of various other scientists, who included Nobel Prize winner Professor Brian Josephson, Dr Michael Persinger of the Psychophysiology Laboratory at Laurentian University, and Doctors Highman and Kurtz, who were both medical doctors.

The results showed that the distribution of power in my EEG spectrum while I was engaged in paranormal activity was quite different from that seen while I was in any of the other states. There was 'a major concentration of energy in the Theta band', which was characteristic of deep sleep. Further tests with a sophisticated computer at the Toronto Hospital for Sick Children revealed that the source of the electrical energy was the limbic system. Whitton concluded that the psychic power coming from it was 'not a random gift, but an innate function and ability in the brain of *Homo sapiens*, a function probably lost or defunct in most people for thousands of years'.[1]

I now wonder if it is any coincidence that the same part of the brain that would seem to be active when I am healing is the same as that involved in the relaxation response and religious experience. It certainly seems to correlate with Herbert Benson's more recent findings. He believes that evolution has equipped us to believe in an 'Infinite Absolute' in order to offset our uniquely human ability to ponder our own mortality. As he puts it, 'To counter this fundamental angst, humans are also wired for God'.[2]

Spiritual Faith and Health

Evidence is now growing that religion or spiritual faith *can* be good medicine. In 1996, researchers led by Dr Dale Matthews of Georgetown University presented the latest evidence of the influence of religious belief on health to the annual meeting of the prestigious American Association for the Advancement of Science. They had reviewed 212 studies and found that 75 per cent showed a positive effect of religious commitment on health.

Also in 1996, 296 doctors were surveyed at the annual meeting of the American Academy of Family Physicians and it was found that 99 per cent of them believed that religious beliefs could heal and that 75 per cent believed that the prayers of others could promote a patient's recovery.[2]

Certainly, even as recently as twenty-five years ago, no self-respecting doctor would have dared to propose controlled studies of something as intangible as prayer, yet there have now been over 1,200 studies on the relationship between religion and health. Western medicine has spent the past 100 years trying to rid itself of the remnants of mysticism, yet today there appears to be a shift towards the view that there may be more to health than blood-cell counts and electrocardiograms and more to healing than pills and scalpels. In other words, people now want medical care that is grounded in spirituality.

Prayer and Healing

Science had always treated the claims made for the power of prayer and healing with great scepticism, but in 2000, Dr John A. Astin of Stanford University School of Medicine published a report on distant healing and prayer which came down heavily on the side of the healers.[3] After reviewing dozens of studies, Astin and his colleagues believe they had found evidence that prayer really does help to reduce pain and accelerate recovery from illness. They were, by their own admission, surprised, as they had not expected to find that spiritual intervention had any effect.

Astin and his medical colleagues had merely caught up with the types of experiment that had been carried out up to forty years previously by other researchers. In 1959, Stephan Figar of Prague found that intense mental concentration by one man could produce a measurable change in the blood pressure of a second one lying at rest some distance away.[4]

In 1966, the *International Journal of Neuropsychiatry* had published a report by Professor Douglas Dean, who was also involved in the Toronto tests in which I took part. He had discovered that when someone thinks hard about a close friend, no matter where they may be, that person registers a measurable change in blood pressure and volume. Using this response as a means of communication, Dean managed to send simple Morse code messages from New Jersey to Florida, entirely without the knowledge of the receiver, who just lay quietly attached to a plethysmograph.[5]

Recent studies have shown that heart patients who were being prayed for did better than those who were not – even without being told about the experiment.[6, 7]

Distant Healing

Dr Elisabeth Targ, clinical director of psychosocial oncology research at the California Pacific Medical Centre in San Francisco, has published the results of a study that she and her colleagues conducted to test whether distant healing, including prayer, had any beneficial effect on health on AIDS when subjects did not know they were receiving treatment.

In the experiment, forty severely ill AIDS patients were randomly selected; half were prayed for or sent distant healing, and half were not. All the patients received standard medical care, but none were told to which group they had been assigned. Blood tests and psychological testing at the beginning of the study, and six months later, assessed the patients. The patients who had been receiving distant healing had experienced significantly fewer new AIDS-related illnesses, had less severe illnesses, required fewer doctor visits and fewer days of hospitalisation. The psychological tests showed that the distant healing effects were not affected by the subjects' beliefs about which group they were in.[8] When asked why the researchers had chosen a disease for which there is no known cure, Elisabeth Targ responded by saying, 'AIDS is perfect. This way the sceptics can't say we picked a disease that was too easy. Besides, healers like a challenge!'

Of course, while these studies have demonstrated the effect of distant healing on sick people, numerous other studies have shown the same effect in a laboratory setting. At the beginning of this book I described how I was able to influence cancer cells in a plastic flask. However, this influence occurred not only when I *held* a flask containing cancer cells, but also when I tried to influence them from a *distance*.[9] In France, Jean Barry, in a controlled test, showed that people could inhibit the growth of a destructive fungus at a distance of one and a half metres, using only mental intentions.[10] His study was successfully replicated by researchers at the University of Tennessee, using the same organism, at distances of one to 15 miles, using student volunteers as 'healers'.[11] Carroll B. Nash carried out a similar study at St Joseph's University in Philadelphia using the common bacterium *E. coli*, with dozens of unskilled volunteers.[12]

I believe that these studies are important for two reasons. As the studies involved *in vitro* samples, in other words non-human, the results cannot be explained away by psychological factors or placebo. It seems also that almost anybody can do it and that you do not have to have belief in yourself as 'a healer'. In my seminars, and during my public healing demonstrations, I have always encouraged participants to think of loved ones or friends who need healing because I know just how effective it is.

For almost forty years, Kari had suffered from fibromyitis, a very painful condition that causes muscle inflammation and degeneration. She had difficulty in doing many simple things for herself. I was doing a healing demonstration at the Oslo Concert House and Kari lives many miles away but, as she said, 'I concentrated on the healing that was going on at the Concert House and suddenly got the shakes. Ever since then I have been full of energy and with much less pain.'

A member of the same audience sat and thought about his friend Harald, who had been involved a year earlier in a car accident that had left him with permanent pain in his neck and shoulders. Later Harald told me, 'The pain is now gone and after the healing demonstration, even though I could not personally be there, my whole body felt lighter. It is as though a big load has gone.'

Perhaps you know someone who is in need of help or healing, in which case you might find the following simple exercise helpful.

EXERCISE: DISTANT HEALING

Begin by taking some deep breaths. Breathe in peace. Breathe out any fear or conflict. Imagine, if you like, that you are filling a balloon with your fears – and let them go. Let a wave of peace and healing move through your body. Perhaps you can imagine it as a colour, or repeat a word like 'relax' or 'peace' to yourself. Let go of any tension in your jaw muscles, and your neck and shoulder muscles.

Imagine someone you want to help, someone in pain, standing in front of you. Sit for a few moments and just look at them. See what they look like, what they are wearing, their complexion. There is no need to do anything. Just get in touch with their appearance.

After a few minutes, begin to feel what it might be like to be them. Imagine what it is like to be in their body, to have their life, their feelings. Try to begin to see it from their perspective rather than yours. Imagine what it would be like to have their problem.

As the wall begins to break down between you and the other person, you might find yourself understanding them a little more and focusing more on them than yourself. As this happens, allow yourself to breathe in their pain. Imagine it, perhaps, as black smoke. Don't worry if you can't see the smoke, it's the idea behind it that is important – the act of breathing in their pain. Then breathe out light to them. Breathe in their pain and breathe out the light. Keep on doing it.

As your awareness begins to meet discomfort, let your body relax and allow sensations to float. Let your hands open to feel the tender sensations that are now arising.

If your mind wanders, don't worry. Just return to the focus point when you can.

Imagine now all the other people around the world who are experiencing the same pain. Sense the woman lying on her side alone in the mud hut, the man unable to get up from his sleepless bed, the child gazing toward the fluorescent ceiling of his hospital room, wondering, 'Why me?'

Feel the joy of being connected and a much greater sense of being at one with all those in discomfort. Feel a new tenderness arising, relating to all pain. Let your mind float. Let the images come and go. Let yourself gently experience them, constantly sharing the healing. Let the breath come. Let the breath go. Feel your heart opening into healing and silently say:

'May they be free of their suffering.'

'May they be at peace.'

The Mystery of Healing Energy

The numerous successful studies of distant healing and prayer perhaps raise more questions than they answer. They certainly raise philosophical issues, such as why a benevolent God or deity would respond only to the prayers of or on behalf of persons in the treatment group when many people in the control group will probably pray for themselves and will be prayed for by friends and loved ones. Similarly, why would a compassionate God or higher power that intends the well-being of all mankind respond only to the needs of those who pray or are being prayed for?

I used to practise distant healing and on several occasions someone would call and thank me profusely for some wonderful healing they said had occurred in a relative or friend after I had been asked to send healing to that person, but I would find no trace of the letter or the individual referred to in my files. A day or two later their letter would arrive. In these cases healing occurred before I even knew of the need for it. So who, or what, was making the healing work? Was it the person writing the letter? Was it an unconscious connection with me? Is the intent sufficient to make healing work, perhaps through the intervention of some higher force? Are requests for help really prayers that are picked up and answered by that force?

However it works, I regard healing energy as an unconditional universal force for good. I have felt its effects as a child, parent, lover and friend. We may not be able to prove its existence scientifically, but that is not the only scale of measurement. We measure love by the effect it has on our lives and we should treat healing in the same way.

A rather nice twist in the research into distant healing and prayer came from an experiment carried out by Catholic priest and psychologist Father Sean O'Laoire. He divided 406 people into 2 groups, one of which received prayer and one which did not. However, he also examined the effects of prayer on the 90 people who were doing the praying. The experiment was a controlled double-blind study in which no one knew who was and was not receiving prayer. The purpose was to study the effects of prayer on 11 measures of self-esteem, anxiety, and depression. O'Laire found that those being prayed for improved on all 11 measures, but he also discovered that on 10 of the 11, those *doing* the praying improved *more* than those being prayed for.[13]

The Worshipper's Reward

There is certainly a growing body of evidence to show that religious and spiritual practice does have an impact on our health. In 1997, the prestigious *International Journal of Psychiatry in Medicine* published a study by Dr Harold Koenig that found a direct association between religious activity and immune functioning.[14]

Another study found that one of the best predictors of survival after open heart surgery was the degree to which the patients said they drew comfort and strength from religious or spiritual belief. Researchers found that none of the 37 'deeply religious' patients died during the 6 months after surgery, while 21 of the other patients did.[15]

In a major report published in the professional journal *Demography* in 1999, researchers found that regular church worshippers live 10 per cent longer than those who never attend services. Life expectancy was found to be 82 for weekly churchgoers, 83 for those who attend more than once a week and 75 for non-churchgoers.[16] The study included Christian and non-Christian worshippers and was also adjusted for respondents' incomes, alcohol and tobacco use, marital status and even weight. So the reward of going to church might be a longer wait for heaven!

Critics have suggested that there may be other explanations for the positive health effects of religious practices and spiritual beliefs, so many of which have now been scientifically demonstrated to promote health and reduce disease:

Healthy behaviour Religious involvement may discourage behaviour that increases health risks, such as tobacco and alcohol consumption, or it may encourage other positive lifestyle choices.

Social support People who regularly attend religious services appear to have larger and denser social networks to provide emotional support and other forms of assistance than less-frequent attendees.

Self-esteem Religious involvement may promote feelings of self-worth and confidence in the ability to control your own affairs and destiny.

Coping skills Prayer, meditation and other religious activities help people deal with stressful events and conditions.

Positive emotions Religious activities may lead to positive emotions, which have been shown to influence immune functions and other physiological factors that influence health.

Healthy beliefs Faith may promote a positive outlook that offers both emotional and tangible means of promoting an individual's health and well-being.

I believe that whether we express our spiritual beliefs by going to church or in some other way, by being positive, always looking for the good in other people and searching for a higher purpose, we can make the world a better, safer place. We may not think it can make any difference, but when that sort of action is taken by millions, it cannot fail to have a beneficial effect. The way we think conditions our actions and gives the world its spiritual energy. If these thoughts are negative, the energy they generate is likely to be destructive. If these thoughts are positive, the energy benefits everyone. When I give healing, it is not necessarily just the person I am working with one to one who gets the benefit. Healing has a ripple effect and the positive energy channelled at the centre flows out to the edges.

I also believe that there are times when healing does not work because in a spiritual context it is not the right time for it to work. It might be that someone is learning in some way or evolving through an experience of illness. A person might have gone as far as they can in this life, and it is time for them to leave it and move on. This too is part of the healing journey.

Chapter 13

PREPARING FOR
THE LAST JOURNEY

A s a healer I have for many years worked with people with serious, life-threatening or terminal illness and I have long believed that my role is, at times, as much to help somebody to die as it is to help them to live. Sometimes their disease is so aggressive that no matter how positive they are, it will make no difference to their survival. But healing is not limited to the body. If I can help someone to die peacefully, free of pain, and in dignity, I feel that is also of value. Dying can itself be a true healing.

Healing should mean returning to some sort of balance, or becoming whole. Sometimes I think that the word is used in an inappropriate way. Doctors and healers may say that the patients who heal are exceptional, but what does that make everybody else? The idea that you are a good person if you are healed makes you a bad person if you die. Who needs to die with a sense of failure? I know that many people have been hurt by the idea that, for example, they are responsible for their illness. You are not responsible for your illness – you are not responsible for your disease. But you are responsible *to* your disease.

In the past, some of my patients have told me that they are not going to give in, or surrender, to their illness. The word 'surrender' is interesting because most people, particularly in the case of illness, equate surrender with defeat. But surrender is letting go of resistance. While my work, and the material I have shared in this book, supports optimism, a sense of control and a fighting spirit, there may come a time when a patient moves from a point of fighting to one of acceptance. When this occurs should be an entirely individual choice and nobody else should tell the person that they should keep fighting. You may find that for a while you fluctuate back and forth in 'resistance-surrender cycle'. Most of my patients, as they come to a certain point in their journey, which usually includes opening to the reality that death might well be in the near future, begin to finish business.

Chris was a very sporty, no-nonsense man in his late forties who had been diagnosed with liver cancer. I was not sure what I could do for him, but at our first meeting I said the same to him as I say to anybody coming to me for treatment the first time: 'Let me have three sessions with you. If nothing happens, maybe I can't do any more.'

Chris came to me on a monthly basis and by the last session it was obvious that his condition was deteriorating. When we had finished, he looked at me and said, 'So, that's my three sessions, is it? You're going to kick me out now, are you, because we're not getting anywhere?' I was shocked and for the first time realised how my attitude must have come across to him, and probably others, as unfeeling and uncaring.

Chris said, 'Let me tell you something. You might think that you're not doing anything. You and I both know that this cancer is getting worse, but what you may not know is that when I leave you it is like walking out on air and I'm completely pain-free for the next two weeks. That's all I'm asking of you. Please don't cast me out. I may not live, but it's the quality of my remaining life that is important to me.'

Against expectations, Chris went on to live for another six months. The last time I saw him he looked absolutely dreadful and I knew that there was nothing more I could do to help him physically. He was his usual honest self and he said to me, 'I know I've only got a few days left now. Come on, hit me with it one more time!'

After the healing session, Chris's wife was a little late in collecting him and we had time to talk. We discussed what we learn from serious illness and death, and about their possible spiritual implications. I mentioned the 'if only' factor and how heavily it seemed to weigh on many bereaved people – 'If only I had said. . .', 'If only I had time to. . .', 'If only I had been there . . .' I told him of cases of impending death which had moved people to resolve conflicts or emotional difficulties with those who were ostensibly closest to them. We can pay a great price if we leave the fundamentals on the back burner for the duration of our lives. If we resolve problems as we go and are mindful of others' needs, there will be no 'if only'.

When Chris got up to leave, he hugged me. We both knew we would not see each other again. A couple of days later his wife telephoned my office and wanted to speak to me. Knowing what she was going to tell me, I was expecting her to sound flat and depressed. On the contrary, in the background I could hear loud music playing and she told me that Chris had died peacefully early the previous evening. After they had left me and driven home, he had taken her into their living room, sat her down and told her that he was about to die. Before this acknowledgement, he had always been full of bravado and plans for the future. A keen yachtsman, he had told her about the races he was going to win and the competitions he was going to enter. She told me that she and her daughter had felt fraudulent because they knew he was not going to make it, but love and loyalty necessitated that they should keep up the charade.

When Chris told his wife he was going to die, she felt as though a great weight had been lifted from her shoulders. Suddenly, and at last, they could be open and honest with each other again. They spent most of the next twenty-four hours looking through their photograph albums and as they did so reminisced about the great shared events in their life: marriage, the birth of their daughter, wonderful holidays and all the other happy occasions. They also held each other and forgave each other for the times when perhaps inadvertently they had caused each other pain or unhappiness. In the last hours of Chris's life they reached the point where there was no unfinished business. Everything of importance to either of them had been discussed and resolved and all that was left was their love.

At the end of our conversation, his wife said, 'I cannot thank you enough for that. I can't tell you how much I will grieve for him and miss him. But although Chris has now gone, for me the healing was actually in that we had time to say goodbye and to say it properly.'

Chris had left behind some specific instructions for his funeral, she told me. He wanted all those attending to go with happy faces and smiles. He wanted his favourite soft rock music to be played and not the standard funereal music. When she said this, I realised that was the music in the background. However, his last instruction had really bemused the undertaker. His body was to be placed in a coffin painted white with blue 'go-fast' stripes (the motif on his racing yacht) down the sides so that when he was brought into the church all his friends could have one last laugh with him. He wanted to go out on a positive note and be remembered that way.

Stephen Levine, author of books such as *Who Dies?*, *A Year to Live* and *Healing into Life and Death,* whose work I greatly admire, tells a story of a woman with whom he worked. She had never had a good relationship with her mother, who had been very judgemental, very unkind and extremely abusive. When her mother became gravely ill, she was the only daughter who would even go and sit at her bedside because her sisters had felt so hurt and judged that they wanted nothing more to do with their mother. Being a Zen student, the woman decided that her work on herself was to be there for her mother. She would sit next to her, wishing her well, and her mother would go into a light sleep and then come out, as people do when they are very ill. On the day that she died, the mother looked up and said, 'I hope you roast in hell. I hope you have the worst possible life.' She died cursing her daughter, but for the daughter, offering loving kindness in return, it was wonderful. She had really finished her business with her mother. The woman who was dying died. The woman sitting next to her was healed. This is an extreme story, but hopefully we can all get a glimpse of what we *could* be.

If Only . . .

Life and death leave a legacy. Each of us can choose what ours will be. Some people are fortunate because they have been able to say their good-byes and find a space for healing, setting free those who are left behind. Others are not so lucky. So often the past holds us back.

Lucy, one of my seminar participants, shared her experience of losing her father. She was born when he was a serving naval officer and as a child never had very much contact or bonding with him because he was so frequently away at sea, often for months at a time. When he had shore leave and came home he was very detached and emotionally undemonstrative. So far as Lucy was concerned, he seemed like a lodger who occasionally came and stayed in the house and as she grew up, she grew apart from him. In later life they had a rather poor relationship because she felt a gulf between them, caused by her sense of abandonment as a child and his aloofness and detachment.

Out of the blue, Lucy received a telephone call with a message that her father had suffered a major stroke and was not expected to live for more than a few hours. Although she had not seen him for some years, she immediately leapt into her car and drove to the hospital that he had been taken to. It was her chance to say goodbye and to say, in the kindest and most compassionate way, all the things that she had always previously wanted to share with him.

Lucy arrived at the hospital, only to find that her father had died twenty minutes before. She was, she said, grief-stricken not only at his loss, but also at the loss of any chance to ever resolve things with him. '*If only* I had made more effort before . . . *If only* I had driven to the hospital that much faster . . .' It seemed too late to heal the wounds.

Some weeks later Lucy wrote her father an extremely long letter, pouring out her heart and writing down everything that she had always wanted to tell him – including that now she was grown up, she could understand so much better her feelings of neglect and of not being loved as a child. As she wrote the letter, she had a strong sense that her father was watching and was aware of everything she had written. She felt that all her emotions of loss throughout her life were now stored, in an almost physical way, in the pages of the letter. What should she do with it?

Lucy reflected on it for a while and then burned the letter, sheet by sheet, until she was left with a pile of ash. It was a cathartic experience, as if, having expressed her innermost feelings, she was now letting them go. Several weeks later she drove to the coast and on a fine spring morning threw the ash of the letter out into the waves. It was, she said, highly symbolic on several levels, and it was her healing.

The Art of Dying

Our culture does not handle dying very well. It is no longer a part of our everyday lives as it was for our ancestors. We don't look upon it as directly as they did, or live with it as closely. Most of us don't participate in it as personally. In his book *How We Die*, Sherwin B. Nuland describes the art of dying as an art often lost in the science of medicine, where advanced technologies can sometimes rescue patients from death, but not always rescue them from the havoc of their final illness.

Long before we became so taken up with medical technology and prolonging the moment of death, we understood the need to create a sacred space for those in the process of dying. Care-givers provided support and help to individuals as they prepared to die. Sadly, we have largely lost these skills, so that the dying person is now too often fearful, isolated, lonely and in denial. When the news comes that you are dying, you are possibly at a loss because we have so little background for knowing what to do.

Five days before William Saroyan, the Armenian-American writer and humanitarian, died in 1981, he called the Associated Press and left a humorous message: 'Everybody has got to die, but I have always believed an exception would be made in my case. Now what?' In the same situation, you may well ask the same question. Traumatic news has rocked your life. Your days on Earth are limited. Although you have always known that, and you have also known that one day we must all die, the truth will now probably strike in a way you have never realised.

Everyone reacts differently when they discover that they have a life-threatening illness. Your reaction will depend on many factors, including your personality, relationship styles, spirituality and religious beliefs, and how you have coped with difficult situations in the past. Your friends or loved ones will want to help you by words and actions. Being able to talk about your death with them may be very difficult. However, it can also bring a growing closeness to your relationship, because you can share your feelings.

Although people who mean well will probably surround you in the end, you must die *your* death. Dying can be considered a journey that you take alone with a crowd, but these pieces of advice may help you in those first few days after you learn the bad news.

Suggestions for Coming to Terms with the News

Be grateful and accept help, from whatever source, graciously
One or two people, probably family members, will make huge personal sacrifices to help you. If you are married, your spouse will probably do this, but don't be surprised if others – a daughter, a brother-in-law or even a friend – come forward to offer extraordinary help.

Understand the way people treat you Family members and especially friends will probably treat you differently and might seem patronising or overbearing. Although it is not always easy, it is best to ignore this and treat them as you always have. They will get back to being their normal selves when they have got over the shock. You know who you are, not whom others think you are. You might find that people expect you to be different in some way because you are dying. You don't have to like the way they treat you, but it will help if you can understand why they are doing it.

Happily accept all gifts from family and friends It will make them feel better and you might receive something you really like and appreciate.

We need time to be by ourselves so do not be afraid to ask to be alone Some family and friends might feel obliged to fill your every waking moment with activities, perhaps because they think they are 'taking your mind off' your impending death. They may also be doing the same for themselves. They are hiding from the one important thing you share – that they, like you, will also die.

Be your own counsel No one, including your doctor, priest, spouse or friends, can understand 100 per cent what you want and need. Remember Immanuel Kant's advice to avoid accepting someone else's authority in place of your own powers of reason. It is you who should be making choices and considering alternatives. You can, and should, ask for advice, but ultimately you should make the decisions.

Avoidance can create an invisible wall between individuals and families You may try to avoid talking about dying so as not to hurt others or make them sad. You may also fear that family and friends will abandon you if you talk about it. The greatest fear of many people who are dying is being abandoned. If they feel shut out from your thoughts and feelings, it tends to increase, rather than decrease, sadness and fear.

Slow down and ask your family and friends to slow down There may not be a lot of time, but there will be enough time, in all but the most extreme cases, to think, plan and prepare.

Trust the process You may not understand all that's happening, or why it's happening, but try to believe that there is a principle at work here. Work under the belief that you are being led towards growth and healing, and day by day your way will become clearer.

Accepting Your Feelings

Your feelings at this time will probably be intense and unpredictable. There may be no order to your emotions, which may appear one at a time, surface in a complete jumble, or sometimes be contradictory. It may be a chaotic time and the pressures may feel enormous. Under these circumstances, unexpectedly powerful emotions are to be expected. You may be sad. You may be angry with yourself, the world or God. You may feel guilty that you have in some way brought this illness on yourself, be despairing or depressed, pretend that everything is normal or calmly accept what is happening. There is no set pattern for these emotions, although they will generally change rapidly in the first few weeks after the prognosis as you begin to adapt to the new reality.

You have permission to feel whatever you feel, even though others may ask you, verbally or non-verbally, to hide or deny your feelings. They may say 'Be strong!' when really they are saying 'Please don't cry.' It can be difficult to be with someone in deep pain. Look for the permission you deserve from those who really understand you, perhaps those who have been around dying people before. You may well find that you need:

Someone or somewhere to talk about death Although there are many things that you may want to share, you may not want to share them all with one person. Talk about whatever you want with whomever you want. Remember that some people, both men and women, have never talked about their feelings, so try to accept that this pattern will probably not change now.

Someone to tell you that you are still beautiful In his book, *Touch: An Exploration*, Norman Autton describes a man who had cancer in the bones of his face. 'He had had surgery which had left a large cavity in his face. He had a prosthesis to cover and protect the cavity but seldom wore it, and as the cancer progressed, it became too small to cover the hole. He was very much comforted by touch and liked the nurses to kiss him on his face to show they did not find him repulsive.'

Someone who can help to restore your hope, within the context of realism about your situation Knowledge can help to reduce fear of the unknown and it can help you to be realistic so that you can prepare for the future. Talk with health professionals or other people who have cared for someone in your situation. It often helps to explain to an understanding person why you feel afraid, because it allows you to think through the reasons for your feelings. Also, talking with an understanding person will show you that other people realise and appreciate how you feel.

The Dress Rehearsal

In just the same way that an athlete can improve their performance by visualising themselves competing successfully before they go out onto the track, or perhaps by listening to the music that will inspire them, so I believe we can prepare ourselves for the act of dying. As with the dress rehearsal of a play, you too can go through your own dress rehearsal before the curtain is lifted and you are alone with the crowd.

We have all, at times, thought about dying and have probably wondered what it will be like. Socrates recommended that we should 'always be occupied in the practice of dying'. So does the Dalai Lama. A few years ago, when asked what he would like to do next, he replied that he was fifty-eight years old and felt that it was time to complete his preparations for death. Stephen Levine likens it to applying for a passport while still uncertain of our destination or time of departure. The following exercise may help you to be prepared for the unknown.

EXERCISE: MEDITATING INTO THE FINAL JOURNEY

I suggest that you find somewhere in your home that you intuitively feel would be a safe place to die. It might also be a good idea to have the means to summon someone, if you practise this exercise alone, in case you get affected by a feeling of reality and fantasy merging.

As you sit in a comfortable position, taking in a few deep breaths, feel the body you breathe in. Feel your body expanding and contracting with each breath. For a few moments, focus your attention on the rising and falling of your abdomen. Be aware of the changing flow of sensation in each inhalation, in each exhalation. Each inhalation is softening the muscles of your abdomen. Thoughts may come and thoughts may go as you start to relax through your breathing. Imagine them floating like bubbles.

As you sit quietly, feel the heaviness and the weight of your body. It's as if gravity wants to pull it towards the ground. Explore this body you inhabit. There is no one exactly like you. There never has been and never will be. You are more than your body. The person you are physically is only one part of who you really are. It is your mind, your heart and your soul that complete you. At this time in your life these other less visible parts of you may become more important than the visible.

Within your physical body is a light body that produces consciousness of the physical vessel and the world around it. That is what experiences life in or out of the body. Try to become aware of the lighter body within. Each breath drawn in through your nostrils is experienced as sensation by the light body within. Become aware of how each breath connects the two together. Each breath you take maintains that connection, allowing life to stay one more moment in the body. Imagine that your body no longer has the strength, the energy, to maintain its connection with the life force.

Take each breath as though it were your last. Imagine that each inhalation is your last. Don't try to conserve your breath to stay in the body. Let it come and let it go. Let each breath be your last. Let that last exhalation go. The last breath of life leaving the physical body behind. The physical body and the light body separating. The end of life, the final breath . . .

Imagine now that you are beginning to experience the process of dissolving out of that body. Sensations from your body are no longer so distinct, melting away . . . dissolving out of the body . . . leaving that heavier form behind. Dissolving into consciousness itself . . .

Gently, gently let go of all that holds you back, of all that tries to pull you back from this moment of transition called death. Your desk may be covered with unanswered letters, unfinished projects. Either someone else will pick them up for you or they will remain undone. It doesn't matter much. Nobody will know that the idea you meant to work out never came to fruition. Then there are the people in your life. If you loved them well, they will miss you and grieve for you. Over time the poignancy of your absence will fade and only a warm remembrance will be left. There may be those for whom you didn't care enough, those you rejected, those with whom there was still some unfinished business. It doesn't matter now. There is nothing you can do about it.

Let go. Let the tasks of the world slip away. Recognise the changing experience of the mind as it separates from the body. Dissolving now into realms of pure light. Allow yourself to float. You feel lighter as you shed the heavy load you have been carrying. Maintain an open-heartedness of being that does not grasp. Let things be as they are without making any attempts to interfere. Grasping at nothing. Let go, gently and without force. Trust the process.

Shining before you is a great light. Enter that light. This shining, luminous light is your true self. It has no birth. It has no death. Go gently into it. Don't be frightened or bewildered. Don't pull back in fear from the immensity of your true being. Now is the moment for liberation. Let go into the light. Light dissolving into light. Space dissolving into space. Let yourself go, radiating out into space. You are the light.

Through meditations like this, we can begin to develop our own understanding of death. Our anxieties about social status and material possessions will no longer seem so important. The most important point about death is that as time runs out, there are no more chances to get it right. So if you live your life 'finishing business' by keeping yourself up to date and clear in your relationships, and if you work to dissolve the barriers to love in your life, your death will be that much easier. All of us can prepare for death in this way at any time.

Writing Your Own Obituary

Another stimulating and more light-hearted way to rehearse your death is to write your own obituary. Imagine that you know you are going to die within days and complete as many of the following sentences as you find suitably provocative:

○ Outside observers would probably say that my main achievement has been . . .

○ For myself, what I am most pleased with and proud of in my life are . . .

❍ One of the most important lessons that I have learnt in my life is . . .

❍ During my life I have used . . . [list three positive personal characteristics, for example imagination, sense of humour and intelligence] through my . . . [list three activities, for example writing, running groups, being a parent] with the underlying vision, I now realise, of helping towards a world in which, one day . . . [describe your long-term Utopia, for example people being kind and sensitive to one another, nature being at ease and magic being alive].

❍ The people I have felt closest to in my life have been . . .

❍ One generalisation I could make about the quality of my relationships with others is that . . .

❍ If I regret anything, it is that . . .

❍ If I had known how short a time I had left to live, I would probably have . . .

Choosing the Right Time

Of course, the above approaches work well when you have already been told that you have a finite time to live. But what happens in the case of sudden death, when perhaps you have not had time to prepare for an unknown destination at the last moment? If you were driving on a motorway tomorrow and suddenly the car beside you had a blow-out and swerved into your vehicle, what famous last words might be forthcoming? Most likely, it would be 'Oh, shit!' – probably the most common last words of those who die in accidents.

A participant at one of my seminars once told me an interesting and amusing account of just such a scenario. He had been driving down a motorway in appalling weather conditions; there was torrential rain and the road was covered in standing water that was being sprayed in great clouds in all directions by motorists who were oblivious of the safety of speed restrictions. To his horror, the car in front hit a sheet of water, aquaplaned and then spun through 180 degrees so that he was approaching it head-on at some speed. He knew there was going to be a very serious collision from which he would be lucky to survive and in the final seconds before impact, as so many people describe, his life flashed before him. His last conscious thought was, 'I am not going to die now. I have paid a great deal of money into my retirement fund and I intend to live to enjoy it!'

Although he spent several days in a coma and many weeks in hospital recovering from serious injuries, he still remembered those last thoughts before the impact and felt that at that point he had been given a decision to live or die.

In November 2000 I was a guest on *The Ruby Wax Show* on BBC Television, together with the journalist and author John Diamond, who in early 1997 had been diagnosed with throat cancer. He had undergone five major operations, the surgical removal and reconstruction of his tongue and eventually the loss of his speech, prolonged radiotherapy and chemotherapy, and several bouts of remission. For four years he wrote of his slow demise through a regular Saturday column in *The Times*. This became a weekly psychological study conveyed with enormous wit.

In February 2001, Diamond's cancer returned to his throat and right lung and he was offered further chemotherapy treatment, but two weeks later he died. He had been admitted to hospital with bleeding in his neck and throat. The next day, he had more arterial bleeding, during which he wrote a note to Peter Rhys Evans, the head and neck consultant who had treated him for the previous three years. It read: 'Please, no more treatment. No more resuscitation.'

Mr Rhys Evans said, 'What was typical about John, what absolutely summed him up, was when at one stage I was telling him that I had to take him back to theatre to tie off the bleeding point, he immediately scribbled a note: "What is the bleeding point?" It took me a moment to get the other meaning of it. It just showed how on the ball he was.'

I suspect that John Diamond became, as many of my patients describe it after years of gruelling treatment, 'battle weary'.

Choosing the Moment

I am sure that, generally, we choose the moment that is right to die. Some dying people realise they will die more peacefully under certain conditions; until those conditions are met, they may delay the timing of their deaths. This differs from knowing when they will die; some people *do* know and *do* indicate when death will happen, others actually choose the moment of death. Some wait until certain people arrive, or until others leave, or until the ones they care about most have the right kind of support.

I have heard numerous stories from people who have been very upset that their loved one died after they had turned their back, sometimes for just a few minutes. Typically, someone has sat with their dying partner for many hours when they decide to nip down the corridor outside to get a cup of tea or coffee from the vending machine. It only takes a couple of minutes but by the time they return to the bedside, their loved one has slipped away. Alternatively, you may have sat for several days and nights with a dying person and the nurses can see that you are extremely tired and desperately need to sleep and rest. 'Go home and come back in the morning. He'll still be here then. He's still got a couple of days to go.' Reassured, you leave their bedside and drive home. As you unlock the front door you can hear the telephone ringing. The hospital is calling to say that the person has just died. This scenario, which is surprisingly common, deeply upsets many people because they feel that they should have been there and that they abandoned their loved one at the most important time. There may possibly be another explanation.

I had been treating Eileen on a monthly basis for a couple of years and had rarely seen such a devoted couple as she and her husband Bob. They would have done anything for one another and their mutual love was quite touching. Bob knew that his wife was dying, but at the end of her life he stayed by her side for several days, hoping against hope that somehow she would rally as she had done so often in the past and be able to come home. Even though she was in a deep sleep, he held her hand for hours, talking to her, praying and telling her how deeply he loved her. To his amazement, she suddenly opened her eyes and looked straight at him. 'Please let me go,' she said to him, 'you're holding me back.' He then realised that his thoughts, energies and love were actually preventing her from being able to die peacefully. At that moment Bob remembered the phrase 'If you love someone, let them go.' He kissed her on the cheek and she slipped away.

I believe that sometimes we actually make the process of dying more difficult for those we love the most simply *because* we love them so much. It then becomes an energy that holds that person back from dying because we do not want to lose them. That is almost certainly why the dying frequently take their last breath and slip away when we have gone to get the cup of coffee. The energy of 'holding on' has moved away and its grip is loosened. It may also spare those closest from witnessing the dying event or the effort of providing the care. Sometimes a dying person is waiting for a particular circumstance or condition, but the person chosen to provide it isn't always a family member.

I know that every year more of my really sick patients are likely to die in the first three weeks of January than at any other time. It is as if they know that this will be their last Christmas, their last New Year's Day, and they hold on until it has passed, either because they want to enjoy it for a final time themselves or because they do not want to spoil someone else's holiday period. We all have significant dates, whether they are birthdays, anniversaries or holidays. Dying people often try to wait for an important date to pass before dying, so as not to spoil it for the family. Others wait until the ones they care most about have the right kind of support.

Maggie was suffering from breast cancer that had metastasised into her bones and her liver and her doctors had given her three months to live. I treated her for almost a year, during which time she never ceased to amaze the doctors and nurses with her determination, strength and humour.

One day Maggie had been dozing on her bed at home when she opened her eyes to see a huge 'light being' above her. She closed her eyes again and when she reopened them, it was still there. 'I knew then that I wasn't imagining it, dear,' she said to me. She took it as a sign that her life was coming to an end and told family and friends that 'A good guest always knows when it is time to leave the party.'

Saying Goodbye

Finally, there comes a time to say goodbye. It can obviously be painful but for friends, families or carers, it can be intensified if they start the process thinking that you will die immediately after you have said goodbye. Sometimes your final breath may be hours or even days later.

So people often say goodbye many times in different forms.

It is believed that as we die the last sense we lose is our hearing. So if you are caring for a dying person, keep talking, even if you think they are asleep or cannot hear you. Touch is also greatly valued. Touch your loved one in a way that is comforting to them by holding hands, stroking a brow or snuggling up together. Your physical presence is a part of what nurtures a place of trust.

GUIDELINES FOR SAYING GOODBYE TO A LOVED ONE

○ Tell your loved one that you love them. If they are unable to respond, then answer for them: 'And I believe you love me too.'

○ Forgive your loved one for any past estrangement, behaviour or words. If they are unable to respond then answer for them: 'And I believe you forgive me too.'

○ Give your loved one permission to let go.

○ If your loved one has a religious faith, tell them that you feel God's love in this place surrounding you both. Let them know your trust is now in God. If you can express your experience of God's love or presence, describe it to them. Tell them that God will continue to support you after they have gone and that you will make it in the future with your faith in God and your belief that they are also at peace with God.

Wendy was one of the people who stepped over the line that separates my friends from my patients. She had breast cancer that spread to her bones and eventually into her liver and brain. She came to me as a patient and by the time she died was much loved by both Gig and myself. She was drawn to the part of Suffolk where Gig and I live and bought a cottage up on the hill near us. Our friendship was characterised by endless talks about life and death over good food and wine. Our shared philosophy was encapsulated by a piece of writing, entitled *Risks*, which Wendy wanted to be read at her funeral:

To laugh is to risk appearing a fool.
To weep is to risk appearing sentimental.
To reach out for another is to risk involvement.
To expose feelings is to risk exposing your true self.
To place your ideas, your dreams before the crowd is to risk
   their loss.
To love is to risk not being loved in return.
To live is to risk dying.
To hope is to risk despair.
To try is to risk failure.

But risks must be taken because the greatest hazard in life is to risk nothing. The person who risks nothing does nothing, has nothing, is nothing. He may avoid suffering and sorrow, but he simply cannot learn, feel, change, grow, love, live. Chained by his certitudes, he is a slave: he has forfeited freedom.

Only a person who risks is free.

Gayathri was another of my patients whose philosophy made a lasting impression on me. Soon after graduating from university, she was diagnosed with systemic lupus, a disease that attacked all her organs, especially her kidneys, finally resulting in total kidney failure. In my book *One Foot in the Stars*, I described how she had attended one of my healing circles in 1996. She was then on daily peritoneal dialysis while she awaited a transplant. The kidney failure had caused her blood pressure to rise, which in turn had resulted in a blood vessel in her retina bursting a few weeks before she was due to join the circle. A specialist at the eye hospital she attended for this additional problem said nothing could be done. Gayathri's mother wrote to me shortly after her daughter had been to my healing circle, telling me that Gayathri woke up the following morning and was able to see perfectly with that eye. Her sight remained, but it was only much later, after she finally died from the disease, that I discovered what a remarkable young woman she was.

Gayathri's original diagnosis had dealt her a severe blow, leaving her shocked and bewildered, but she had the courage to build a new life around her illness. She had by then joined the Civil Service, but her illness forced her to give this up. Later she worked in the Astrophysics Department at Oxford University, where her Head of Department valued her work so much that some of the research she did for him was published in her own name. Being at Oxford enabled her to be treated at the John Radcliffe Hospital by Professor Ledingham. He looked after her for thirteen years and became almost a father figure. But in spite of all his persuasion, and that of her family and friends, she refused to accept a kidney transplant, saying that others' needs were greater than hers. At first she also refused dialysis, but was persuaded to accept this and it kept her going for many years.

When Professor Ledingham retired, Gayathri moved to Scotland. She loved Scotland and liked the peace and quiet of Scottish rural life. She became acutely ill not long after I last saw her at the beginning of 2001, but refused to go to hospital until her dog was safely sent to kennels. It was a delay that may have cost her her life, because she died before she could get to hospital, at the tragically early age of forty-one. At the service to celebrate her life, an extract from Victor Hugo's *Toilers of the Sea* was read:

I am standing upon that foreshore. A ship at my side spreads her white sails to the morning breeze and starts for the blue ocean. She is an object of beauty and strength and I stand and watch her until at length she hangs like a speck of white cloud just where the sea and sky come down to mingle with each other. Then someone at my side says, 'There! She's gone!' 'Gone where?' 'Gone from my sight, that's all.' She is just as large in mast and spar and hull as ever she was when she left my side; just as able to bear her load of living freight to the place of her destination. Her diminished size is in me, not in her. And just at that moment when someone at my side says, 'There! She's gone!' there are other eyes watching her coming and other voices ready to take up the glad shout, 'Here she comes!' And that is dying.

But that is another journey.

References

Chapter 2

1. D. L. Lefkowitz, M. P. Gelderman, S. R. Fuhrmann, S. Graham and J. D. Starnes, 1999. 'Neutrophilic myeloperoxidase-macrophage interactions perpetuate chronic inflammation associated with experimental arthritis', *Clinical Immunology* 91: 145–55.
2. R. W. Bartrop, L. Lazarus, E. Luckhurst, L. G. Kiloh and R. Penny, 1977. 'Depressed lymphocyte function after bereavement', *Lancet* 834–39.
3. S. J. Schliefer, S. E. Keller, M. Camerino, J. C. Thornton and M. Stein, 1983. 'Suppression of lymphocyte stimulation following bereavement', *Journal of the American Medical Association* 250: 374–77.
4. P. Ekman, 1984. 'Expression and the Nature of Emotion', *Approaches to Emotion*, eds. K. Scherer and P. Ekman (Hillsdale, NJ: Lawrence Erlbaum).
5. N. R. S. Hall, M. O'Grady and D. Calandra, 1994. 'Transformation of personality and the immune system', *Advances* 10, no. 4: 7–15.
6. G. F. Solomon, L. Temoshok, A. O'Leary and J. Zich, 1987. 'An intensive psychoimmunologic study of long-surviving persons with AIDS', *Annals of the New York Academy of Sciences* 496: 647–55.
7. R. Bauer and H. Wagner, 1991. 'Echinacea species as potential immunostimulatory drugs', *Econ. Med. Plant Res.* 5: 231–53.
8. M. Erhard et al., 1994. 'Effect of echinacea, aconitum, lachesis, and apis extracts, and their combinations on phagocytosis of human granulocytes', *Phytotherapy Res.* 8: 14–17.
9. A. Wildfeuer and D. Meyerhofer, 1994. 'Study of the influence of phyto-preparation on the cellular function of bodily defence', *Arzneim Forsch* 44: 361–66.
10. P. Pohl, 1969. 'Therapy of radiation-induced leukopenia by Esberitox', *Med. Klin.* 64: 1546–47.

Chapter 3

1. D. Spiegel, J. R. Bloom, H. C. Kraemer and E. Gottheil, 1989. 'Effect of psychosocial treatment on survival of patients with metastatic breast cancer', *Lancet* 2: 888–91.
2. F. I. Fawzy, N. W. Fawzy, C. S. Hyun, R. Elashoff, D. Guthrie, J. L. Fahey and D. L. Morton, 1993. 'Effects of an early structured psychiatric intervention, coping and affective state on recurrence and

survival six years later', *Archives of General Psychiatry* 50: 681–89.
3. L. Temoshok, B. W. Heller, R. W. Sagebiel, M. S. Blois, D. M. Sweet, R. J. Di Clemente and M. L. Gold, 1995. 'The relationship of psychosocial factors to prognostic indicators in cutaneous malignant melanoma', *Journal of Psychosomatic Research* 29: 139–54.
4. S. Greer, T. Morris and K. W. Pettingale, 1990. 'Psychological response to breast cancer and fifteen-year outcome', *Lancet* 1: 49–50.
5. S. Greer, T. Morris and K. W. Pettingale, 1979. 'Psychological response to breast cancer: effect on outcome', *Lancet* 2: 785–87.
6. G. F. Solomon, L. Temoshok, A. O'Leary and J. Zich, 1987. 'An intensive psychoimmunologic study of long-surviving persons with Aids', *Annals of the New York Academy of Sciences* 496: 647–557.
7. J. W. Pennebaker, 1993. 'Putting stress into words: health, linguistic, and therapeutic implications', *Behavioural Research and Therapy* 31: 539–48.
8. D. Spence, 'The Paradox of Denial', *The Denial of Stress*, ed. S. Bresnitz.
9. A. Schmale and H. Iker, 1966. 'The effect of hopelessness and the development of cancer in women with atypical cytology', *Psychosomatic Medicine* 5: 714–21.
10. S. M. Levy, J. Lee, C. Bageley and M. Lippman, 1988. 'Survival hazards analysis in first recurrent breast cancer patients: seven-year follow up', *Psychosomatic Medicine* 50: 520–28.

Chapter 4

1. J. Itami et al., 1994. 'Laughter and immunity', *Shinshin-Igaku* 34: 565–71.
2. K. M. Dillon, B. Minchoff and K. H. Baker, 1985–86. 'Positive emotional states and enhancement of the immune system', *International Journal of Psychiatry in Medicine* 15: 13–17.
3. K. B. Thomas, 1987. 'General practice consultations: is there any point in being positive?', *British Medical Journal* 294: 1200–2.
4. J. D. Levine, N. C. Gordon and H. L. Fields, 1978. 'The mechanism of placebo analgesia', *Lancet* 2: 654–57.
5. J. M. Mossey and E. Shapiro, 1982. 'Self-rated health: a predictor of mortality among the elderly', *American Journal of Public Health* 72: 800–807.
6. G. E. Vaillant, 1979. 'Natural history of male psychologic health: effects of mental health on physical health', *New England Journal of Medicine* 301 (23).
7. C. Peterson and M. E. Seligman, 1987. *Journal of Personality and Social Psychology* 55 (2): 237–65.

8. C. Peterson et al., 1993. *Learned Helpless: A Theory for the Age of Personal Control* (New York: Oxford University Press).

9. T. Elliott et al., 1991. 'Negotiating reality after physical loss: hope, depression, and disability', *Journal of Personality and Social Psychology* 61, 4.

10. T. Maruta, R. C. Colligan, M. Malinchoc and K. P. Offord, 2000. 'Optimists vs pessimists: survival rate among medical patients over a 30-year period', *Mayo Clinic Proceedings* 75 (2): 133–34.

11. J. S. House, K. R. Landis and D. Umberson, 1988. 'Social relationships and health', *Science* 241: 540–45.

12. J. Greene, 1997. 'Prescribing a healthy social life: a robust social life is important in healing – & staying well', *Journal of the American Medical Association* 277: 1940–4.

13. E. Maunsell et al., 1995. 'Social support and survival among women with breast cancer', *Cancer* 76: 631–37.

14. D. E. Morisky, D. M. Levine, L. W. Green, S. Shapiro, R. P. Russell and C. R. Smith, 1983. 'Five-year blood pressure control and mortality following health education for hypertensive patients', *American Journal of Public Health* 73: 153–62.

15. A. Rosengren et al., 1993. 'Stressful life events, social support, and mortality in men born in 1933', *British Medical Journal* 304: 164–8.

16. P. Moen, D. Dempster-McClain and R. M. Williams, 1989. 'Social integration and longevity: an event history analysis of women's roles and resilience', *American Sociological Review* 54: 635–47.

17. *Lancet,* 1951, 224: 420.

18. D. C. McClelland and C. Kirshnit, 'The effect of motivational arousal through films on salivary immune function', unpublished manuscript.

Chapter 5

1. D. Phillips, T. Ruth and L. Wagner, 1993. 'Psychology and survival', *Lancet* 342: 1142–45.

2. L. Appleby et al., 1997. *British Medical Journal,* 314: 932.

3. Blackburn et al., 1986. *Journal of Affective Disorders* 10: 67–75.

Chapter 6

1. D. E. Stewart, A. M. Cheung, S. Duff, F. Wong, M. McQuestion, T. Cheng, L. Pudy and T. Bunston, 2001. 'Attributions of cause and recurrence in long-term breast cancer survivors', *Psycho-Oncology* 10: 179–83.

2. B. Andersen, 1998. 'Stress and immune responses after surgical treat-

ment for regional breast cancer', *Journal of the National Cancer Institute* 90 (1): 30–36.

3. S. E. Sephton, 2000. 'Stress hormone linked to earlier death in women with breast cancer', *Journal of the National Cancer Institute* 92: 994–1000.

4. D. Mohr, 1998. 'Correlation between stress and disease activity in multiple sclerosis', paper presented to annual meeting of the Society of Behavioural Medicine.

5. W. T. Boyce et al., 1995. 'Psychobiologic reactivity to stress and childhood respiratory illnesses: results of two prospective studies', *Psychosomatic Medicine* 57: 411–22.

6. B. McEwen, 1993. 'Stress and the individual: mechanisms leading to disease', *Archives of Internal Medicine* 153: 2093–101.

7. R. Genco and L. Tedesco, 1999. 'Relationship of stress, distress and inadequate coping behaviours to periodontal disease', *Journal of Periodontology* 70: 711–23.

8. J. K. Kiecolt-Glaser, L. D. Fisher, P. Ogrocki, J. C. Stout, C. E. Speicher and R. Glaser, 1987. 'Marital quality, marital disruption, and immune function,' *Psychosomatic Medicine* 49: 13–34.

9. J. K. Kiecolt-Glaser, R. Glaser, E. C. Strain, J. C. Stout, K. L. Tarr, J. E. Holliday and C. E. Speicher, 1986. 'Modulation of cellular immunity in medical students', *Journal of Behavioural Medicine* 9: 5–21.

10. R. H. Rosenman, R. J. Brand, C. D. Jenkins, M. Friedman et al., 1975. 'Coronary heart disease in the Western Collaborative Study: final follow-up experience of eight and one-half years', *Journal of the American Medical Association* 223: 872–77.

11. C. Nordstrom, K. M. Dwyer, N. Bairey Merz, A. Shircore, P. Sun, W. Sun and J. H. Dwyer, 1999. 'Stress in the workplace and early arteriosclerosis', paper at American Heart Association conference.

12. T. G. Vriijkotte, L. J. P. Van Doornen and E. J. C. De Geus, 1999. 'Work stress and metabolic haemostatic risk factors', *Journal of Psychosomatic Medicine* 61: 796–805

Chapter 7

1. H. Morowitz, 1975. 'Hiding in the Hammond Report', *Hospital Practice,* August, 35–39.

2. G. F. Solomon and R. H. Moos, 1965. 'The relationship of personality to the presence of rheumatoid factor in asymptomatic relatives of patients with rheumatoid arthritis', *Psychosomatic Medicine* 27: 350–60.

3. G. F. Solomon, L. Temoshok, A. O'Leary and J. Zich, 1987. 'An

intensive psychoimmunologic study of long-surviving persons with AIDS', *Annals of the New York Academy of Sciences* 496: 647–55.

Chapter 8

1. D. Lobstein, B. J. Mosbacher and A. H. Ismail, 1983. 'Depression as a powerful discriminator between physically active and sedentary middle-aged men', *Journal of Psychosomatic Res.* 27: 69–76.
2. M. Lappe, *The Tao of immunology: a revolutionary new understanding of our body's defences,* 146.
3. D. Nieman, D. Henson, G. Gusewitch, B. Warren, R. Dotson, D. Butterworth and S. Nehlsen-Cannarella, 1993. 'Physical activity and immune function in elderly women', *Medicine and Science in Sports and Exercise* 25 (July): 823–31.
4. L. Bernstein, B. Henderson, R. Hanisch, J. Sullivan-Halley and R. Ross, 1994. 'Physical exercise and reduced risk of breast cancer in young women', *Journal of the National Cancer Institute* 86 (September): 1403–7.
5. R. E. Frisch, G. Wyshak, N. Albright et al., 1987. 'Lower lifetime occurrence of breast cancer and cancer of the reproductive system among former college athletes', *American Journal of Clinical Nutrition* 45: 328.
6. G. S. Ginsburg, 1996. 'Effects of a single bout of ultra endurance', *Journal of the American Medical Association* 276: 221–25.
7. J. E. Manson, Frank B. Hu et al., 1999. 'A prospective study of walking as compared with vigorous exercise in the prevention of coronary heart disease in women', *New England Journal of Medicine* 341: 650–58.
8. T. Chou, 1992. 'Wake up and smell the coffee: caffeine, coffee, and the medical consequences', *West J. Medicine* 157: 544–53.
9. M. G. Montiero et al., 1990. 'Subjective feelings of anxiety in young men after ethanol and diazepam infusions', *Journal of Clinical Psychiatry* 51: 12–16.
10. J. H. Wright et al., 1978. 'Glucose metabolism in unipolar depression', *British Journal of Psychiatry* 132: 386–93.
11. S. K. Bhattacharya and S. K. Mitra, 1991. 'Anxiolytic activity of panax ginseng roots: an experimental study', *Journal of Ethnopharmacology* 34: 87–92.
12. F. Scaglione et al., 1990. 'Immunomodulatory effects of two extracts of panax ginseng', *Drugs Exp. Clin. Res.* 16: 537–42.
13. B. Bohn, C. T. Nebe and C. Birr, 1987. 'Flow-cytometric studies with eleutherococcus senticosus extract as an immunomodulatory

agent', *Arzneimittel-Forsch.* 37: 1193–96.

14. K. Allen and L. Golden, 1997. 'Listening to music of choice lowers stress in out-patient eye-surgery patients', paper presented to American Psychosomatic Society annual meeting.

Chapter 10

1. M. J. Stampfer, F. B. Hu, J. A. E. Manson, E. B. Rimm and W. C. Willett, 2000. 'Primary prevention of coronary heart disease in women through diet and lifestyle', *New England Journal of Medicine* 343/1: 16–22.

2. H. Kiesewetter et al., 1991. 'Effect of garlic on thrombocyte aggregation, microcirculation, and other risk factors', *International Journal of Clinical Pharmacology and Toxicology* 29: 151–55.

3. S. Richer, 1996. 'Antioxidants halt macular degeneration', *Ocular Surgery News*, June.

4. J. A. Mares-Perlman et al., 1995. 'Serum antioxidants and age-related macular degeneration in a population-based case-control study', *Archives of Ophthalmology* 113: 1518–22.

5. V. Watson, 1997, 'Wine consumption decreases risk of age-related blindness', *Medical Tribune* 7, June.

6. B. K. Butland, A. M. Fehily and P. C. Elwood, 2000. 'Diet, lung function, and lung function decline in a cohort of 2,512 middle aged men', *Thorax* 55: 102–8.

7. R. Swank, 1970. 'Twenty years on a low fat diet', *Archives of Neurology* 23: 460.

8. R. Swank, 1988. 'Multiple sclerosis: the lipid relationship', *American Journal of Clinical Nutrition* 48: 1387.

9. P. R. Fortin et al., 1995. 'Validation of a meta-analysis: the effects of fish oil in rheumatoid arthritis', *Journal of Clinical Epidemiology* 48: 1379–90.

10. H. Iso, K. M. Rexrode, M. J. Stampfer, J. O. E. Manson, G. A. Colditz, F. E. Speizer, C. H. Hennekens and W. C. Willett, 2001. 'Intake of fish and omega-3 fatty acids and risk of stroke in women', *Journal of the American Medical Association* 285: 304–12.

11. A. Belluzi et al., 1996. 'Effect of an enteric-coated fish-oil preparation on relapses in Crohn's disease', *New England Journal of Medicine* 334 (24): 1557–60.

Chapter 11

1. D. R. Miller et al., 1998. 'Phase I/II trial of the safety and efficacy of

shark cartilage in the treatment of advanced cancer' *Journal of Clinical Oncology* 16(11): 3649–55.

2. E. Cameron and L. Pauling, 1976. 'Supplemental ascorbate in the supportive treatment of cancer: prolongation of survival times in terminal human cancer', *Proceedings of the National Academy of Sciences* 73: 3685–89.

3. A. Murata, F. Morishge and H. Yamaguchi, 1982. 'Prolongation of survival times of terminal cancer patients by administration of large doses of ascorbate', *International Journal for Vitamin and Nutrition Research* Supplement 23: 101–13.

4. E. T. Creagan et al., 1979. 'Failure of high-dose vitamin C (ascorbic acid) therapy to benefit patients with advanced breast cancer, a controlled trial', *New England Journal of Medicine* 301: 687–90.

5. C. G. Moertel et al., 1985. 'High-dose vitamin C versus placebo in the treatment of patients with advanced cancer who have had no prior chemotherapy. A randomised double-blind comparison', *New England Journal of Medicine* 312: 137–41.

6. L. Tschetter et al., 1983. 'A community-based study of vitamin C in patients with advanced cancer', *Proceedings of the American Society of Clinical Oncology* 2: 92.

7. K. J. Helzlsouer et al., 2000. 'Vitamin E may guard against prostate cancer', *Journal of the National Cancer Institute* 92: 44–49.

8. M. W. Yu et al., 1999. *American Journal of Epidemiology* 150: 367–74.

9. P. Knekt et al., 1998. 'Low selenium and lung cancer risk', *American Journal of Epidemiology* 148: 975–82.

10. L. C. Clark, 1996. 'Selenium and cancer prevention', *Journal of the American Medical Association.*

11. E. Giovannucci, M. J. Stampfer, G. A. Colditz, D. J. Hunter, C. Fuchs, B. A. Rosner, F. E. Speizer and W. C. Willett, 1998. 'Multivitamin use, folate, and colon cancer in women in the nurses' health study', *Annals of Internal Medicine* 129: 517–24.

12. G. Jasienska and I. Thune, 2001. 'Lifestyle, hormones, and risk of breast cancer', *British Medical Journal* 322: 586–87.

13. N. Simonsen, P. van't Veer, J. J. Strain et al., 1998. 'Adipose tissue omega-3 and omega-6 fatty acid content and breast cancer in the EURAMIC study', *American Journal of Epidemiology* 147: 342–52.

14. D. Bagga, S. Capone, H. Wang et al., 1997. 'Dietary modulation of omega-3/omega-6 polyunsaturated fatty acid ratios in patients with breast cancer', *Journal of the National Cancer Institute* 89: 1123–31.

15. H. Senzaki, S. Iwamoto, E. Ogura et al., 1998. 'Dietary effects of fatty acids on growth and metastasis of kpl-1 human breast cancer

cells in vivo and in vitra', *Anticancer Research* 18: 1621–28.

16. M. Holmes-McNary and A. S. Baldwin, 2000. 'Chemopreventive properties of trans-resveratol are associated with inhibition of activation of IkB Kinase', *Cancer Research* 60: 3477–83.

17. Z. L. Zhang, 1990. 'Hepatoprotective effects of Astralagus root', *Journal of Ethnopharmocology* 30: 145–49.

18. *Cancer Treatment Rep.* 62 (1978): 887–91.

19. *Cancer Letter* 57 (1991): 121–29.

20. T. Nagoa et al., 1981. 'Chemo-immunotherapy with Krestin (PSK) in acute leukaemia', *Tokai Journal of Experimental Clinical Medicine* 6: 141–46.

21. M. Torisu et al., 1990. 'Significant and prolongation of disease-free period gained by oral PSK administration after curative surgical operation of colorectal cancer', *Cancer Immunology Immunotherapy* 31: 261–68.

22. V. Kupin and E. Polevaia, 1986. 'Stimulation of the immunological reactivity of cancer patients by eleuthercoccus extract', *Voprosy Onkologii* 32: 21–26.

23. *Carcinogenesis* 7 (1986): 1197–201.

24. *Free Radic. Res. Commun.* 1 (1986): 387–94.

25. H. A. Nieper, 1976. 'Bromelain in der Kontrolle malignen Washtums', *Krebsgeschehen* 1: 9–15.

26. G. Gerard, 1976. 'Therapeutique anti-cancereuse et bromelaines', *Agressologie* 3: 261–74.

27. T. Hajto, 1986. 'Immunomodulating effects of Iscador: a Viscum album preparation', *Oncology* 43, Supplement 1: 51–65.

28. T. Hajto and G. Lanzrein, 1986. 'Natural killer and antibody-dependent cell-mediated cytotoxicity activities and large granular lymphocyte frequencies in Viscum album-treated breast cancer patients', *Oncology* 43: 93–97.

29. N. Bloksma et al., 1979. 'Cellular and humoral adjuvant activity of a mistletoe extract', *Immunobiology* 156: 309–19.

Chapter 12

1. J. Whitton, 1974. 'Ramp functions in EEG power spectra during actual or attempted paranormal events', *New Horizons Journal.*

2. H. Benson, *Timeless Healing* (New York: Fireside, 1996).

3. J. A. Astin, E. Harkness and E. Ernst, 2000. 'The efficacy of distant healing: a systematic review of randomised trials', *Annals of Internal Medicine* 132: 903–10.

4. S. Figar, 1959. 'The application of plethysmography to the objective study of so-called extra sensory perception', *Journal of the Society for Psychical Research* 38: 1.

5. E. D. Dean, 1966. 'Plethysmograph recordings as ESP responses', *International Journal of Neuropsychiatry* 2: 10.

6. W. S. Harris, M. Gowda, J. W. Kolb, C. P. Strychacz, J. L. Vacek, P. G. Jones et al., 1999. 'A randomised, controlled trial of the effects of remote, intercessory prayer on outcomes in patients admitted to the coronary care unit', *Archives of Internal Medicine* 159: 2273–8.

7. R. C. Byrd, 1988. 'Positive therapeutic effects of intercessory prayer in a coronary care unit population', *Southern Medical Journal* 81, no. 7: 826–29.

8. F. Siher et al., 1998. 'A randomised double-blind study of the effect of distant healing in a population with advanced AIDS: report of a small-scale study', *Western Journal of Medicine* 169, no. 6: 356–63.

9. W. Braud, G. Davis and R. Wood, 1979. 'Experiments with Matthew Manning', *Journal of the Society for Psychical Research* 50: 199–223.

10. J. Barry, 1968. 'General and comparative study of the psychokinetic effect on a fungus culture', *Journal of Parapsychology* 32, no. 4: 237–43.

11. W. H. Tedder and M. L. Monty, 1981. 'Exploration of long-distance PK: a conceptual replication of the influence on a biological system', *Research in Parapsychology 1980*, eds. W. G. Roll et al. (Metuchen, NJ: Scarecrow Press), 90–93.

12. C. B. Nash, 1982. 'Psychokinetic control of bacterial growth', *Journal of the Society for Psychical Research* 51: 217–21.

13. S. O'Laoire, 1997. 'An experimental study of the effects of distant, intercessory prayer on self-esteem, anxiety, and depression', *Alternative Therapies* 3, no. 6: 39–53.

14. H. G. Koenig et al., 1997. 'Attendance at religious services, inter-leukin-6, and other biological parameters of immune function in older adults', *International Journal of Psychiatry in Medicine* 27.

15. T. E. Oxman et al., 1995. 'Lack of social participation or religious strength and comfort as risk factors for death after cardiac surgery in the elderly', *Psychosomatic Medicine* 57: 5–15.

16. R. Hummer, R. Rogers, C. Nam and C. G. Ellison, 1999. 'Religious attendance and mortality in the US adult population', *Demography*.

Reading List

Autton, Norman, *Touch: an Exploration*. Darton, Longman & Todd, 1989.

Bach, Richard, *Illusions*. Delacorte Press, 1977.

Benson, Herbert, *Timeless Healing*. Simon & Schuster, 1997.

Campbell, Don, *The Mozart Effect*. Avon, 1997.

Campbell, Joseph, *The Hero with a Thousand Faces*. Princeton University Press, 1949.

Champion, Bob, *Champion's Story*. VGNG, 1981.

Cousins, Norman, *The Anatomy of an Illness*. Bantam, 1979.

Cousins, Norman, *The Healing Heart*. Bantam, 1985.

Goldhor-Lerner, Harriet, *The Dance of Anger*. Harper & Row, 1997.

Hirshberg, Caryle, & Barasch, Marc Ian, *Remarkable Recovery*. Riverhead Books, 1995.

Holford, Patrick, *The Optimum Nutrition Bible*. Piatkus, 1998.

Kant, Immanuel, *Critique of Pure Reason*. 1781.

Levine, Stephen, *Who Dies?* Anchor Doubleday, 1982.

Levine, Stephen, *Healing into Life and Death*. Anchor Doubleday, 1989.

Levine, Stephen, *A Year to Live*. Thorsons, 1997.

Manning, Matthew, *One Foot in the Stars*. Element, 1999.

Northrup, Dr Christiane, *Women's Bodies, Women's Wisdom*. Piatkus, 1998.

Nuland, Sherwin, B., *How We Die*. Vintage Books, 1993.

Picard, Lynn, *The Elephant's Rope and the Untethered Spirit*. Robert D. Reed, 2000.

Roet, Brian, *A Safer Place to Cry*. Macdonald Optima, 1989.

Siegel, Bernie, *Love, Medicine and Miracles*. Random House, 1986.

Siegel, Bernie, *Peace, Love and Healing*. Random House, 1990.

Seligman, Martin, *Learned Optimism*. Knopf, 1998.

Simonton, Carl & Stephanie, *Getting Well Again*. Bantam, 1978.

Weil, Andrew, *Spontaneous Healing*. Unapix, 1996.

Resources

Matthew Manning can be contacted at:
PO Box 100
Bury St Edmunds
Suffolk IP29 4DE
Tel: 01284 830222; Fax: 01284 830228; E-mail: healing@keme.co.uk;
Website: www.matthewmanning.com

Organisations

Ainsworth's Homoeopathic Chemist
36 New Cavendish Street
London W1G 8UF
Tel: 020 7935 5330

Association of Hypnotists and Psychotherapists
12 Cross Street
Nelson
Lancs BB9 7EN
Tel: 01282 699378

Bristol Cancer Help Centre
Grove House
Cornwallis Grove
Clifton
Bristol BS8 4PG
Tel: 0117 980 9500

British Association for Counselling (BAC)
1 Regent Place
Rugby
Warwickshire CV21 2PY
Tel: 01788 578328

British Medical Acupuncture Society
67–69 Chancery Lane
London WC2A 1AF

The British Wheel of Yoga
25 Jermyn Street
Sleaford
Lincs
NG34 7RU
Tel: 01529 306851; Fax: 01529 303233; E-mail: office@bwy.org.uk

Hypnotherapist
Dr Brian Roet
2 The Mews
6 Putney Common
London
SW15 1HL
Tel: 020 8780 2284

The Institute for Optimum Nutrition
Blades Court
Deodor Road
London SW15 2NU
Tel: 020 8877 9993; E-mail: allion@ion.ac.uk;
Website: www.optimumnutrition.co.uk

The National Federation of Spiritual Healers
Old Manor Farm Studio
Church Street
Sunbury-on-Thames
Middlesex TW6 6RG
Tel: 01932 783164; Fax: 01932 779648; E-mail: office@NFSH.org.uk

Support Services

BACUP (British Association of Cancer United Patients)
(Information, counselling, leaflets and research information)
3 Bath Place
Rivington Street
London EC2A 3YR
Tel: 020 7613 2121

Cancerlink
7 Britannia Street
London WC1X 9YN
Tel: 020 7833 2451
Young people's line: 0800 591028

The Compassionate Friends
(Self-help group of parents who have lost a child of any age)
53 North Street
Bristol BS3 1EN
Tel: 0117 953 9639

Cruse
(Bereavement counselling)
126 Sheen Road
Richmond TW9 1UR
Tel: 020 8332 7227

National Cancer Alliance
PO Box 579
Oxford OX4 1LB
Tel: 01865 793566

Index